POVERTY AND LOW INCOME IN THE NORDIC COUNTRIES

Poverty and Low Income in the Nordic Countries

Edited by
BJÖRN GUSTAFSSON
University of Göteborg, Sweden

PEDER J. PEDERSEN
University of Aarhus and Centre for Labour Market and Social Research, Denmark

LONDON AND NEW YORK

First published 2000 by Ashgate Publishing

Reissued 2018 by Routledge
2 Park Square, Milton Park, Abingdon, Oxon OX14 4RN
711 Third Avenue, New York, NY 10017, USA

Routledge is an imprint of the Taylor & Francis Group, an informa business

Copyright © Björn Gustafsson and Peder J. Pedersen, selection of editorial matter; individual chapters, the contributors 2000

All rights reserved. No part of this book may be reprinted or reproduced or utilised in any form or by any electronic, mechanical, or other means, now known or hereafter invented, including photocopying and recording, or in any information storage or retrieval system, without permission in writing from the publishers.

Notice:
Product or corporate names may be trademarks or registered trademarks, and are used only for identification and explanation without intent to infringe.

Publisher's Note
The publisher has gone to great lengths to ensure the quality of this reprint but points out that some imperfections in the original copies may be apparent.

Disclaimer
The publisher has made every effort to trace copyright holders and welcomes correspondence from those they have been unable to contact.

A Library of Congress record exists under LC control number: 99073697

ISBN 13: 978-1-138-70301-8 (hbk)
ISBN 13: 978-1-138-70297-4 (pbk)
ISBN 13: 978-1-315-20341-6 (ebk)

Contents

Preface   ix

1. **Introduction**   1
   BJÖRN GUSTAFSSON AND PEDER J. PEDERSEN

   1.1 The Subject and Outline of the Book   1
   1.2 The Nordic Countries – Some Characteristics and Patterns of Change   5
   1.3 Concepts and Measurement   15
       1.3.1 The framework   15
       1.3.2 Defining a poverty line at one point in time   16
       1.3.3 Updating the poverty line   17
       1.3.4 Poverty index   17
       1.3.5 The duration of poverty   18
       1.3.6 Assessing whether a household is poor or not   18
   References   20

2. **Low Incomes in Denmark 1980-1995**   21
   PEDER J. PEDERSEN AND NINA SMITH

   2.1 Introduction   21
   2.2 Some Earlier Danish Studies   23
   2.3 Data   24
   2.4 The Poverty/Low Income Line   27
   2.5 The Low Income Share in Denmark 1980-1995   29
   2.6 Low Income Groups in Denmark   32
   2.7 Redistribution through Income Taxes   39
   2.8 Is Low Income Status Permanent?   40
   2.9 Concluding Remarks   57
   2.10 Appendix   60
   References   62

3.	**Income Poverty in Finland 1971-1995**	**63**
	MARKUS JÄNTTI AND VELI-MATTI RITAKALLIO	
	3.1 Introduction	63
	3.2 Economic and Social Developments in Finland 1971-1995	64
	3.2.1 Macroeconomic conditions	66
	3.2.2 Social policy and other institutional developments	72
	3.3 Previous Research on Poverty in Finland	75
	3.4 Data	77
	3.5 Trends in the Distribution and Incidence of Poverty	79
	3.5.1 Overall developments	79
	3.6 Poverty Risks in Selected Population Groups	86
	3.6.1 Age of household reference person	86
	3.6.2 Household type	89
	3.6.3 Region	92
	3.6.4 Socio-economic status	93
	3.7 Concluding Comments	97
	References	98
4.	**Poverty in Iceland**	**101**
	STEFÁN ÓLAFSSON AND KARL SIGURÐSSON	
	4.1 Introduction: General Background and Previous Research	101
	4.2 Poverty in Perspective: The Level of Living Environment in Contemporary Iceland	103
	4.3 The Data	110
	4.4 The Total Poverty Level	113
	4.5 The Net Poverty Level 1995: Total and disposable family earnings compared	119
	4.6 Conclusions	121
	4.7 Appendix: Trends in Poverty Ratios by Socio-Economic Groups, 1986-1995	123
	References	129
5.	**Extent, Level and Distribution of Low Income in Norway 1979-1995**	**131**
	ROLFE AABERGE, ARNE S. ANDERSEN AND TOM WENNEMO	
	5.1 Introduction	131
	5.2 Measuring Poverty	133
	5.3 Previous Research in Norway	135
	5.4 Data	137

	5.5	Definition of Low Income/Poverty Lines	139
	5.6	The Pattern of Poverty in Norway 1979-1995	141
	5.7	Income Composition among the Poor	148
	5.8	Poverty in Different Population Groups	150
		5.8.1 Age	150
		5.8.2 Gender	151
		5.8.3 Type of household	152
		5.8.4 Region	153
	5.9	Chronic Poverty	154
	5.10	Summary and Conclusions	161
	5.11	Appendix I	163
	5.12	Appendix II	166
		5.12.1 Variance of FGT indices	166
		References	168

6. Poverty in Sweden: Changes 1975-1995, Profile and Dynamics — 169
BJÖRN GUSTAFSSON

	6.1	Introduction	169
	6.2	The Literature on Poverty in Sweden	171
		6.2.1 Contributions by sociologists	172
		6.2.2 International comparisons of income poverty	173
		6.2.3 A native tradition	174
	6.3	Data and Assumptions	175
	6.4	The Development of Poverty	177
	6.5	Poverty in Different Categories of the Population	182
	6.6	Gender and Poverty	192
	6.7	Designing a Study of Swedish Poverty Dynamics	194
	6.8	Results on Poverty Dynamics	196
	6.9	Conclusions	201
	6.10	Appendix	203
		References	204

7. Conclusions — 207
BJÖRN GUSTAFSSON AND PEDER J. PEDERSEN

	7.1	The Study	207
	7.2	The Development of Poverty over Time	208
	7.3	The Poverty Profile	209
	7.4	Dynamic Aspects of Poverty	211
	7.5	Concluding Remarks	212

Presentation of the Authors 213

Presentation of Nordiska Ministerrådet 215

Preface

The initiative for this book stems from a dialogue between the Nordic Council and the Nordic Council of Ministers. This lead to a research project in which social scientists from Denmark, Finland, Iceland, Norway and Sweden co-operated in order to address a number of questions: How has the number of people living below a predetermined poverty line changed over time in the Nordic countries? Who are the poor in the various Nordic countries? How does poverty or low income at the individual level appear when the observation period is extended to cover a longer period of years?

There are at least two fundamental reasons why results from research on poverty in the Nordic countries could be of considerable interest for readers outside these countries as well. Firstly, the Nordic countries are well known for their ambitious social policies. Therefore, knowledge about poverty in the Nordic countries helps to suggest what would lie in store for other countries if their social policy ambitions increased. Secondly, in contrast to the situation in many other countries, data on household income have been collected using consistent methods in the Nordic countries over decades, making it possible to conduct analyses covering long periods of time. Data available in Denmark, Norway and Sweden make it possible also to investigate the dynamic aspects of poverty at the household level.

Questions on poverty and low income have, of course, previously been addressed on the basis of the experience from individual Nordic countries. The new aspect of this book is that it co-ordinates the statistical analyses. This has allowed the application of a more comparative framework than is usually possible in studies covering many countries and years. The results make it possible to compare the development of the extent of poverty and the poverty profile across the various Nordic countries. A comparative approach to poverty in the Nordic countries is particularly interesting as they have experienced rather different profiles of unemployment during recent decades.

The project was funded by the Nordic Council of Ministers as well as the Swedish National Board of Health and Welfare, where Annika Puide co-ordinated it. In an earlier report, Puide, A. (Editor) *Den nordiska fattigdomens utveckling och struktur*, Köbenhavn, Nordiska Ministerrådet (TemaNord 1996:583) results were reported using Danish, Swedish, English and Norwegian in the different chapters. The report was presented at a seminar in Stockholm in autumn 1996. We would like to thank Claes Örtendahl, Else Öyen and Hans Hansen for giving us valuable comments on that occasion. The seminar also inspired us to continue the work and make the findings accessible to people not proficient in the Nordic languages.

In the continuation of the project we have taken several approaches. Firstly, authors of the various country chapters have updated the empirical descriptions by using newer data. This makes it possible to bring the analysis and description forward up to the middle of the 1990s. Secondly, all country chapters have been revised by their respective authors. Thirdly, we have rewritten and extended the introductory chapter, as well as adding a concluding chapter. Thus, while the book clearly builds on its predecessor, it also differs from it in many respects.

Björn Gustafsson   *Peder J. Pedersen*
Göteborg, Sweden   Aarhus, Denmark

1 Introduction

BJÖRN GUSTAFSSON AND PEDER J. PEDERSEN

1.1 The Subject and Outline of the Book

Poverty is a long-standing social issue in Denmark, Finland, Norway, Iceland and Sweden. For centuries, large parts of the population in the Nordic countries had to struggle hard for survival as, until the last hundred years, the general standard of living was low in these predominantly agrarian economies. The public provision of income support was only rudimentary and consisted of stringently means-tested poor relief to the destitute who could not work.

However, industrialisation, in the second half of the last century, brought widespread change and rapid economic growth. At the turn of the century, GNP per capita in the Nordic countries was significantly lower that the average among the OECD countries. During this century, GNP per capita rose more rapidly in the Nordic countries than the average for the OECD area (cf. Maddison 1991, pp. 6-7). One of the results of this rapid growth was a reduction of poverty in the absolute sense of the word.

During this century, other forces reduced the importance of the issue of poverty in the Nordic countries. Unemployment was very high in the Nordic countries in the inter-war years, but became a much smaller social and political problem after World War II. Unemployment remained low in the Nordic countries, except Denmark, until around 1990, in contrast to most other Western European countries, which experienced a growing problem of unemployment from the mid-1970s.

Ever more ambitious social security programmes materialised during the long period of full employment. The public sector grew rapidly, especially during the 1960s and 1970s. As a consequence of these changes, poverty moved down on the agenda of social policy in the Nordic countries. The discontinuity with the past was also marked by the renaming of programmes for poor relief.

Not only from a historical perspective but also from an outsider's point of view, poverty in the absolute sense of the word in the contemporary Nordic countries can be considered as a not very serious subject. When the World Bank counts the poor in the world in its World Development Report their figures do not include inhabitants of the Nordic countries. However, when the frame of reference is narrowed from a global perspective to that of the industrialised countries, poverty or low income also exists in the Nordic countries.

2 Poverty and Low Income in the Nordic Countries

Recently, the statistical authority of the European Union, Eurostat, published estimates of poverty in EU 12, excluding the three fairly new member states: Austria, Finland and Sweden. (Eurostat, 1997). According to the criteria employed by Eurostat, poverty is reported to exist in Denmark, the only Nordic country covered. However, at the same time, the Danish poverty rate is lower than for any other country reported. Another study of the EU covering all the Nordic countries except Iceland presents further evidence (Vogel, 1997). This study too finds that the population in Denmark is less poverty prone than in all other non-Nordic EU countries. However, the findings for Finland, Norway and Sweden are actually very similar to those from Denmark. Thus, from an EU perspective, poverty in the Nordic countries exists, but appears to be relatively small.

The starting point for this book, therefore, is that there is a low level of poverty in this group of countries. But even in the prosperous Nordic countries with their large and comprehensive social programmes, some people are less well off than others. The purpose of this book is to study how poverty has developed.

There are several reasons why the problems of the less fortunate have once again become of interest to policy makers and the general public in the Nordic countries and thus provided a motivation for our book. Starting first and gradually in Denmark during the 1970s and abruptly at the beginning of the 1990s in Finland and Sweden, unemployment has increased to much higher levels than previously. The wide expansion of the welfare state came to an end during the 1980s (at least temporarily). Finland and Sweden have even experienced sizeable cuts in welfare programmes during the 1990s. Average income has mainly been increasing during the last 15-20 years, the period covered in the present study. However, not everyone has benefited from increasing economic growth. The proportion of people living on means-tested social assistance has expanded in the various Nordic countries, at the same time as average income has increased to an all time high (Eardley et al., 1996).

The first question we address in this book is how the extent of poverty or low income has changed over time in the Nordic countries. To answer this question, we work with micro data sets for each of the countries. This makes it possible to report time series on the extent of poverty in Denmark 1980 - 1995, Finland 1971 - 1995, Iceland 1986 - 1997, Norway 1979 - 1995 and Sweden 1975 - 1995. We define a person as poor if the disposable income of the household in which he or she lives is below a given poverty line, specified either as an absolute or a relative measure. The development according to the time series can be compared across the countries since central concepts have been harmonised. Even though we have attempted to construct the variables in the same way in all the countries, the collection of data and the concepts used differ between the countries to an extent that prevents perfect comparability.

The second question we address in this book is who the poor are in the various Nordic countries. We report on the poverty profile for each of the five countries. We do this not only for one point in time, but for longest period for which data is available in each of the countries. Knowledge of the poverty profile and changes within it is very useful when discussing social policy measures. Have the Nordic countries been particularly successful in reducing poverty for some particular categories? Which categories in the Nordic countries are poverty prone during the 1990s? The answers to these questions define the challenges for contemporary welfare policy.

Most poverty studies are based on the situation of the household as it appears during a period of, usually, no more than one year. However, the economic situation of households is not static. In some households members change from not working to taking up a work and in others the reverse happens. Often household members change their hours of work from one year to the next. Wages and salaries increase for many people from one year to the next, while the reverse can also happen. Further causes of change in poverty status are changes in the receipt of transfer payments and altered household composition.

The third and final question we address in this book is how poverty at the individual level appears when the observation period is enlarged to cover a larger number of years. This leads to several subsequent questions, such as to what extent poverty is chronic or transitory; for which categories poverty-mobility is high or low; and what events make people move into or out of poverty.

Answering questions about poverty-mobility places a high demand on data. This explains why poverty profiles have been reported for many countries, whereas knowledge about poverty-mobility and the duration of poverty is concentrated in fewer countries. There is no official panel survey designed to monitor poverty dynamics for a Nordic country. Based on the data sets developed for the present book, we are, however, able to report results on poverty dynamics for Denmark, Norway and Sweden.

Before proceeding any further, some words about the limitations of the present book should be offered. Due to the problems of comparability, in spite of our attempts to harmonise as much as possible, it is not a central issue to compare poverty or low income shares across the Nordic countries at a specific point in time in order to investigate whether the extent of poverty is larger or smaller in one country than in another. One reason for this is that studies addressing such questions in a broader frame had already been begun elsewhere when we planned the present project and we saw no point in duplicating the work of others. The Luxembourg Income Study (LIS) has been successful in bringing together data sets from many countries including the four large Nordic countries and in harmonising definitions to some degree. A limitation of this approach is that data is collected differently in different countries. An important step in overcoming that problem was taken by the launching of the European Household Panel by Eurostat. Today, data for Denmark and Finland have been collected in this unified system which also covers other EU-countries. There are also data sources (the Surveys on Living Conditions) which are similar for Norway and Sweden.

Another characteristic of the present study which should be emphasised at the outset is that we work only with an economic definition of poverty based on the disposable income of a household. We think there are good reasons to limit the concept "Poverty" to the economic sphere and separate the concept from a wider concept of "Level of living". This means that policy implications from our study are clearest for those policies which affect the disposable income of households. Examples of such policies are found in the field of social security and income taxes. There is much evidence of poor people being worse off also in other spheres of life. Often they are reported to be disadvantaged regarding housing and on average to have more health problems than others However, we have chosen – partly dictated by data availability – not to focus on these matters in this book.

Following the present introductory chapter, the book consists of five country chapters and a concluding chapter. Chapter 2 by Peder J. Pedersen and Nina Smith reports on poverty in Denmark while poverty in Finland is addressed by Markus Jäntti and Veli-Matti Ritakallio in Chapter 3. Stefan Olafsson and Karl Sigurdsson report on poverty in Iceland in Chapter 4 while Rolf Aaberge, Arne S. Andersen and Tom Wennemo address poverty in Norway in Chapter 5 and Björn Gustafsson poverty in Sweden in Chapter 6. We draw together the findings in the various chapters in the concluding Chapter 7. We use the rest of this introductory chapter to set the stage for the various country chapters. In the next section we outline characteristics of the Nordic countries which seem to be important for understanding the poverty situation and how it has changed in the Nordic countries. In Section 3 we shift to the literature on conceptualising and measuring poverty in order to put our study of Nordic poverty in a larger perspective of poverty studies and to discuss the central concepts.

1.2 The Nordic Countries – Some Characteristics and Patterns of Change

The Nordic countries differ in area and in the size of their populations. By area, Sweden at one end, is one of the biggest countries in Europe, and Denmark, at the other end, one of the smaller European countries. The Nordic countries have a population of around 23 million, with a big variation from 8.5 million in Sweden to 0.3 million in Iceland. Though different by area and population, the Nordic countries share a number of similar characteristics that tend to make the problem of poverty or low income relatively small. In this subsection, we shall briefly summarise a number of these characteristics and their possible importance to low income problems.

The populations in the Nordic countries have until the most recent decades been fairly homogeneous, including in language, where the national languages are understood in the other Nordic countries, with the exception of Finnish. During the most recent 30-35 years, the countries have been exposed to immigration in very different degrees. At one extreme, Sweden has received many immigrants during these years and the proportion of the population born abroad is currently about 10 per cent. This proportion is significantly smaller in Denmark and Norway, and Finland and Iceland at the other extreme have had very few immigrants.

Since 1954 there has been free mobility between the Nordic labour markets. The major intra-Nordic migration flow was from Finland to Sweden in the 1960s and the 1970s. When the income gap between the two countries narrowed in the 1980s, it was followed by a major return migration to Finland.

Immigration of non-Nordic citizens was, back in the 1960s, dominated by people moving to take up a job. Many have remained and have been joined by their families. In the 1980s and 1990s, immigration came to be dominated by refugees, many coming from overseas countries, and by family reunions. This latter wave of immigrants have found large problems in entering the labour market.

Although the countries share many similarities, there have until recently been differences in their level of industrial and economic development and in their natural resource base. Industrialisation began at different times in the countries. Finland was the late-comer in this respect. Now, Finland has caught up with the other three Nordic neighbours, and – with Norway on top – GNP per capita is at approximately the same level in the Nordic countries. The 'catch up' in Finland occurred during the 1980s, i.e. the period covered by the present study.

The natural or resource bases differ considerably between the Nordic countries. Traditionally, the Danish economy was based on agriculture and food processing industries, the Norwegian on shipping, fishing and timber, the Swedish on metal and wood-processing industries, the Finnish on timber and pulp, and that of Iceland on fishery. All this has changed in recent decades. It has changed least in Iceland, where fishery is still the dominant activity, implying that changes in catch and in prices have very great macroeconomic repercussions. In the other Nordic countries, the industrial base has been very much broadened in the recent decades.

The biggest changes have occurred in Finland and Norway. Finland was not hit economically like the other OECD countries after the first oil price shock in 1974, as it had at that time an agreement on balanced trade with the Soviet Union who supplied the Finnish energy import. Energy prices rose less for Finland than for the other OECD countries and resulted in a boost in export demand to the Soviet Union due to the balanced trade agreement. The external trade relations meant, on the other hand, that Finland was hit extremely hard when the Soviet Union collapsed around 1990. A major part of the country's export was wiped out at one stroke and unemployment rose at a speed hardly ever experienced by any other country, cf. Figure 1.1.

Norway has, since the 1970s, undergone major macroeconomic changes due to the extraction of large oil and natural gas reserves in the North Sea. The country has become a major energy exporter. This has boosted national wealth and GNP per capita in Norway, but has at the same time created a heavy macroeconomic dependence on the big price volatility in the energy market.

Turning to the labour markets, the Nordic countries have the same characteristics in many respects, cf. the comprehensive studies in Wadensjö (ed., 1996). The labour markets are highly unionised. In Denmark, Finland, Iceland and Sweden unemployment insurance is organised based on what is known as the Ghent-principle, i.e. insurance coverage is closely related to union membership. As a consequence, unionisation in those countries is about 80 per cent, and it has been increasing during the most recent 25 years. This development is, as is well known, quite contrary to the fairly low, and mostly declining level of unionisation in most other OECD countries. In Norway, unemployment insurance is part of the comprehensive system of state-run transfer incomes. Unionisation is somewhat lower than in the other Nordic countries, but still high compared with most other OECD countries.

On the industrial relations side, negotiations in the Nordic countries have typically been considered highly centralised, cf. for example, the ranking found in Calmfors and Driffil (1988). Only recently has there been a tendency in the Nordic countries too towards a more decentralised approach in collective bargaining. The low inequality in the distribution of wages is one of the probable results of the combination of centralised negotiations and highly organised labour markets, cf. OECD (1993). Both the skill and the regional differences in wages are small. Female labour force participation is among the highest in the OECD area. There is a gender wage gap also in the Nordic countries, but smaller than in most other industrial economies, cf. Asplund et al. (1996). Finally, adult minimum wages are relatively high, reducing the risk of finding any major group of working poor.

Another common characteristic of the Nordic countries is the existence of ambitious and comprehensive social programmes, both directed to people in the core groups in relation to the labour market and to the young and the elderly. Services provided by public authorities at no or very low cost include hospitals, primary and secondary schools and university education. At subsidised prices, day care for children is widely available, reflecting that the typical family with children is one in which both parents participate in the labour market. Housing subsidies are available for low income groups, i.e. single parents and pensioners without significant private pension incomes.

The high level of publicly provided goods at low or no cost for the users is a common characteristic for the Nordic countries, and at the same time constitutes a difference between them and most other Western European countries. Regarding income transfers from the public sector, the Nordic countries have comprehensive systems. In this area there is, however, no difference relative to many other European countries when the comparison is made using a summary measure like total income transfers relative to GNP. There may be greater differences concerning the composition of transfers and thereby differences regarding their impact on the income distribution and the prevalence of poverty.

Income transfers to families include allowances – some means-tested and some not – to families with children, means-tested rent subsidies, and programmes to replace all or part of the income loss at child birth. As mentioned, two-earner families are widespread in the Nordic countries, few families have more than three children, and families with children are typically in the core age groups where unemployment is fairly low. These characteristics, along with the transfer programmes, reduces the risk of children living in poverty in the Nordic countries.

Young adults typically stay longer in their parents' households in the south of Europe compared to the Nordic countries. Furthermore, parents in many European countries are morally, and sometimes also legally, responsible for providing for their adult children in the case of need. Things are different in the Nordic countries where most young adults live in separate households and where the parents are not legally obliged to provide for them in the case where the adult children have no or low incomes themselves. This feature makes young adulthood in the Nordic countries a more problematic life phase for those without a job than outsiders might expect.

From a historical perspective, poverty in the Nordic countries has predominantly been a problem among old people. Before the establishment of the present comprehensive welfare states, old people had to rely for their survival on savings from their active age or on support from children or other relatives. Often those sources were insufficient, and old people formed a major proportion of the group receiving poor relief. However, the building of comprehensive pension systems has been a central element in the expansion of the welfare state, and has contributed to reducing the old age poverty problem. Furthermore, eligibility for the state funded basic old age pension system is not dependent on the extent of the pensioners' previous participation in the labour market. Besides the basic public old age pension system, labour market pensions and private pension plans cover an expanding number of the pensioners. For people below the official retirement age, there has been a development of different programmes for early retirement for health or labour market related reasons, along with programmes in some of the countries where eligibility depends only on labour market experience and a specific age limit. The overall impact of this development has been that few people in the older age groups retire early without having an income from one of those different programs or retirement plans.

Unemployment insurance benefits are fairly generous in the Nordic countries. Eligibility rules and coverage differs between the countries, but for those unemployed who are not covered or eligible, means-tested social welfare benefits are available. The maximum duration of unemployment insurance benefits differs between the countries and has been changing over time. The insurance system is, however, combined with programmes for active labour market policies. People in long-term unemployment eventually reaching the maximum duration of unemployment insurance benefits are eligible for entry into a programme in which they continue to receive an income. For the period considered in the present book, people could remain in the insurance-programme system for an indefinite period, unless they refused to enter a programme. In this way, most adults have been able to gain an income even in long periods when they have not had an ordinary job.

Many institutions and characteristics are thus similar across the Nordic countries. This is also true concerning the political environment, where social democratic parties – although almost never having an absolute majority – have played a major role in shaping the policies to reduce the incidence and duration of poverty. In foreign and defence policy the Nordic countries differ. Three of them, Denmark, Iceland and Norway being NATO members, and Denmark, (since 1972), and Finland and Sweden, (since 1995), are members of the EU. Despite these differences, there are, however, many factors to justify treating the Nordic countries as a relevant analytical entity.

Next we turn to a brief quantitative survey of the development in some macroeconomic and labour market related factors of relevance for the subject of the present book. We limit the attention to the maximum period coinciding with the micro data sets used in the subsequent chapters.

The Nordic countries, like most other OECD countries, were hit by the oil price shock in 1974 and the subsequent recession. In the following years, macroeconomic trends differed, however, between the Nordic countries. In the following we will concentrate on some aspects of special relevance for the low income problem.

Unemployment has traditionally been seen as an important factor behind poverty or low income problems. In this area there have been big differences between the experience in the Nordic countries in the most recent 25-30 years, cf. Figure 1.1 showing unemployment rates in the five Nordic countries for the period 1971 to 1997.

10 *Poverty and Low Income in the Nordic Countries*

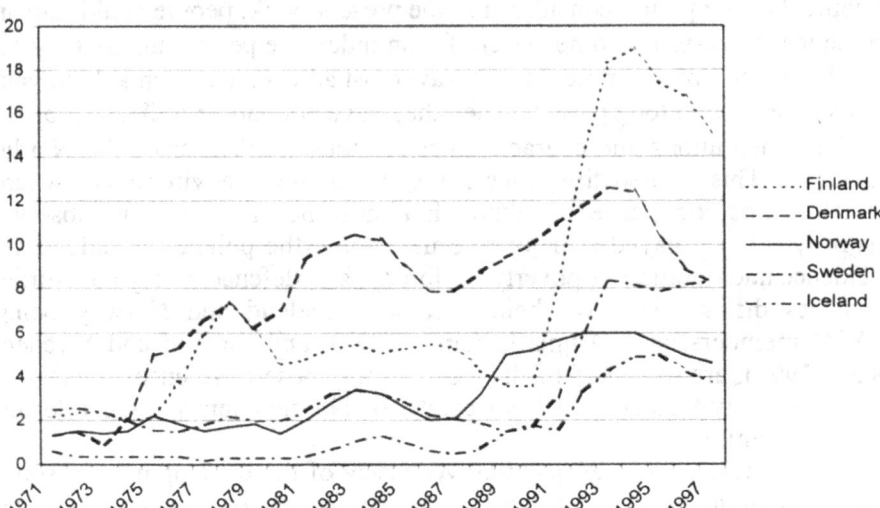

Figure 1.1 Unemployment rates in the Nordic countries, 1971-1997

Before 1990 unemployment was practically non-existent in Iceland. This has changed in the 1990s, but still leaves Iceland with an unemployment rate at a very low level compared to other European countries. Our comments will therefore concentrate on the experience of the four other countries. During the second half of the 1970s unemployment increased dramatically in Denmark. The same increase occurred, although at a more gradual rate in Finland. Full employment remained intact in Norway and Sweden. During the 1980s the picture changed. In all countries except Finland unemployment reacted to the second oil price shock and the subsequent international recession in the early 1980s. Thereafter, the unemployment profiles differed between the countries. For more than a decade Denmark had the highest – and mostly increasing – level of unemployment. Finland entered the decade with falling unemployment and came out close to full employment at the end of the decade. The reverse oil price shock in 1986 had negative effects for Norway as a big energy producer and unemployment went up in the late 1980s.

Norway and especially Sweden were, until the end of the 1980s, considered as success stories – islands of full employment in a European environment with an increasing trend of unemployment. The international literature, e.g. Layard et al. (1991) emphasised the importance of specific labour market institutions as decisive for this situation. At the same time it was emphasised, e.g. by Atkinson et al. (1995) that the Nordic countries realised a highly equal distribution of incomes in this period compared to many other countries. The development in Denmark during the same period, however, cautions against drawing any direct conclusions about a narrow relationship between low unemployment, equality in the income distribution and implicitly a low poverty share. Denmark with much higher unemployment until the early 1990s experienced the same low level of income inequality as the other Nordic countries and a low poverty rate around a falling trend.[1]

From 1990 Figure 1.1 shows the well known dramatic changes in unemployment in the Nordic countries with an explosive increase in Finland of a magnitude hardly experienced in such a short span of time by any other country. Swedish unemployment increased to the same level as in Denmark. Only in Norway did unemployment stablilise, although at a higher level than in the 1980s. Even Iceland experienced unemployment for the first time in the 1990s.

The immediate impact of unemployment on the distribution of factor incomes and the poverty share is more or less neutralised by compensations from unemployment insurance or social welfare systems. Another compensating mechanism is an increase in the participation rate. A higher participation rate reduces the proportion of people with no or very little income and dampens the impact if a member of the household becomes unemployed. It is evident from Figure 1.2 that there have been very big changes in the participation rates in the period under study.

---

[1] Evidence for the lacking direct relationship between unemployment and inequality in the income distribution is the topic in Aaberge et al. (1997).

12 *Poverty and Low Income in the Nordic Countries*

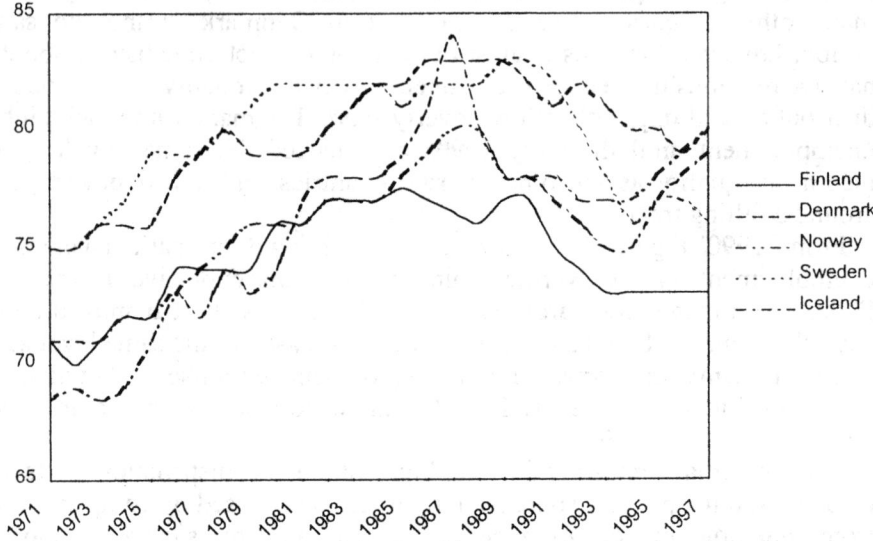

Figure 1.2 Labour force participation rates in the Nordic countries, 1971-97

In the early 1970s participation rates were stable in the Nordic countries. A strong increase occurred from the time of the first oil price shock in all five countries lasting until the late 1980s. The increase occurred at two levels, with the highest level in Denmark and Sweden. The other three countries experienced a similar increase but at a common lower level. This trend definitely dampened the impact of unemployment on the distribution of incomes in Denmark and Finland in the period until 1990. In Norway and Sweden the most important effect was to reduce the proportion of people of labour market active age with little or no individual income.

The increase in participation rates was reversed from the late 1980s. In all the Nordic countries participation rates decrease until 1994/95 where they tend to stabilise. The most dramatic decline is observed in Sweden, with a drop of almost 5 per cent. Participation rates went down at the same time as unemployment went up dramatically in Finland and Sweden. This would *cet.par.* increase the low income shares in the affected countries. On the other hand, some of those people who leave the labour force or delay entry have entered labour market policy programmes where they are entitled to an income, but statistically are classified as being outside the labour force. There is, however, no doubt that part of the decline in the participation rates is real in the sense that a number of people no longer have a labour market related income but are being provided for by their family.

Income transfers from the public sector are, as already mentioned, an important factor dampening the impact of unemployment on disposable incomes in the households. This factor is obviously of major importance regarding the low income or poverty share. An indicator for this aspect in the period we study is found in Figure 1.3, showing total transfers to households relative to GDP. Overall, relative transfers increase from a level around 10-15 per cent to a level of 15-30 per cent at the end of the period. Note, that Figure 1.3 is only illustrative in the sense that it does not distinguish between the automatic reaction to a recession and the effects from changes in the individual transfer rates. In Sweden and Finland, transfer rates were reduced in the 1990s so that an automatic cyclical reaction with the initial rates maintained would have meant an even stronger increase in the transfer/GDP ratio.

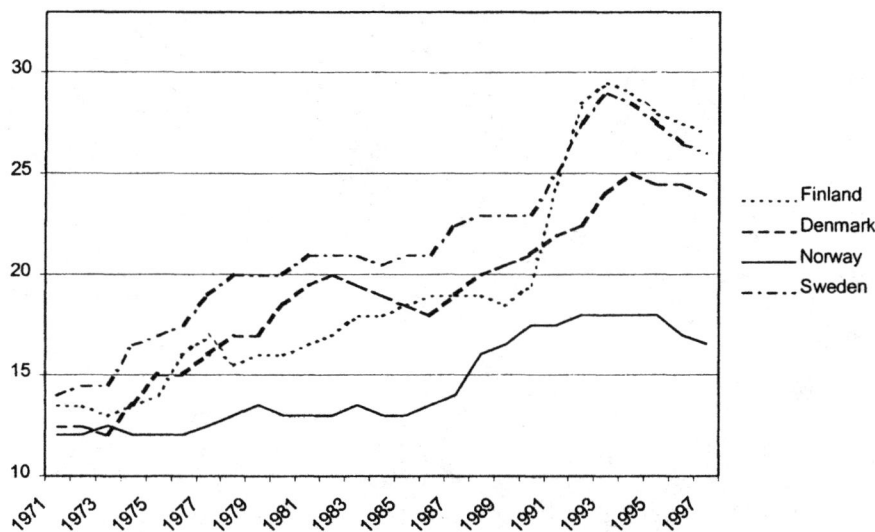

Figure 1.3 **Total transfers to households relative to GDP, 1971-97**

The income transfers shown in Figure 1.3 are the sum of expenditures in a big number of programmes, i.e. pensions, unemployment benefits, sickness benefits, child benefits, early retirement pensions, social welfare benefits and rent support. The national levels and profiles over time therefore reflect a mixture of cyclical reactions, political decisions and structural changes. There is an increasing trend in the transfer ratio in all the countries. Cyclical reactions to changes in unemployment are visible in

Denmark and Norway before 1990. In Finland and Sweden, the trend is dominant until the explosive increase in unemployment in 1990. Part of the development in Figure 1.3 is also indirectly related to unemployment. For instance, in the case of Denmark the increase in unemployment in the late 1970s motivated the introduction of a new programme for early retirement before the normal pension age. The programme was not rolled back when unemployment went down and in this way created a permanent increase in income going to those aged between 60 and 66. The impact is clearly visible in the low income share for this age group, cf. Chapter 2.

The counterpart of the strong increase in the transfer ratio is a need for higher revenues in the public sector. Figure 1.4 shows the development from 1971 to 1997 in the ratio between public sector revenue and GDP, i.e. a measure of the aggregate tax pressure in the economy.

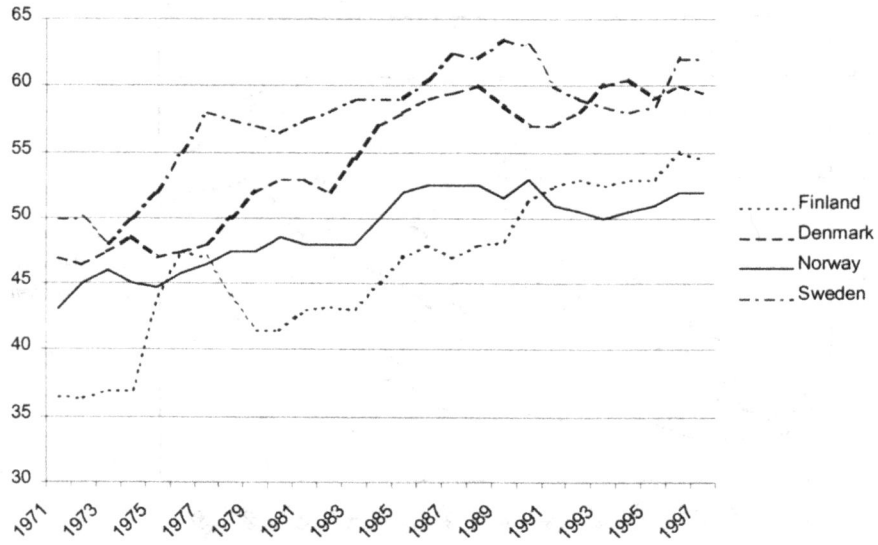

Figure 1.4   Public sector revenue relative to GDP, 1971-97

In Finland we observe a strongly increasing trend from a level of 35 per cent to a level of about 55 per cent. The initial level is much higher in the other three countries, where the overall tax ratio stabilises from the mid-1980s. The decline in Sweden in the early 1990s reflects the severity of the cyclical downturn, implying a fall in real GDP. Figures 1.3 and 1.4 combined signal potential long term problems in financing the welfare state with the implications this could have for the hitherto highly equal distribution of incomes and low poverty share in the Nordic countries.

1.3 Concepts and Measurement[2]

Opinions on how to conceptualise and measure poverty differ widely. Many problems are discussed in the literature. The aim of this section is to place the present study of poverty and low income in the Nordic countries into a wider frame and thereby illuminate some characteristics of the approach taken.

1.3.1 The framework

Poverty assessments start from micro-units which are aggregated to macro-units. Resources are assumed to be equally distributed within the micro-unit (households or families), but not outside it. In reality, the extent to which sharing between individuals occurs is not known. Thus we impose errors of two types when defining households or families as the unit for the assessment. Equal sharing within a specific unit might not be an appropriate assumption and resources might be shared between units.

Problems with defining the micro-unit in the available data are discussed in several of the country chapters. The assumption of equal sharing is critical when assessing the relation between gender and poverty. In the chapter on Sweden we report on an attempt to evaluate the standard assumption of equal sharing within a household. The conclusion resulting from questions posed to respondents is that equal sharing is a reasonable good first approximation which, however, is not applicable to all couples.

The definition of the relevant macro-unit is not always self-evident. Poverty assessments are often made to evaluate policies, and the macro unit can therefore be defined according to different purposes. For decisions about development aid the entire world is the adequate macro-unit, and thus it is reasonable to work with a world-wide poverty line as in the World Development Report. But for country-specific policies it makes sense to have a country-specific poverty line. From the Nordic perspective, country-specific poverty lines obviously represent a much higher standard of living in absolute terms than that used when assessing poverty from a global perspective.

The approach of using poverty lines which are specific for each of the five countries we study is not the only possibility when assessing poverty and low income in the Nordic countries. An alternative would be to apply the same poverty line for the entire territory of the Nordic countries.

---

[2] This section draws on Gustafsson (1995) which includes a number of references.

However, there is an important objection: even if a Nordic perspective is relevant in policy making, it is almost always subordinated to the national perspectives. In addition, for people living in Denmark, Finland and Sweden it would probably be equally relevant to view poverty from a EU perspective, and thus apply a common poverty line for all EU members.[3]

1.3.2 Defining a poverty line at one point in time

The definition of the poverty line is obviously central to any assessment of poverty. However, there are several issues to consider, and in this subsection we begin by discussing how a poverty line should be defined at a given point in time. The main issue is how to define a poverty line for a reference person and the choice of an equivalence scale.

The approaches in defining a poverty line at a point in time vary widely. It can be helpful to characterise various approaches of defining a poverty line using the terms 'endogenously determined poverty lines' and 'exogenously determined poverty lines'. The former are constructed from the analysed data only, the second need other sources. The biggest advantage of the first approach is that a poverty line can always be constructed just from the data. This might be the major reason why this approach has recently spread to studies of poverty in a single country and now seems also to dominate recent cross-country research. In the present book we follow this approach and define for each country the poverty line at 50 per cent of the median for equivalent disposable income.

A disadvantage with an endogenous poverty line is that its meaning is far from concrete. Therefore it can be of interest to use also exogenous poverty lines. In the chapter on Denmark there is a discussion on how the relative poverty line relates to minimum levels utilised in various programmes for income support. In the chapter on Norway the level of the minimum pension is used as an alternative poverty line. In Sweden there is something of a tradition of basing the poverty line on central recommendations regarding guidelines used when processing applications for social assistance in the municipalities. Therefore there are, in the Swedish chapter, also results derived from applying such an approach.

We have chosen to use the same equivalence scale for all the countries covered, thus assuming economies of scale to be the same in all Nordic countries. Although this assumption is very often used in international

---

[3] An additional argument for not using a common Nordic poverty line is based on measurement problems. There are problems with comparability across the data sets used for the various country studies as documented in Zamanian (1993). Also for this reason is a common Nordic poverty line difficult to determine.

comparisons, other approaches are possible. We have applied the equivalence scale used by the OECD in a number of publications. According to this, the needs of an adult living alone are set to 1.0 units. Each additional adult is set at 0.7 units and for each child 0.5 units are added. Assessments of who are considered poor will be affected by the equivalence scale used.

1.3.3 Updating the poverty line
The issue of how to update the poverty line has attracted relatively little attention in the literature although approaches differ widely. One alternative is to redefine the poverty line each time poverty is assessed. "Poverty" then becomes an aspect of the distribution of income. Another alternative applied, for example, when officially assessing poverty in the United States, is to update the poverty line according to how consumer prices have changed. This means that the poverty line represents a constant purchasing power.[4] In this sense "Poverty" is defined as an absolute concept. Time series based on the two alternatives can be expected to result in entirely different pictures of how poverty changes during periods of large changes in average income.

We have chosen to apply both approaches to update the poverty line for the various country chapters. For all countries we present series based on relative poverty lines which are redefined at each point of measurement. But in the chapters on the four larger Nordic countries we have also derived time series based on poverty lines representing a constant level of purchasing power.

1.3.4 Poverty index
Given data and a poverty line, it is easy to determine the number of households and individuals falling under the poverty line. But poverty can be represented in other ways too. There is the further issue of how poor the poor (on average) are and how poverty is distributed among the poor. A seminal paper, Sen (1976), was the starting point for many efforts to include aspects of poverty other than the proportion of poor measured by a summary poverty index.

We have chosen in all chapters concerning the larger Nordic countries to use the same indices which belong to a family suggested by Foster et al.(1984). This family of indices uses for each poor unit its normalised poverty gap, which is a number indicating how far below the poverty line income falls on a scale bounded by 0 and (in case of no negative incomes)

---

[4] Recently the method of defining the official poverty line in the United States has been evaluated by a group of scientists, cf. Citro and Michael, eds. (1995).

1. Those gaps are raised by a positive parameter before the average is taken. Higher values of the parameter give increasing weight to large poverty gaps, and thus indicate greater "poverty aversion". An advantage with this family of indices is that it is additively decomposable by population sub-groups. Thus total poverty can be interpreted as the weighted sum of poverty in mutually exclusive sub-groups. In the literature it has not yet been a common practice to estimate the sampling variance for the poverty estimates reported. The contributions in the chapter on Finland and Norway are innovative in this respect.

1.3.5 The duration of poverty

It is not self-evident over which period of time poverty should be measured, since the choice of period depends on the specific issue. It seems to be a common opinion that it makes sense to apply periods longer than one year. For example, analyses on a yearly basis typically show a disproportionate fraction of those below the poverty line being students, who during later periods have incomes considerably over the poverty line. This result appears as less alarming than one which shows old people to be poverty prone. Chronic poverty is generally perceived as a more serious problem than transitory poverty.

What can be said on the duration of poverty? An analysis of this question requires access to panel data in which individuals and households can be followed over time, and such data sets are scarce. Due to this, most studies on poverty dynamics in industrialised countries build on data from the United States. Studies of the dynamics of poverty give rise to new methodological issues. For example, the work by Bane and Ellwood (1986) shows the usefulness of defining the experience of poverty as spells of poverty, distinguishing between incidence and duration of a state with low income. Another insight is that although many people leave poverty, their exit is often not permanent (Stevens, 1994). In this book we are able to report studies of poverty dynamics in the chapters on Denmark, Norway and Sweden.

1.3.6 Assessing whether a household is poor or not

What should be considered when classifying a household as poor or non-poor? Opinions vary on this too. We follow an often-used strategy of using the disposable income of a household, and nothing else. However, as discussed in the chapter on Norway, the definition of disposable income is far from self evident. To focus only on disposable income can give misleading results. There are attempts to incorporate more aspects in the literature. There are efforts to consider, for example, the wealth position of the households, and to consider whether low income is an outcome of personal choice or not. However, we have chosen to consider only the disposable income of a household, as there is no generally approved method to include the other aspects. In addition, data availability limits what can be achieved in this respect.

References

Aaberge, R., Björklund, A., Jäntti, M., Pedersen, P.J., Smith, N. and T. Wennemo (1997). Unemployment shocks and income distribution. How did the Nordic countries fare during their crises? Statistics Norway. *Research Department. Discussion Paper No. 201.*

Asplund, R. Barth, E. Smith, N. and Wadensjö, E. (1996). The Male – Female Wage Gap in the Nordic Countries in Wadensjö, E. (Ed) *The Nordic Labour Markets in the 1990s,* North Holland, Amsterdam.

Atkinson, A., Rainwater, L. and Smeeding, T. (1995). Income Distribution in OECD Countries, Paris: *OECD, Social Policy Studies No 18.*

Bane, M.J. and Ellwood, D. (1986). Slipping Into and Out of Poverty: The Dynamics of Spells, *Journal of Human Resources, 21, 1 - 23.*

Calmfors, L. and Driffill, J. (1988). Bargaining structure, corporatism and OECD macroeconomic performance. *Economic Policy 6: 15-61.*

Citro, C. and Michael R. (eds) (1995). *Measuring Poverty. A New Approach,* Washington D.C. National Academy Press.

Eardley, T. et al (1996). Social Assistance in OECD Countries: Synthesis Report, London: *HMSO Department of Social Security Research Report No 46.*

Eurostat (1997). Income Distribution and Poverty in EU12 - 1993, *Statistics in Focus. Population and social conditions 6,* Luxembourg.

Foster, J., Greer, J. and Thorbecke, E. (1984). A Class of Decomposable Poverty Measures, *Econometrica, 52: 761 - 766.*

Gustafsson, B. (1995). Assessing Poverty – Some Reflections on the Literature, *Journal of Population Economics, 8, 361 - 381.*

Layard, R., S. Nickell and Jackman, R. (1991). *Unemployment. Macroeconomic performance and the labour market.* Oxford University Press.

Maddison, A. (1991). *Dynamic forces in capitalist development.* Oxford University Press.

OECD. (1993). *Employment Outlook.* Paris.

Sen, A. (1976). Poverty: An Ordinal Approach to Measurement, *Econometrica, 44, 219 - 231.*

Stevens, A.H. (1994). The Dynamics of Poverty Spells: Updating Bane and Ellwood, *American Economic Review, 84, 34 - 37.*

Vogel, J. (1997). Living Conditions and Inequality in the European Union 1997, *Eurostat, Working Papers. Population and social conditions E/1997-3.*

Wadensjö, E. (ed.) (1996). *The Nordic labour markets in the 1990s.* North Holland. Amsterdam.

Zamanian, M. (1993). Jämförande nordisk inkomststatistik II, Köbenhavn: Nordisk statistisk sekretariat, *Tekniske rapporter 58.*

2 Low Incomes in Denmark 1980-1995

PEDER J. PEDERSEN AND NINA SMITH

2.1 Introduction[1]

When compared internationally, incomes in Denmark are very equally distributed. Nevertheless, the rather few existing studies of poverty or low incomes have often aroused strong reactions, both from the politicians and from the social science community. One of the main objectives in the creation of the Danish welfare state throughout the last century has been an equalisation through redistribution of incomes and the prevention of poverty. It therefore follows that analyses of poverty or low income, depending on one's political standpoint, could be interpreted in two different ways: as an implicit attack or critique against those who built the welfare state for not having succeeded in one of the most important areas – or, alternatively, as a redundant scientific preoccupation with a non-existing problem, cf. Hansen (1989) and Abrahamson (1992). This is in strong contrast to the situations found in the other Nordic countries. Finland and Sweden in particular have seen many contributions in the field of low income and poverty during the 1980s, in spite of the fact that these countries did not experience the same problems of unemployment and marginalisation as did Denmark during this period.

Poverty or low income can be defined in many different ways. The Danish research tradition in this field has often differed from the approach chosen in the other Nordic countries because it has attempted to include aspects other than the strictly economic in the definition of poverty, cf. Halleröd et al. (1996) and Abrahamson (1992). Whether or not it is sufficient to rely on strictly economic variables in the definition of poverty must depend on the purpose of any specific analysis, cf. the comprehensive discussion of this problem by Hansen (1989) and Kangas and Ritakallio

---

[1] We are grateful for research assistance from Deniz Arikan and for comments on this and an earlier version of the paper from Erik J. Hansen and Björn Gustafsson and from participants at a seminar at the Aarhus School of Business and University of Gothenburg.

(1995). As an alternative to income, a number of studies have concentrated on consumption as the relevant concept in studies of poverty, cf. e.g. Jorgenson (1998). In the present analysis, poverty is defined only through economic criteria, i.e. defined with reference to low incomes in the household, using a number of alternative measures of income. This is partly determined by the limitations of the data. The consequence of this choice is that the interpretation of the results presented below is restricted to the purely economic concept of poverty. As a result, some households will be placed in the poverty/low income class even though they might be well functioning and have ample resources in other respects, while the opposite might be the case for some of the households classified as non-poor by the economic criterion. Therefore, we chose to use the concept "low income" or "economic poverty" in the following instead of the broader concept of poverty.

In the present study, we analyse the prevalence of low incomes in Denmark during the period from 1980 to 1995. The relatively few previous Danish studies have mostly been cross-sections for a single year. In contrast to this, we analyse a fairly long and turbulent period, including periods of strongly increasing and decreasing unemployment occurring around a fairly high average level of unemployment. We are thus able to follow how these cyclical changes have influenced the incidence of low income.

In Section 2 we survey briefly some earlier studies of low income in Denmark. Section 3 describes our data, while Section 4 discusses the methods used to delimit the concept of economic poverty. In Section 5 we survey the aggregate development in the low income share, while Section 6 goes into more detail concerning the development in the low income rate for different sub-groups in the population, i.e. by age, gender, family status and individual unemployment. Most of the study builds on the use of disposable equivalent income as the most relevant concept in the present context. In Section 7, however, we include a short description of the development when gross income is used as a supplement to the use of disposable income. Thereby we gain some indirect evidence on the importance of net taxes and tax rules for the profile of the low income share over time. In Section 8 we use the longitudinal structure of our data to explore whether low income is a predominantly short term problem experienced by many individuals or a long term problem mainly related to a small group of people. Finally, Section 9 provides a conclusion.

2.2 Some Earlier Danish Studies

As mentioned in the introduction, the extent of research into the prevalence of low income in Denmark is fairly restricted. Based on an initiative from the European Commission, the Danish National Institute for Social Research made a comprehensive study of poverty, (Friis (1981)), which showed that 13 per cent of the Danes were poor in 1977, when poverty was defined as having an income below 50 per cent of the average income in Denmark. For the member states of the European Economic Community – at that time – the average share of the population living in poverty was 12.6 per cent. Cross-country comparison of the distribution of income is fraught with difficulties, but it would hardly be controversial to claim that incomes in Denmark were more equally distributed at that time than on average in the rest of the Community countries. The finding of the same share of the population living in poverty was therefore controversial and caused a major debate concerning the relevance of the poverty line in the EU-study. It is evident from the following that results are quite sensitive to even minor changes in the definition of the poverty line.

In 1986 E.J. Hansen published a study on living conditions in Denmark. Based on a more restrictive concept of poverty, Hansen concluded that 3 to 4 per cent of the population between 29 and 79 years in the mid-1980s were poor by this criterion. In contrast to Friis (1981), E.J. Hansen used an absolute rather than a relative poverty line. An absolute poverty line in this sense is determined as an exogenous concept, i.e. one determined by factors outside the income distribution under study. The absolute poverty line in the study by Hansen (1986) was defined by a double criterion, i.e. the family gross income should be lower than 100,000 DKK per year and at the same time a person was classified as living in poverty if she or he had less than 1,000 DKK per month to provide for daily consumption.[2]

A more recent study by F.K. Hansen (1990) also applies an absolute poverty line on a cross-sectional data set. F.K. Hansen classifies a person as living in poverty if the available monthly amount for daily consumption is less than 1,000 DKK. In contrast to E.J. Hansen (1986) who uses the annual family gross income as the dominating criterion, F.K. Hansen applies only

---

[2] This study also caused strong critique and debate in Denmark. A group of Finnish and Swedish researchers in the field commented on the Danish discussion as follows: "This discussion can, in a Nordic perspective, be seen as typically Danish and is an example of the fact that the study of poverty has been much more politicised in Denmark than in the other Nordic countries", Halleröd et al. (1996).

the criterion related to monthly expenditure per person. The consequence is a much higher estimate, that 14 per cent of all Danish families live in poverty. F.K. Hansen uses survey data for 1988 and is able to combine the survey information with register data on income for the same individuals for the years 1982, 1984 and 1986. In this way, it is possible to study to what extent poverty is an enduring situation. An indicator of this was the finding that 4 per cent of the individuals in the survey had a disposable income under the lowest quartile of the distribution for all four years for which data were available.

According to the poverty studies by the European Commission (1994) 2.5 per cent of the Danish population was below a poverty line defined as 50 per cent of the average expenditure per individual in the households calculated on the basis of an equivalence scale. For each member country the European Commission used a poverty line defined as 50 per cent of the national average expenditures per individual. For the European Union as a whole it was found that 10 per cent were below the national poverty lines defined in this way.

The Ministry of Economic Affairs presented a study of economic poverty in 1993 using a poverty line set at 50 per cent of the median. This analysis was made for a representative sample using the OECD equivalence scale to correct for variations in the size of households. The main result was that 6.7 per cent of the families were below the poverty line in 1993. In sensitivity analyses it turned out that the share in economic poverty with the poverty line set at 40 and 60 per cent of the median was 4.4 and 9.8 per cent of the families respectively.

Summing up, the existing evidence on the prevalence of low income or economic poverty in Denmark presents a somewhat confusing picture. The estimates of the low income shares are based on cross-sections for a rather small number of years and the variability of the estimates reflects an unknown mixture of the impact from specific circumstances in the year of any given study and the use of different poverty lines. Below, the same kind of poverty line is applied to each year over a period of 16 years. Firstly, however, we will describe the data set used in the following sections.

2.3 Data

The present analysis is built on register data for individuals for the period 1980-1995. We use a longitudinal sample of 0.5 per cent of the Danish population aged between 18 and 75. The data we use is a sub-sample of the 5 per cent longitudinal sample at the Centre for Labour Market and Social

Research (CLS) at the University of Aarhus and the Aarhus School of Business. The data base is built from administrative registers in Statistics Denmark. They cover the whole country and as the same people are monitored during the whole period, the data are highly relevant for the present study of low incomes, as they make it possible to perform dynamic analyses, which is not usually the case in this area. The fact that data is built on administrative registers does, on the other hand, have some drawbacks. As discussed below, the household definition is not ideally suited for the present purpose and some components of transfer incomes which are relevant for the analysis are not captured by the registers. This problem is also discussed below.

A household is defined as consisting of one or two adults along with the number of children below the age of 18 living with one or both of their parents. If a household consists of two adults who are formally married, we have information on income and wealth for both. For people who are cohabiting without being legally married, the data do not include information on the income of a cohabiting partner outside the sample. We therefore have to treat these people as singles, i.e. we are forced to make the implicit assumption that two cohabiting partners have completely separate individual incomes and expenditure, which, of course, is unrealistic in most case.[3] Individuals who are 18 or above and who live with one or both of their parents are – due to data restrictions – treated as independent households, i.e. we have had to assume implicitly that their incomes and expenditure are completely separable from the rest of the family with whom the live.[4] This will tend to result in an upward bias in the estimate of the share of young people with low incomes, as a part of this group is still living at their parents' homes and is being fully or partially supported by their parents.[5] It is not possible to distinguish between

---

[3] However, if there are children in this type of household, we assume that the burden of supporting the children is split evenly between the two adults, see below.

[4] The definition of households used in the present study differs from the one used by the Ministry of Economic Affairs (1993). The data used by the Ministry made it possible to include people between 18 and 26 with their family if they lived at home, and to treat cohabiting couples in the same way as legally married couples.

[5] In 1990, 8.5 per cent of the households had adult children living at the parents' home. On the other hand, about 1200 households consisted of children younger (continued) than 18 who lived by themselves. Both numbers have been decreasing during the period we study.

children under 18 who live with their parents and those who live by themselves. Therefore, the sample is restricted to individuals who are 18 or above. Further, as the primary purpose of the data set we use is to analyse labour market problems, individuals who are 76 or above do not appear in the sample.

The sample contains information on a number of income variables, i.e. gross income, (subdivided into earnings and capital income), taxable income, unemployment insurance benefits, pensions and social assistance (bistandshjælp).[6] Based on these individual income data, the tax rules in each year have been applied to calculate taxes paid and child benefits. Finally, disposable income in the household is calculated as the difference between the sum of gross income and transfers and taxes paid.

Some of the cash transfers from the public sector are not covered by this data. This is true of housing benefits as well as a variety of individual benefits to pensioners. Benefits in this area are means-tested, but in such a complicated way, including criteria concerning the size and the gross rent of the apartment, and partly based on discretionary administrative decisions, that it is impossible to "reconstruct" by use of an algorithm. We are therefore forced to exclude them from the analysis below. The consequence of this is an underestimate of the consumption potential of households in the lower part of the income distribution, i.e. pensioners without supplementary capital income and households having social assistance as their main source of income. The estimates of the poverty or low income shares presented below are therefore biased upwards.

We use an equivalence scale to correct for differences in household size. The weights in the scale come from the equivalence scale used by the OECD, i.e. the first adult has the weight 1, the second 0.7 and each child has a weight of 0.5. The disposable income per equivalent individual in the household is calculated as household disposable income divided by the equivalence-scale-weighted number of individuals in the household.

As mentioned above, we do not know the income of the cohabiting partner of a person included in the sample, and, as a consequence, these people are treated in the analysis as households consisting of one adult plus the number of children. Typically, there will be two incomes in these

---

[6] The distinction between pensions and social assistance is not available in the primary data set. It is made using an algorithm modelling the main rules in the area.

households and the provision for any children will be shared between the partners. To avoid a downward bias in the estimate of disposable income per person in those households, we have chosen to apply half the normal weight, i.e. 0.25, to children in cohabitation households.

In the subsequent sections, the individual and not the household is the unit of analysis, while the household is the unit used to calculate disposable income per equivalent person.

2.4 The Poverty/Low Income Line

The available methods for drawing a poverty or low income line fall into two broad groups. Either they are based on some absolute measure of a poverty line, or they are based on a certain fractile in the distribution of incomes resulting in a relatively low income line valid at a specific point in time.[7]

When an absolute poverty line is used, the definition of the line is typically based on data on household expenditure budgets from which a minimum consumption expenditure is derived, defining the poverty line regarding disposable income. There are a number of technical and conceptual problems connected with the use of an absolute measure. On the technical side, it is necessary to have access to reliable expenditure data, updated at not too infrequent intervals. On the conceptual side, an element of subjectivity is unavoidable. A person or an institution has to decide which goods and services, and in which quantities, should be included in a minimum budget. Goods that were considered luxuries a generation ago tend to be necessities today. An example could be TV sets. In this way it becomes difficult to maintain that the poverty line is an immutable constant through time.

The alternative is to use a low income line defined relative to the current distribution of incomes, e.g. set at 50 per cent of the median income. This would solve the subjectivity problem mentioned above, as the low income line in this situation is generated from a distribution that is exogenous to the problem being studied. A relative measure, on the other hand, raises other conceptual problems, or problems related to the interpretation of the results. It could rightfully be claimed that the result is not necessarily evidence of the extent of economic poverty, but simply a reflection of the variance in the income distribution. In this sense, what we measure is inequality, which

---

[7] More detailed discussions of this issue can be found in Barr (1993) and Gustafsson (1995).

is different from poverty in the traditional meaning of the term. Even in the most affluent country, part of the population would be classified as "poor", insofar as there are people who fall below 50 per cent of the median.

In the present analysis the choice has been to use a primarily relative poverty/low income line, i.e. 50 per cent of the median income at any given time with the restrictions implicit in this choice. To give a perspective on the use of this measure, a number of sensitivity analyses are presented showing the results of varying the 50 per cent limit. Furthermore, we present the results from calculations using alternative absolute measures of low income. The choice of an absolute low income line is difficult, as no explicit estimates of minimum budgets are available for Denmark. As implicit measures, one could use the level of social assistance to a person living alone or the base level of the national old age pension.

Neither of these measures is without problems, however, cf. Table 2.A.1 in the Appendix, as the base level of social welfare is regulated in discrete jumps reflecting political decisions in this area. Furthermore, until the mid-1980s social welfare was, in principle, discretionary at the individual level, with decisions being made by the local social administrations in each case. Therefore, it is problematic to use the term "base level" for this period. The amounts shown in Table 2.A.1 are the upper limit effective after receipt of discretionary individual benefits for a nine-month period until the mid-1980s. During the period under study there are also a number of changes of the rules concerning housing benefits, which further complicate the use of the base level social assistance as a low income line.

The development of the base level of the national old age pension is more stable, although not very gradual from year to year. Due to the problems inherent in these two measures, we have chosen to use a third – and partly absolute – measure for the low income line, i.e. an average of 50 per cent of the median income in each of the years from 1979 to 1995, measured in each of the respective year's prices. The specific procedure is as follows. First, the median income in each year is deflated to 1979 prices using the consumer price index. Next, the average for the whole period of the annual median incomes is calculated in 1979 prices. Finally, this overall fixed price average is re-calculated for each year in current prices using the consumer price index. The advantage of using this measure is that it is insensitive to temporary fluctuations in total income and in the variance in the distribution of incomes. Fundamentally, the measure is derived from the data, but the calculation results in an "absolute" low income line that is reasonably independent of data in the individual years.

2.5 The Low Income Share in Denmark 1980-1995

On average, the unemployment level has been high throughout the period under study in the present analysis. There have, however, been strong cyclical movements in unemployment and employment. Two big recessions occurred, the first lasting until 1983 and the second lasting from 1987 to 1993. Between 1983 and 1987, the Danish economy experienced an extremely high increase in employment, especially in the private sector. Since 1993, there has again been a strong cyclical upswing in the economy, of which only the first phase is covered by the data used here.[8]

Our prior expectation was that a long period with average unemployment at a high level would result in an increasing share of the population belonging to the low income group. This should especially be the case if the low income line is the absolute measure discussed above. The low income or poverty lines using both the relative measure and the absolute measure are shown in Table 2.A.1 in the Appendix, where the main difference between the two low income lines appears in the very last years of the period, with a somewhat stronger increase in the relative low income line.

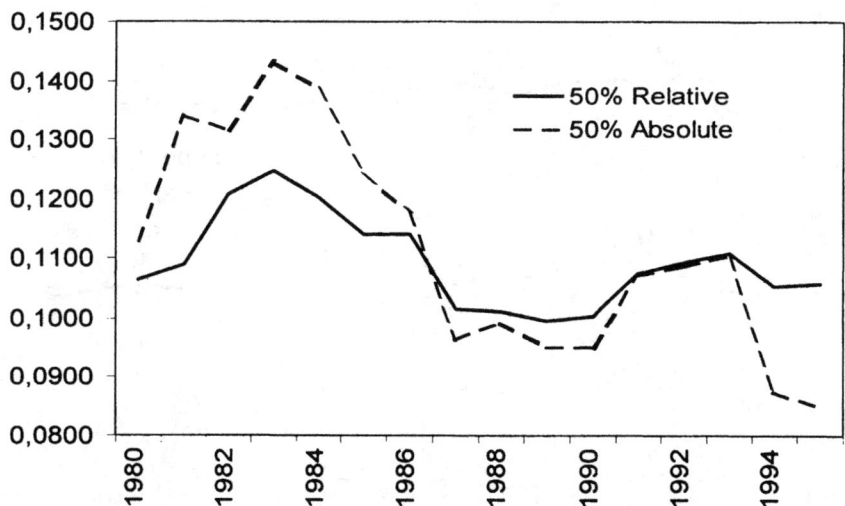

Figure 2.1 The share of the population aged 18-75 with low income in Denmark, 1980-1995. Relative and absolute low income lines

---

[8] Our data set builds on information from administrative registers and the tax registers are completed for a specific year with a lag of two years.

Figure 2.1 shows the development in the low income share for the population in the age group 18 to 75 using both the relative and the absolute low income lines. Looking first at the results using the relative measure, we find a quite small variation between a high of 12.5 per cent in 1983 and a low of 10.0 per cent in 1989. Contrary to prior expectations, the trend in the share does not increase.

There is a certain reflection of the cyclical variations, with a declining share in the boom years in the mid-1980s, an increase in the early 1980s recession and a somewhat smaller increase in the early 1990s recession. It is interesting to note that both the level of and the increase in unemployment is higher in the early 1990s than in the early 1980s. In spite of this, the low income share is lower and the increase is smaller during the later of the two recessions.

The use of the absolute low income line results, as expected, in a stronger decline in the low income share from a high of 14.3 per cent in 1983 to a low of 8.5 per cent in 1995. Thus, the use of the absolute low income line results in much stronger cyclical variations in the low income share. In the following, however, we will use the relative low income line, defined as 50 per cent of the contemporary median of disposable income per equivalence-weighted person in the households.

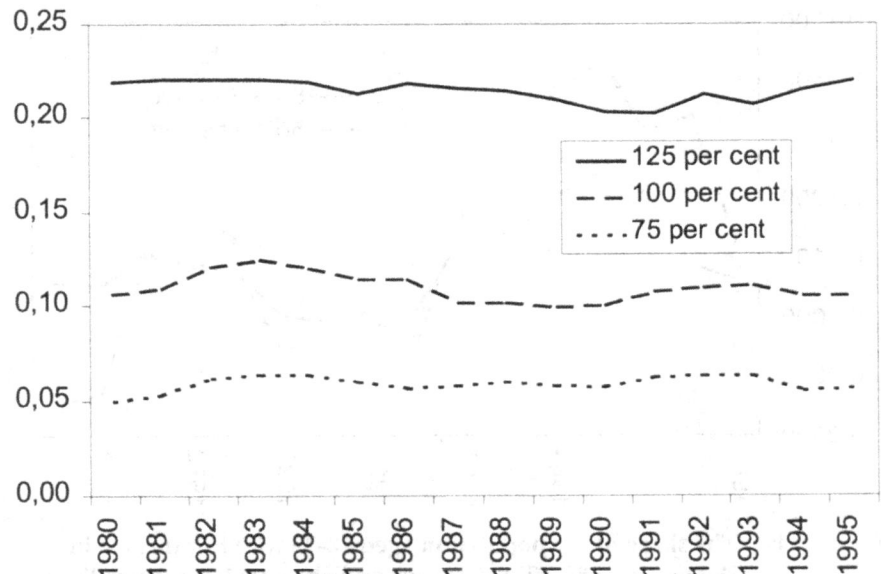

Figure 2.2 The share of the population aged 18-75 with low income using alternative low income lines 25 per cent above and below 50 per cent of the median income

To evaluate the sensitivity of the low income share relative to the somewhat arbitrary choice of cut off point at 50 per cent of the median income, we show, in Figure 2.2, the low income shares if the cut off point is increased or decreased by 25 per cent, i.e. Figure 2.2 shows the low income shares using low income lines set at 75 per cent, 100 per cent and 125 per cent of half the median income.

A reduction of the low income line results in the finding that 5 to 6 per cent of the population have disposable incomes below this level. On the other hand, we find about 10 to 12 per cent of the population with incomes between 50 per cent of the median and a cut off point 25 per cent above this level. In 1995, 5.7 per cent had incomes below 75 per cent of the main low income line, 10.6 per cent were below the line and 22.0 per cent had incomes below a level of 125 per cent of the main low income line.

Calculations of the share of people below a certain low income line do not provide clear information about the distribution of the lowest incomes in the economy. Therefore, calculations of low income shares are usually supplemented with a poverty or low income index which includes information about that part of the income distribution below the low income line. The index which is probably most widely used is the Foster-Greer-Thorbecke index (Foster et al., 1984)

$$P_\alpha = \frac{1}{n} \Sigma (\frac{z-y_i}{z})^\alpha$$

where n is the number of people in the population, z is the low income line and y_i is the disposable income for person i and the summation is taken from all observations with $y_i < z$. The parameter α indicates the weighting of low incomes in the index. The greater the value of α, the greater the emphasis put on low incomes. For an α set at 0, the index P_0 is the share of the population below the low income line shown in Figures 1 and 2. For an α set at 1, the index P_1 measures the average gap between the low income line and the actual income for people in the low income group, i.e. it indicates how far the low incomes in the distribution fall below the line. More precisely, we have $P_1 = P_0(1 - M(z)/z)$, where $M(z)$ is the average income for people below the low income line and the expression in parentheses measures the poverty or low income gap. Finally, values of α above 1, e.g. $\alpha = 2$, result in an index P_2, where the gap between individual incomes and the low income line is squared, thereby emphasising the very low incomes in the distribution. The results from the calculations of the three indices are shown in Figure 2.3, with the initial value of each index set at 100 in 1980.

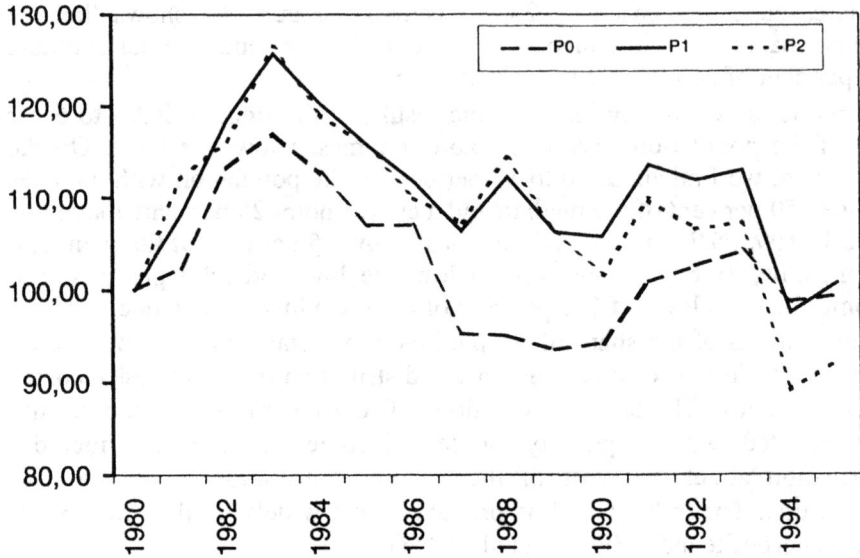

Figure 2.3 The development in alternative poverty indices 1980=100

As mentioned, the index P_0 is the same as that shown in Figures 1 and 2. P_1, measuring the poverty gap, lies above P_0 in all the years since 1980, except for the two latest years of the cyclical upswing in the 1990s, where both indices return to the initial level. The low income share and the low income gap show the same cyclical patterns. It is interesting to note that P_2, which gives more weight to the very low incomes, shows the strongest decline from a high in 1983 to a low in 1994 and with a terminal level below the initial level in 1980.

2.6 Low Income Groups in Denmark

The purpose of this section is to investigate the composition of the low income group. Who are the main subgroups? It could be primarily students or the unemployed, women, single mothers or pensioners. If the low income group is dominated by students or pensioners, then the problem regarding low incomes is different from that in which low incomes are primarily a phenomenon among people in the most labour-market-relevant age groups (which, at the same time, covers the majority of households with dependent children). For students and other young people involved in education, low income will typically be a temporary state, followed by an above average income.

In Table 2.1 we show the low income share in a number of occupational groups for selected years. The self-employed have a slightly falling share with low incomes during the 1980s, while the share goes up in the 1990s, at the same time as the number of the self employed and assisting spouses in the sample goes down. Note, however, that the recording of incomes is more uncertain and the cyclical sensitivity is higher for this group than among wage and salary earners. For the three groups of wage and salary earners with the most stable attachment to the labour market, the low income shares are very small and, except for skilled workers, decline through the 1980s. The falling share for unskilled workers may reflect that this group includes many women and the part-time share of women has been decreasing since the early 1980s. The cyclical upswing between 1990 and 1995 is reflected in a further decrease in the low income share among salaried employees and skilled workers. The group of "Other wage earners" with a looser attachment to the labour market has a higher and increasing share during the 1980s. The decrease between 1990 and 1995 is presumably a reflection of the cyclical upswing.

Table 2.1　Low Income Shares by Occupational Status (per cent)

	Self employed	Salaried employees	Skilled workers	Unskilled workers	Other wage earners	Pensioners	Others	Students
1980	5.48	1.86	1.20	4.11	11.74	16.73	28.48	88.35
1985	4.49	1.95	1.31	3.45	12.02	17.77	25.10	86.71
1990	4.50	1.81	2.81	3.08	14.18	5.60	41.26	81.94
1995	8.96	1.31	2.21	3.15	10.92	6.11	33.02	78.73

The group "Pensioners" consists mainly of people who have taken early retirement with a public pension to which they are eligible for social or health reasons, people in a labour market related early retirement program, and people aged 67 to 75 receiving the national old age pension, under which everybody is eligible for a base amount.[9] The changes have been most pronounced for pensioners, with a decline to nearly one third of the initial level in the low income group in 1980. The low income share is high

---

[9] Except for individuals who are employed as wage earners after the age of 67.

in the residual occupational group "Others", which includes long term recipients of social assistance. The terminal level is still high for this group in 1995. The vast majority of students are expected to be only temporarily in a low income state.

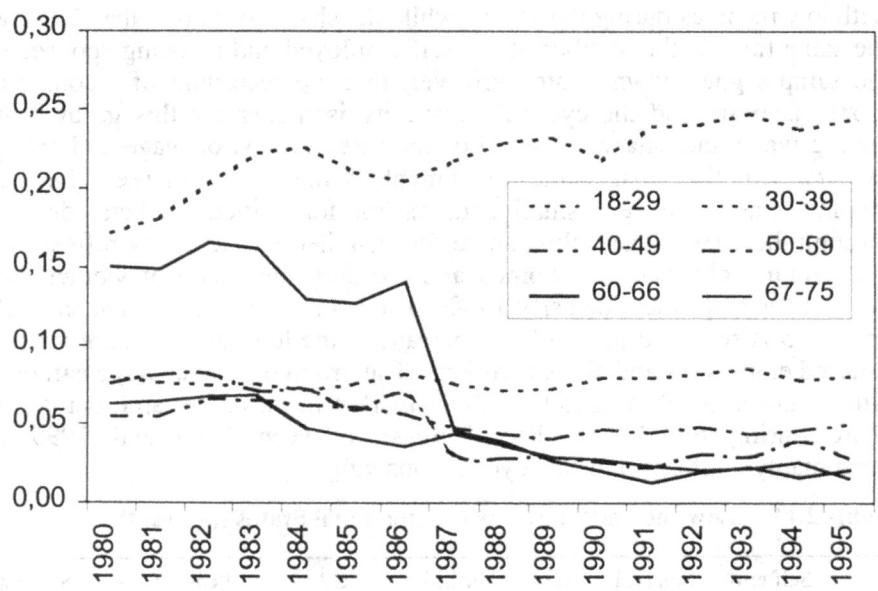

Figure 2.4   The share in the low income group by age, 1980-1995

In Figure 2.4 we show the shares in the low income group for different age groups. In 1995, the low income share is below 10 per cent for all age groups over 30, and the share falls as we move up through the age groups. Throughout the period, the low income shares have been nearly constant for people between 30 and 49. In contrast, there is a rising trend in the low income share from 17 per cent to 24 per cent in 1995 for the youngest age group. The development for this group reflects, among other things, an increasing propensity to stay longer in the educational system, cf. the result for students in Table 2.1. Thus, it cannot be interpreted directly as a deterioration of the position of this age group in terms of the long-run distribution of factor incomes.

For the age group above 50, the share in the low income group declined dramatically during the period, ending at a level of about 2 per cent, i.e. the low income problem was almost negligible in 1995. The decline is most spectacular in the age group between 60 and 66.[10] The falling trend is related to changes in labour market and social policy during the period. The existence of a labour-market-related early retirement programme since 1979, the reforms of early retirement pensions for social or health reasons in the mid-1980s, and the *de facto* unlimited duration of fairly generous unemployment benefits until the early 1990s have implied that many people in this age group have improved their income position significantly. In particular, many married women in this age group who - at an earlier date - would have left the labour market without an income, have instead become eligible for an income from one of the early retirement programmes.

In the oldest age group, 67 to 75, practically nobody falls into the low income group in 1995. The improved position during the period is related to a number of factors. The ratio of the national old age pension to the average income from work has increased. At the same time, there has been an increasing trend in private pensions, to which an increasing number of people from the age of 67 are eligible. The increasing importance of private pensions has had a similar effect on disposable incomes for the 60 to 66 year olds.

As in many other countries, the proportion of women in the low income group is higher than the proportion of men, cf. Table 2.2. Part of this difference might, however, relate to the problems regarding the definition of households, cf. the above discussion. Some of the women on low income may cohabit with non-poor men, and the impact of this might not be fully captured by the procedure we use to counter this problem.

For men, the low income share has been nearly constant during the period. For women, the share declined during the 1980s, but this decline came to an end during the first half of the 1990s. The falling female share during the 1980s occurred in spite of the fact that female unemployment went up relative to that of males in this decade. Part of the explanation of this pattern could be that female participation was still increasing, and that the part-time frequency had declined since 1982. Finally, the strong decline in the number of pensioners in the low income group had the highest impact on women, who form a majority of the older part of the population. Part of the explanation for the increase in the female low income share

---

[10] However, the drop between 1986 and 1987 may be exaggerated because we are not able to include the tax effect of all of the special tax rules favouring people in these age groups. Thus, the poverty rate for these age groups may be overvalued before 1987.

from 1990 to 1995 might be the introduction of leave schemes compensated with benefits which are typically lower than the unemployment insurance benefits and mainly used by women, see Pedersen and Pedersen (1998).

Table 2.2   The Relative Share in Low Income by Gender and Region (per cent)

	Men	Women	Copenhagen	Provinces
1980	8.92	12.36	10.50	10.73
1985	9.19	13.63	12.85	10.61
1990	8.92	11.18	10.80	9.63
1995	9.06	12.11	10.81	10.45

During the 1980s a shift occurred in the low income shares inside and outside the Copenhagen metropolitan area. The low income share was marginally lower in Copenhagen than outside in 1980. However, the cyclical boom in the mid-1980s had its primary impact outside Copenhagen. Since then, the low income share returned to the initial level in Copenhagen, and by 1995 the share was marginally lower outside.

One group that is usually expected to have a high share with low income is that of single parents, of which the great majority are mothers. Their situation is shown in Figure 2.5, along with the situation for a number of other household types. For the group of single parents with 1 or 2 children, the low income share has increased through the period, from about 25 per cent to about 30 per cent. There are few single parents with 3 or more children in the sample. The low income share for this group was in the interval from 67 to 94 per cent in the period, with the average level being higher in the 1990s (87 per cent) than in the 1980s (79 per cent). For this group, we should emphasise the upwards bias in the low income share due to the unavailability of information on rent support, which is especially important for this group. For married and cohabiting couples with children, the low income share in 1995 was 5.8 per cent for those with 1 or 2 children and 20.2 per cent for those with 3 or more children. For both groups, the shares increased during the 1990s. The increase was small for households with 1 or 2 children, but significant for those with 3 or more children. For married and cohabiting couples without children, the low income share is close to the level of married and cohabiting couples with 1 or 2 children.

Another traditional explanation of why people can enter the low income group is unemployment. The Danish unemployment insurance system

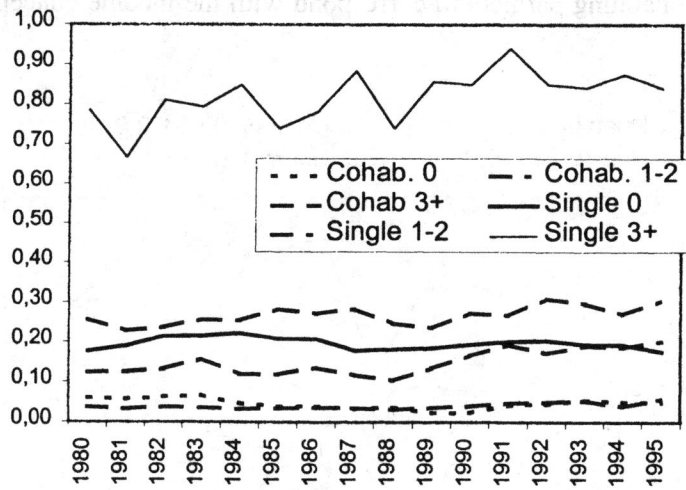

Figure 2.5 Share in the low income group by different household types regarding marital status and number of children, 1980-1995

offers comprehensive coverage. About 80 per cent of the labour force are members of insurance funds, and the benefits are 90 per cent of previous earnings up to a maximum amount which is, however, significantly below the average earnings of an unskilled worker. Those unemployed who are not eligible for unemployment insurance benefits, and who are without alternative means to provide for themselves, are eligible for social assistance.[11] The nominal maximum amount of unemployment benefits was kept constant from 1982 to 1987. In combination with the high level of unemployment, the prior expectation would be that an increasing share of the people found in the low income group were people receiving either unemployment insurance benefits or social assistance. To cast light on this matter, Figure 2.6 shows the low income shares depending on what is called the "degree of individual unemployment", i.e. the part of the year spent unemployed. The figure covers individuals who are members of an unemployment insurance fund and individuals who receive social

---

[11] The level of permanent social assistance, i.e. benefits after 9 months duration, is shown in Table 2.A.1 in the Appendix.

assistance due to unemployment, but not those who receive assistance for other reasons. Unemployment is measured as the individual degree of unemployment for people living alone and as average unemployment for two married or cohabiting partners to correspond with the income concept we have adopted.

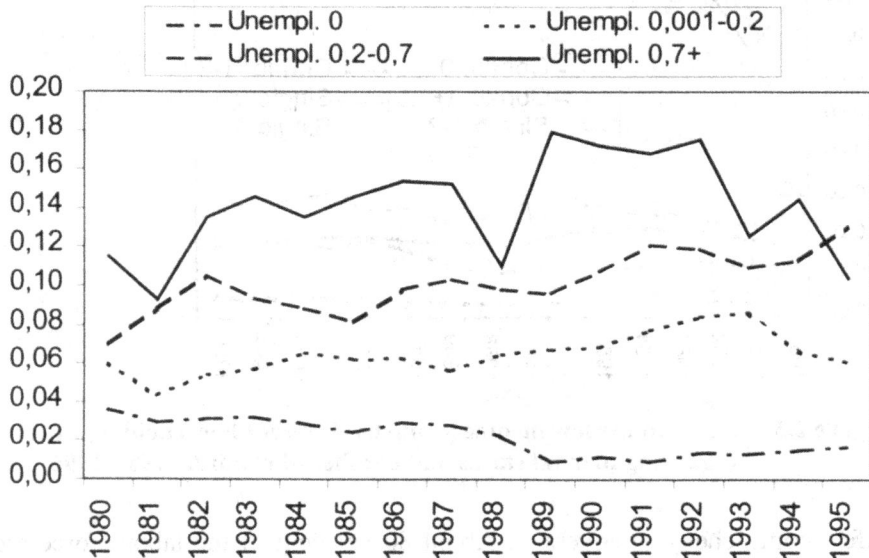

Figure 2.6 Low income shares distributed by average annual degree of unemployment

Figure 2.6 shows clearly how unemployment increases the risk of falling into the low income group. For people with periods of unemployment, and the more so the longer the unemployment, the low income risk increased throughout the period until the cyclical upswing from 1993/94. People without periods of unemployment, including married and cohabiting people where neither of the partners experience unemployment, show a quite different profile, with a decline in the low income risk to about 2 per cent in the late 1980s. The decline for this group is probably related to the increase in female participation and to the decrease in female part time work being replaced by full time work – and thus eligibility for full time unemployment insurance benefits. In 1995 the low income risk was three times higher for the group with short term unemployment than for the group who did not experience unemployment, while it was seven times higher for those unemployed for more than 20 per cent of the year. Looking at the whole period from 1980 to 1995, the "winners" are those without unemployment, where the low income risk declines to half the initial level. The "losers" on the other hand are the group with intermediate unemployment, 20 to 70 per cent of the year, where the low income risk doubles over the period. For the short and the long term unemployed the respective risks in 1995 are at the same level as initially. The relationship between unemployment and low income risk is analysed further below where we report the results of a number of Logit estimations relating the low income risk to individual (and couple related) background factors.

2.7 Redistribution through Income Taxes

The central concept in the present analysis is disposable income on a household basis converted to the individual level by using an equivalence scale. In this section we digress briefly to assess the extent of the redistribution occurring through the income tax system. Personal income tax is the main generator of public sector revenue in Denmark and for that reason too, we find it relevant to consider the sensitivity of the low income share to the use of a gross income concept instead of the disposable income concept used until now. The gross income concept includes market incomes before tax, i.e. wages and salaries and income from independent business, along with pensions and unemployment insurance benefits and imputed social assistance.[12]

Figure 2.7 shows the low income shares in relation to disposable income and gross income respectively, with the low income line set at 50 per cent of the median disposable and gross income respectively.

The low income share relative to gross income was fairly stable at 18 to 20 per cent until 1994. The very strong decline in 1994 reflects a major tax reform where a number of previously tax free benefits were made taxable and increased at the same time to maintain their after tax value on average, cf. the note at the beginning of this section. As these benefits are mainly targeted at people with low incomes, the obvious effect is a decline in the low income share relative to gross income. The gap between the two curves reflects a mixture of the equalising impact of progressive taxation,

---

[12] Unemployment benefits and the major part of pension incomes are taxable in Denmark. In-kind welfare benefits are not registered. Cash benefits are imputed to individuals using an algorithm simulating the rules in this area. Cash benefits were only partly taxed until the tax reform in 1994. Part of the reform was an increase in cash benefits, which were then made taxable along with other personal incomes.

differences in the cyclical impact on the two income distributions and finally changes in tax laws as illustrated most dramatically by the 1994 incident. The gap jumps to a higher level in the years after 1987 reflecting both another tax reform enacted in 1987 and, presumably, the impact from the long recession between 1987 and 1993, which most probably had a greater impact on the low income risk relative to gross income than to disposable income.

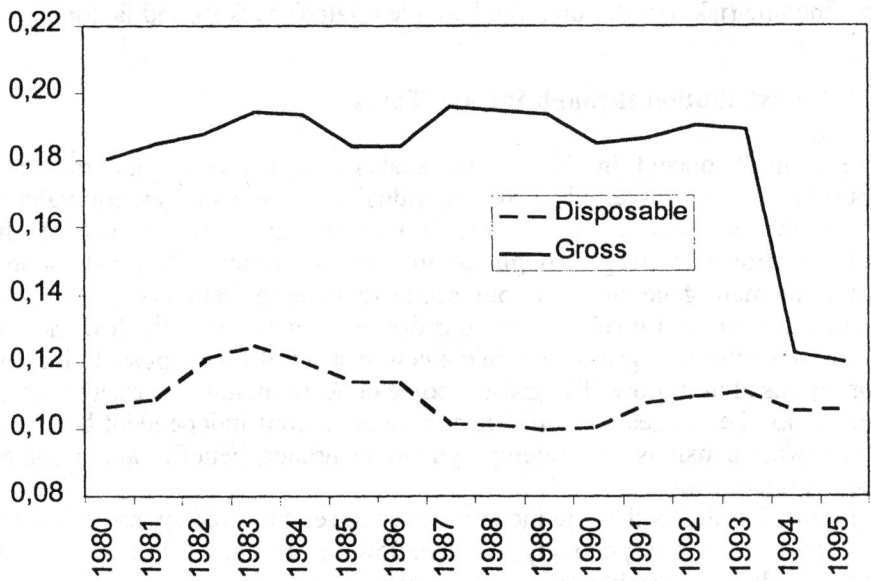

Figure 2.7 The share of individuals below 50 per cent of the median gross income and 50 per cent of the median disposable income, 1980-1995

2.8 Is Low Income Status Permanent?

The duration of spells of poverty or low income is an important element in discussions of the severity of the poverty or low income problem. The problem appears less severe if mobility out of the state with low income is high, and especially if the problem mainly occurs at an early stage of the lifecycle before people have to provide for children. In relation to economic and social policy this situation is very much different from a case where poverty or low income is restricted to a small group with a low exit rate to better income prospects.

The possibility of studying these questions based on a panel of individuals followed during a rather long period was used by Ingerslev (1990) in a study based on Danish register data. A 10 per cent sample of the population was followed in the years 1981 to 1987. The income concept used in the study was disposable income adjusted with the OECD equivalence scale. The main purpose of Ingerslev (1990) was to study the development in the disposable real income for a number of typical families. The low income line was set at a disposable income equal to the lower quartile in the distribution. Concerning duration, one result of Ingerslev was the finding that 7 per cent of the population had a disposable income below this line in each of the years between 1981 and 1987.

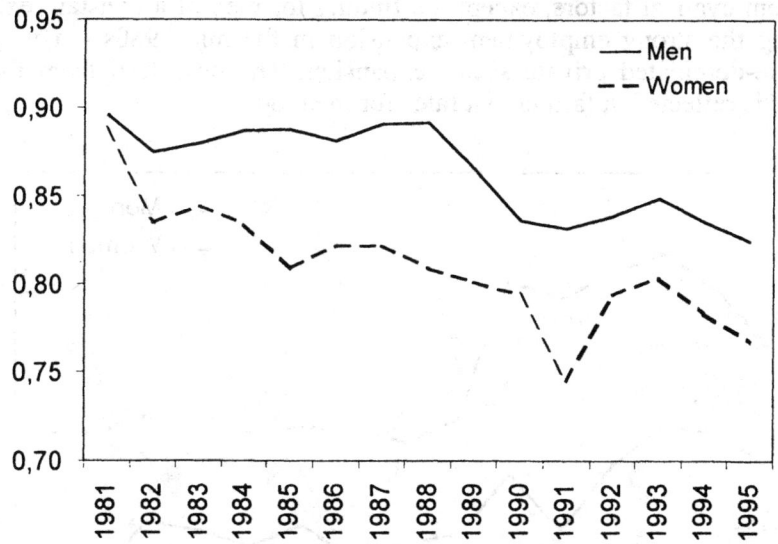

Figure 2.8 The annual exit rate from low income for women and men, 1981-1995

The sample used in the present study is also a panel, so we have the possibility of studying the mobility to and from a state of low income with the year as the time unit. In Figures 2.8 and 2.9 this has been illustrated for the period 1980 to 1995 for the whole sample for women and men separately. The annual exit rate shown in Figure 2.8 is calculated as the number of people leaving the low income group between year t-1 and t relative to the number of people with low income in year t-1. The annual entry rate in Figure 2.9 is calculated in the same way as the flow of people entering low income relative to the number of people with incomes above the low income line in the preceding year.

The annual exit rate follows a falling trend during the period with a level around 0.8 to 0.9. A stationary exit rate of 0.8 would imply that the average duration of a spell of low income would be around 1/0.8, i.e. 1.25 years - a person experiencing low income in the sense defined here would, on average, leave the state again after 15 months. Throughout the period we find a lower exit rate for women, and the nearly unbroken decline in the female exit rate results in women having an exit rate which is about 5 percentage points lower than men at the end of the period - or rephrased in expected durations, women would on average spend a couple of months more in the low income state than men. There is not much evidence of any impact from cyclical factors, except the finding for men of a constant exit rate during the strong employment expansion in the mid-1980s - a very much male-dominated private sector expansion. The downturn from the late 1980s is reflected in falling exit rates for men too.

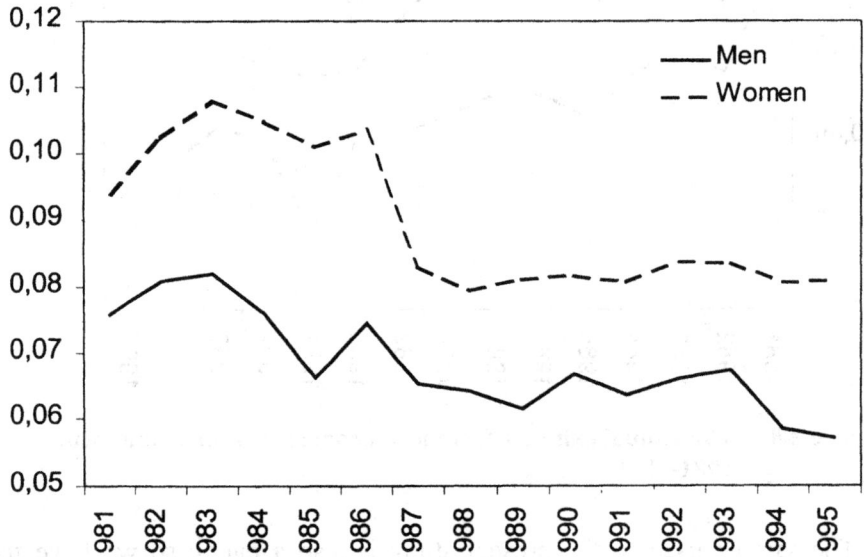

Figure 2.9 The annual entry rate to low income for women and men, 1981-1995

Concerning the entry rates in Figure 2.9, we find the reverse pattern regarding gender, i.e. the entry rate for men is consistently lower than for women. The general impression from Figure 2.9 is a decline to a lower level for the entry rate in the mid-1980s, more pronounced for women than for men, but only small signs of cyclical sensitivity since then.

The overall conclusion from Figure 2.1 was that the aggregate low income share was cyclically sensitive, but stationary over the 15 years from 1980 to 1995. Based on the findings in Figures 2.9 and 2.10 we find that this stationarity is the outcome of a more complex dynamic situation. The falling exit rate tends to increase the duration of spells with low income. At the same time, however, the entry rate to, or incidence of, low income has also been declining and the net outcome is the overall stationarity of the share of the population living in a low income state. In policy setting, stationarity resulting from stationary entry and exit rates is different from the finding of stationarity as the net result of declining exit and entry rates to low income.

To analyse this problem more deeply, we proceed to report results from a number of Logit estimations made annually where the low income risk is related to a number of background factors. The purpose is twofold, both to analyse the separate influence from the background factors reported partially in Section 6, and to study the possible changes in the impact of unemployment in particular over time.

The Logit estimations are reported separately for labour market participants and non-participants. The motivation for this distinction is to enable us to study the impact of unemployment, which is registered only for labour market participants. Furthermore, the distinction is relevant in relation to the discussion in the literature of the eventual occurrence and size of a group of "working poor". The distinction between participation and non-participation is made annually by Statistics Denmark based on criteria regarding the composition of income as between income from work or work related income transfers relative to income from non-work related transfers.

Table 2.3 reports the results from a Logit estimation for the year 1995. The dependent variable is the individual status relative to the low income group, with the value set at 1 if the individual income, adjusted with the equivalence scale, is below the low income line, and set at 0 otherwise. The explanatory variables are as follows:

Lagpoor	Dummy variable set at 1 if the person was in the low income group in the preceding year
Woman	Dummy variable set at 1 for women
Couple	Dummy variable set at 1 if the person is married or cohabiting
Dchild1	Dummy variable set at 1 if the person has one child
Dchild2	Dummy variable set at 1 if the person has 2 children

Dchild3   Dummy variable set at 1 if the person has 3 or more children
Unempl   Average degree of unemployment in the household, annual variation between 0 and 1000, with unemployment during the whole year set at 1000
Educat   Education measured in years
DA12   Dummy variable set at 1 for self-employed and assisting spouses
DA4   Dummy variable set at 1 for skilled workers
DA56   Dummy variable set at 1 for unskilled workers and residual group of "other wage earners"
DA3   Salaried employees, excluded group
D36-45   Dummy variable set at 1 for age 36-45
D46-55   Dummy variable set at 1 for age 46-55
D56-65   Dummy variable set at 1 for age 56-65
D26-35   Age 26-35, excluded group

Results are shown in Table 2.3 for the whole group and also separately for women and men. The Logit estimations have been made for each of the years 1980 to 1995. We comment on the results for the years prior to 1995 below. The results in Table 2.3 refer only to labour market participants in the core age group 26-59, because the variable measuring individual unemployment is only relevant for individuals in the labour force. We report below the results from corresponding Logit estimations for the group of non-participants in the broad age group 18 to 75.

For participants in the core age groups in 1995 we find no impact on the low income risk from the lagged status relative to the low income line, and we find no gender difference in the low income risk. Being married or co-habiting has a significant dampening impact on the risk, more pronounced for women than for men. The low income risk increases with the number of children, and here too is most pronounced for women. Unemployment has a significant positive coefficient, implying a higher low income risk the higher the average unemployment is in the household. Also here, the risk at a given level of household unemployment is higher for women.

The low income risk is lower for women the higher their level of education is, while no impact is found for men. Compared with the excluded group of salaried employees, the self-employed and assisting spouses have a higher risk, while skilled workers have a lower risk. Workers who are 46 or older tend to have a lower risk than people in the excluded age group 26-35.

It was mentioned earlier that unemployment insurance benefits were fixed in nominal terms and thus declines in real terms between 1982 and 1987. It is of interest, then, to examine whether this is reflected in any way

Table 2.3 Logit Estimation of the Individual Low Income Risk, Labour Market Participants, 26-59 Years, 1995

	All		Women		Men	
Variable	Coeff.	St. dev.	Coeff.	St. dev.	Coeff.	St. dev.
Constant	-3.162*	0.546	-2.993*	0.856	-3.572*	0.756
Lagpoor	-0.246	0.266	0.0761	0.351	-0.698	0.478
Woman	0.258	0.168	–	–	–	–
Couple	-2.243*	0.209	-2.510*	0.258	-1.129*	0.365
Dchild1	1.672*	0.273	2.087*	0.448	0.631	0.430
Dchild2	2.904*	0.269	3.590*	0.445	1.390*	0.408
Dchild3	4.442*	0.301	4.993*	0.504	3.340*	0.402
Unempl	2.310*	0.277	3.074*	0.397	1.532*	0.455
Educat	-0.089*	0.036	-0.127*	0.056	-0.043	0.050
DA12	1.897*	0.216	1.257*	0.376	2.231*	0.314
DA4	-0.882*	0.449	0.182	0.631	-1.510*	0.757
DA56	0.353	0.202	0.293	0.263	0.462	0.348
D36-45	-0.684*	0.175	-0.354	0.229	-1.124*	0.297
D46-55	-0.511*	0.235	-1.241*	0.499	-0.335	0.293
D56-65	-0.799	0.503	-13.020	343.7	-0.529	0.533
No. of obs.	6,888		3,214		3,674	
-2logL	1384		659		665	
P0	86.7 per cent		90.7 per cent		85.1 per cent	
P1	11.9 per cent		8.1 per cent		13.3 per cent	

Note: Significance at a 5 per cent level is indicated by *.

in the annual estimates of the coefficient to unemployment. This is done in

Figure 2.10, which shows the significant coefficients to unemployment in the year and gender specific estimations for women and men.

For women, the profile is fairly clear, with predominantly significant positive coefficients to unemployment at a higher level in the latter part of the period. For men, the coefficients are significantly positive from the late

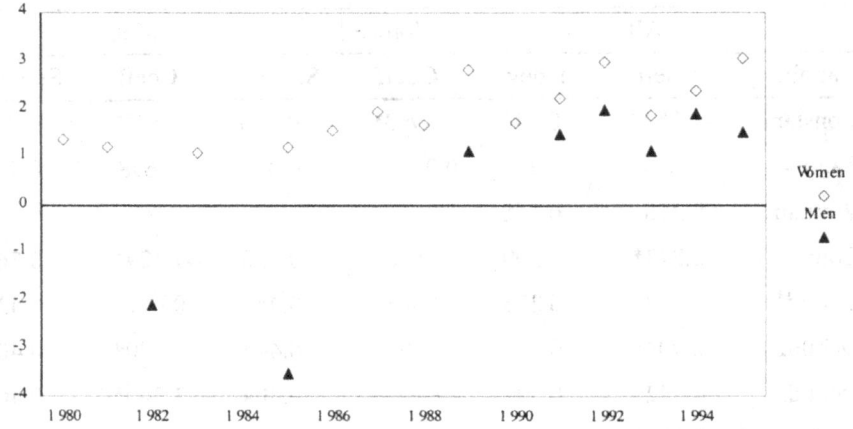

Figure 2.10 Significant coefficients to average household unemployment in annual logit estimations for women and men of the low income risk, 1980-1995

1980s, but at a lower level than that found for women. Prior to that, coefficients are insignificant for men except for two significantly negative coefficients in 1982 and 1985. It is important to remember, however, that the unemployment variable used is the average household unemployment and not the individual unemployment.[13]

---

[13] We have experimented using different specifications of the unemployment variable entered into the Logit estimations. With the preferred approach reported above, there is correspondence between the income concept and the unemployment concept, as both are defined as the household averages. The same approach, but not restricted to the core age group, results in predominantly positive coefficients to unemployment for women from the mid-1980s. For men, the coefficient is significantly positive in the early 1990s and insignificant otherwise. Using individual unemployment instead in estimates for the core age group results in big differences compared with use of average household unemployment. For men, 12 out of 16 coefficients are significantly positive, while for women we find 4 significantly negative coefficients with the remaining

A summary of the profiles for the coefficients in the annual estimations is presented in Table 2.4 for women and men separately.

Table 2.4 **Characteristics of the coefficients to the explanatory variables in gender and year specific logit estimations of the low income risk, labour market participants, 26-59, 1980-1995**

Variable		Significantly positive	Significantly negative	Insignificant
Lagpoor	Women	3	0	13
	Men	0	0	16
Woman		2	0	14
Couple	Women	0	16	0
	Men	0	13	3
Unempl	Women	14	0	2
	Men	6	2	8
Educat	Women	0	10	6
	Men	0	3	13
D36-45	Women	0	7	9
	Men	0	5	11
D46-55	Women	0	6	12
	Men	0	4	12
D56-65	Women	0	0	16
	Men	2	2	12

For participants in the core age groups there is obviously no autocorrelation in the low income risk, and a gender difference is also largely absent. In contrast, we find a strong impact from being married or cohabiting throughout the period. The pattern regarding the coefficients to unemployment has been discussed above. Regarding education, there is a clear gender difference, with the low income risk for women being much

(continued) being insignificant. The explanation for this difference seems to be a weak relationship between average household income and individual unemployment for the woman in the couple compared with the relationship for men.

more sensitive to education. People in the age group 36-55 tend to have a lower risk than the 26-35 group. However, in most of the years the difference is not significant.

In Table 2.5 we present some corresponding results from a Logit estimation of the low income risk in 1995 for non-participants aged 18-75.

Table 2.5 **Logit estimation of the individual low income risk, non-labour market participants, 18-75, 1995**

	All		Women		Men	
Variable	Coeff.	St.dev.	Coeff.	St.dev.	Coeff.	St.dev.
Constant	-1.198*	0.366	-0.313	0.482	-2.386*	0.584
Lagpoor	0.464*	0.167	0.555*	0.222	0.299	0.267
Woman	-0.214	0.121	–	–	–	–
Couple	-0.789*	0.131	-1.120*	0.165	-0.303	0.231
Dchild1	0.741*	0.197	0.504*	0.222	1.104*	0.438
Dchild2	1.549*	0.206	1.278*	0.248	1.934*	0.400
Dchild3	2.415*	0.264	1.993*	0.309	3.717*	0.575
Educat	0.019	0.029	-0.032	0.038	0.092	0.047
DA089	0.576*	0.158	0.333	0.211	0.908*	0.252
D18-25	1.874*	0.168	1.645*	0.220	1.975*	0.266
D36-45	-0.832*	0.179	-0.586*	0.223	-1.589*	0.337
D46-55	-1.026*	0.207	-1.064*	0.278	-1.426*	0.337
D56-65	-1.796*	0.236	-2.077*	0.318	-1.981*	0.362
D66-75	-2.555*	0.277	-3.481*	0.447	-2.226*	0.378
No. of obs.	3418		1965		1453	
-2logL	2083		1225		805	
P_0	90.2 %		90.4 %		90.8 %	
P_1	9.2 %		9.0 %		8.2 %	

Note: Significance at a 5 per cent level is indicated by *

The variable DA089 is a dummy set at 1 for people who are students or who belong to an unclassified non-participating group. The excluded group is pensioners, DA7. The variables D18-25 and D66-75 are set at 1 for people between 18 and 25 and 66 and 75 respectively. The excluded age group is D26-35, 26-35, as in Table 2.3. Compared with the results for participants in Table 2.3, we find a significant history dependence regarding the low income risk for non-participants. The gender variable is also insignificant for non-participants. In contrast to the result for participants, education is insignificant for non-participants. This, presumably, reflects the inclusion of students in the non-participants group, i.e. a group with fairly long education and fairly low incomes. The age pattern in the low income risk is very clear with a significantly higher risk for the youngest age group and significantly lower risk for the age groups older than 35, cf. the separate discussion of the age related differences in risk profiles below. Regarding the separate results for women and men, the impact from the lagged status relative to the low income line is only found for women. Furthermore, the reduction of the risk for married and cohabiting people is found only for women. Regarding the impact of having children and the age related age profiles, we find the same qualitative results for women and men. We return to the question of the time profiles in the estimated coefficients below.

As mentioned above, the age specific risks differ much more among non-participants. In Figure 2.11 we show the profile over time for the significant coefficients to the age dummies taken from the annual Logit estimations using the whole sample of participants as well as non-participants aged 18-75 along with the results for non-participants aged 18-75.[14] We include also the significant coefficients to the 46-55 age dummy D46-55 found in the estimations of labour market participants in the core age group.

It is evident from Figure 2.11 that the age-related differences in the low income risk are a non-participant phenomenon. For all three age dummies, the non-participant coefficient estimates track the estimates for the whole sample very closely. At the same time, the 8 significant coefficients to D46-55 found in estimations of participants in the core age group are numerically smaller than the coefficients found for non-participants.

In Table 2.6 we have collected evidence regarding the profile over time in the coefficients to a number of the explanatory variables used in the annual Logit estimations for non-labour-market participants. In contrast to the 1995 findings in Table 2.5, there is little evidence of a significant impact from lagged low income status. In 6 of the years, being a woman implies a significantly *lower* risk of low income. This is an interesting

---

[14] The results from these estimations of the whole sample are not presented here, but are available on request to the authors.

contrast to the finding for labour market participants of two significantly positive coefficients, indicating a higher risk for women in 2 of the 16 years while the remaining 14 coefficients were found insignificant, cf. Table 2.4. Being married or cohabiting represents the same safeguard against low income for non-participants as for participants. Regarding education, non-significance is completely dominant, reflecting the composition of the non-participants

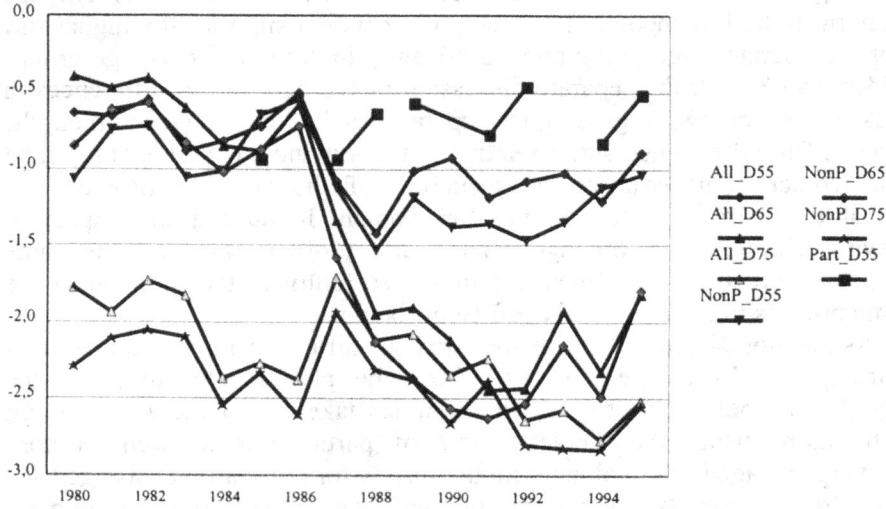

Figure 2.11 Significant coefficients to age dummies in year specific logit estimations of the low income risk for all in the sample, and for non-participants and participants, 1980-1995

Note: All_D55, All_D65 and All_D75 coefficients to D46-55, D56-65 and D66-75 in estimations of all in the sample. NonP_D55, NonP_D65 and NonP_D75 coefficients to D46-55, D56-65 and D66-75 in estimations of non-participants. Part_D55 coefficient to D46-55 in estimation of participants in core age group.

group. Looking at the age dummies, the risk is significantly higher for both women and men younger than 26. For the oldest group, 66-75, the low income risk is significantly lower than for the excluded 26-35 group for both women and men. For the intermediate group, 36-65 years old, the age dependent risk is reduced more relative to the 26-35 year old reference group compared with the finding for participants.

Until now we have analysed the low income risk in a sequence of cross sections. Next, we go on to utilise data to analyse the incidence of low income over longer periods of time. The preceding analyses are consistent with different scenarios regarding the possible combinations of incidence and duration of spells of economic poverty. A fairly small group of people could, perhaps, enter into and exit from a state of low income often, but judged over a long period of time, these people would spend a considerable part of their life in a state of economic poverty. A sequence of cross sections would miss this point. To examine these questions, we proceed to analyse low income from a more long-run perspective.

Table 2.6 Characteristics of the coefficients to the explanatory variables in year specific logit estimations of the low income risk, non labour market participants, 18-75, 1980-1995

Variable		Significantly positive	Significantly negative	Insignificant
Lagpoor	Women	4	0	12
	Men	0	0	16
Woman		0	6	10
Couple	Women	0	16	0
	Men	0	15	1
Educat	Women	0	0	16
	Men	1	0	15
D26-35	Women	16	0	0
	Men	13	0	3
D36-45	Women	0	11	5
	Men	0	8	8
D46-55	Women	0	16	0
	Men	0	8	8
D56-65	Women	0	15	1
	Men	0	14	2
D66-75	Women	0	16	0
	Men	0	16	0

For each individual in the sample, we calculate the average annual disposable income in the years for which observations are available. Next, we calculate the median in the distribution of these individual average annual disposable incomes. All incomes are deflated with the consumer price index to make them comparable over the 1980-1995 period. Individuals observed for less than 5 years are excluded, but their income observations are used in the calculation of the median. Finally, for individuals who by this procedure remain in the sample, we define a variable "Poor" set at 1 if the average annual income is less than 50 per cent of the median and otherwise set at 0.

This procedure has been followed for labour market participants and non-participants separately.[15] In the Logit estimations of the probability of having "long-term-low incomes" (Poor = 1) presented in Table 2.7, the explanatory variables are the individual average values of the variables described above. For labour market participants in the core age group 26-59, the results are shown in Table 2.7, both for all in the group and for women and men separately. For those who have been participants for the whole period, the dependent variable is set at 1 if the individual average disposable income for 1980-1995 is less than 50 per cent of the median income. For people who have been participants 5 - 15 years, the individual average disposable income is calculated for the years in which they were participants, and the dependent variable is set at 1 if this average is less than 50 per cent of the overall median income common for all participants.

For labour market participants, the column for all in the relevant sample in Table 2.7 shows that women do not have a higher risk of long term low income than men. The significant reduction of the risk of long term low income from being married or cohabiting is also the same for women and men. Regarding unemployment, the significantly positive coefficient found in the estimation for all reflects a significantly higher risk for women, while no impact is found in the separate estimations for men. The unemployment variable is the household average corresponding with the income concept such as the one used in the cross sections above.[16] The number of years of

---

[15] Consequently, to be included in the analysis of participants, an individual has to have been a labour market participant for 5 years or more. A parallel rule applies to non-participants. A person with, for example, 7 years in the labour force and 9 years as a non-participant is thus present in both analyses in the following.

[16] Here too, the results are sensitive to the choice of unemployment variable. If average household unemployment is replaced with individual unemployment, we get results different from those in Table 2.7, i.e. a significantly negative coefficient for women and a significantly positive coefficient for men. The counter-intuitive negative coefficient for women presumably reflects a higher

Table 2.7 Logit estimation of the probability of having an average income below 50 per cent of the median income for the period 1980-1995. Labour market participants, 26-59

	All		Women		Men	
	Coeff.	St. dev.	Coeff.	St. dev.	Coeff.	St. dev.
Constant	-2.820*	0.362	-3.997*	0.492	-1.856*	0.547
Woman	0.139	0.106	–	–	–	–
Mdcouple	-5.035*	0.152	-4.782*	0.179	-4.379*	0.374
Mdchild1	3.354*	0.185	4.325*	0.279	1.671*	0.417
Mdchild2	5.476*	0.203	6.589*	0.292	3.210*	0.488
Mdchild3	6.697*	0.211	6.700*	0.332	6.320*	0.387
Munempl	2.377*	0.267	3.463*	0.336	0.010	0.581
Meducat	-0.269*	0.028	-0.258*	0.037	-0.262*	0.043
MDA12	2.153*	0.154	2.003*	0.241	1.935*	0.225
MDA4	-0.513	0.281	–	–	-0.168	0.332
MDA56	0.525*	0.138	0.858*	0.164	0.083	0.278
MD36-45	-0.219*	0.108	0.036	0.146	-0.545*	0.178
MD46-55	0.960*	0.128	1.464*	0.210	0.601*	0.168
MD56-65	1.419*	0.327	1.751*	0.366	-13.13	843.2
No. of obs.	57.249		25.958		30.839	
-2log L	4788		2845		2162	
P0	86.8 per		88.5 per		86.1 per	
P1	8.0 per		5.9 per		9.0 per	

Note: The prefix M to explanatory variables indicates that the average value of the variable is used in the years for which the person is included in the sample. Significance at a 5 per cent level is indicated by *.

education has the same significant impact for both women and men. For women, in contrast to men, unskilled workers and the residual group of

(continued) average unemployment for married or cohabiting women. If we use average household unemployment without the restriction on the core age group as in Table 2.7, we find significantly positive coefficients to unemployment for both women and men. Generally, however, a lack of correspondence between the income concept and the unemployment concept makes it complicated to interpret the results from estimations using individual unemployment.

54 *Poverty and Low Income in the Nordic Countries*

other wage earners have a higher risk of long term low income. Finally, regarding the age profiles, we find that the lower risk for those 36-45 years old, compared with the 26-35 year old excluded reference group, is found only for men, while the higher risk for those 56-59 years old is found only for women. Overall, then, the lowest age-dependent risk for long term low income among labour market participants is found cet.par. for men aged 36-45 years.

Next, Table 2.8 presents the results for non-participants. Here, we find a significantly *lower* risk for women than for men, while once again the impact of being married or cohabiting is the same for women and men. Regarding education, the results differ from the findings among labour market participants. Among non-participants, longer education implies a significantly lower risk of long-term economic poverty among men, while no significant effect is found for women. The age dependence of the risk also differs very much between non-participating women and men. The age-dependent risk profile is U-shaped for women, i.e. the youngest and the oldest age groups have higher risks and the middle aged lower risks than the 26-35 year old reference group. For men, the profile is not age-dependent until the mid-50s, reflecting that only few men are non-participants, at least among those older than 25. Non-participating men aged 56-65 have a higher risk, while the risk is lower for men who are 65 or older. The difference in the age dependence between women and men in the oldest group - where the great majority are non-participants – presumably reflects a higher coverage through supplementary pension arrangements among men. Among the current generation of 66-75 year olds, labour market experience and, consequently, experience-related pension benefits, are higher among men, a fact which is reflected in the different signs to MD66-75.

Table 2.8 Logit estimation of the probability of having an average income below 50 per cent of the median income ("Poor"=1) for the period 1980-1995. Non labour market participants

	All		Women		Men	
	Coeff.	St. dev.	Coeff.	St. dev.	Coeff.	St. dev.
Constant	-0.629*	0.178	-2.606*	0.234	0.922*	0.267
Woman	-0.611*	0.051	–	–	–	–
Mcouple	-2.479*	0.075	-2.577*	0.102	-2.471*	0.116
Mdchild1	1.412*	0.119	1.286*	0.135	0.752*	0.313

(Table 2.8 continued)

Mdchild2	2.233*	0.125	1.969*	0.141	2.721*	0.279
Mdchild3	3.594*	0.130	3.439*	0.148	3.973*	0.312
Meducat	-0.166*	0.017	-0.043	0.023	-0.299*	0.026
MDA089	0.806*	0.070	0.450*	0.099	1.176*	0.100
MD26-35	0.267*	0.069	0.387*	0.091	0.080	0.109
MD36-45	-0.318*	0.084	-0.548*	0.114	-0.115	0.126
MD46-55	-0.190*	0.087	-0.563*	0.128	0.062	0.121
MD56-65	-0.197*	0.083	-0.872*	0.123	0.268*	0.113
MD66-75	0.140	0.103	0.803*	0.148	-0.439*	0.146
No. of obs.	35269		21525		13744	
-2log L	14099		7499		6400	
P_0	80.0 %		82.4 %		77.3 %	
P_1	18.9 %		16.1%		21.6 %	

Note: The prefix M to explanatory variables indicates that the average value of the variable is used in the years for which the person is included in the sample. Significance at a 5 per cent level is indicated by *.

Another way to illustrate the incidence of long term economic poverty, as defined here, is shown in Table 2.9. For labour market participants who are 26-59 years old the two columns in Table 2.9 show the mean values for a number of variables in the two groups "Poor" and "Non-Poor".

While Table 2.9 is informative regarding the differences in mean characteristics between the two groups, it illustrates at the same time the danger inherent in drawing reliable conclusions from cross-tabulations. The share of women is much higher in the Poor group but, cf. Table 2.7, being a woman does not in itself imply a higher risk of long-term economic poverty. The differences in the other mean characteristics are in accordance with the findings in Table 2.7, i.e. the two groups differ considerably concerning family status, unemployment, education, occupational composition and, finally, the non-poor are on average 3.5 years older.

Table 2.9 Mean values for background variables among labour market participants 26-59, 1980-1995

Variable	"Non-Poor"	"Poor"
Woman	0.458	0.669
Couple	0.706	0.441
Unemployment	0.073	0.198
Education, years	11.61	10.20
Self-employed and assisting spouses	0.134	0.217
Salaried employees	0.500	0.275
Skilled workers	0.110	0.041
Unskilled workers and residual group	0.256	0.466
Age, years	41.03	37.69
No. of observations	76532	1210

Note: The two categories are defined by the size of average annual income relative to 50 per cent of the overall median income, cf. the text to Table 2.7.

Table 2.10 shows the mean characteristics for non-participants. Here, it is worth noting that although the share of women does not differ between the groups, being a woman does imply a lower risk of long-term economic poverty in this case when the impact of other background factors is included, cf. Table 2.8.

Overall, 1.56 per cent of the observations among participants and 8.58 per cent among non-participants are in a state of long-term economic poverty: 4.1 per cent in total. However, it is important to remember that this is an unbalanced sample in the sense that individuals with observations for less than 5 years are excluded from the analyses.

Table 2.10 Mean values for background variables among non labour market participants, 1980-1995

Variable	"Non-Poor"	"Poor"
Woman	0.611	0.589
Couple	0.475	0.220
Education, years	10.06	10.35
Pensioner	0.551	0.307
Age, years	52.53	37.34
No. of observations	40438	3796

2.9 Concluding Remarks

The macroeconomic background of the present study has been big cyclical movements in unemployment around a high level. The prior expectation was that this macroeconomic setting would tend to result in an increasing inequality in the distribution of incomes and along with this an increase in the share of the population living in economic poverty.

For the period we have studied, 1980-1995, this prior expectation did not turn out to be true. Based on the use of average disposable income in the household, using an equivalence scale, the low income line was defined as 50 per cent of the median income. Overall, we found a low income share of around 10 to 12 per cent without any increasing trend. The share shows a certain cyclical sensitivity, which was lower in the latter part of the period in spite of the fact that both the level of, and the changes in, unemployment were higher during this period.

Calculations of poverty indices to supplement the information inherent in the low income share show a poverty gap with the same cyclical sensitivity as the low income share, but it mostly lies above the low income share when using 1980 as the base year. On the other hand, we find a strong decline in a poverty index giving high weight to the lowest incomes in the distribution.

The analytical approach in the paper took three directions. First, a descriptive approach where the low income share for the 16 years was calculated on the basis of a number of background variables for the population. Next, a multivariate analysis consisting of annual cross sections using year specific Logit estimations to identify the impact on the low income risk from the different background factors. The analyses were made separately for labour market participants in the core age group and for non-participants, in each case with separate estimations for women and men. Finally, the panel property of the data was used to estimate the relationship between the risk of long-term low income and the different background factors. These analyses were also made separately for participants and non-participants, and with separate estimations for women and men in the two groups.

The descriptive part demonstrated that the aggregate stability in the low income share was the outcome of quite big disaggregate differences and changes that more or less cancelled out to result in overall stability. Among the most spectacular changes was a strong decline in the low income risk for people older than 50, and especially so for the oldest age group in the study, 66-75 years old. This development implies that poverty as an old age phenomenon has practically disappeared. At the same time, the low income share has been increasing among young people, partly as a consequence of an increase in time spent in education.

Women had a somewhat higher risk, but the gender difference was fairly small, with an average low income share of 12 per cent for women and 9 per cent for men. Regarding the family structure, we find a tendency to an increasing risk of low income for families with children in the 1990s.

The prior expectation was that unemployment would prove to be an important factor. In the partial cross section analysis this expectation was confirmed. For the whole period, the low income risk for people without unemployment was initially small, and furthermore it was reduced to half the initial level during the period. On the other hand, for those who were unemployed between 20 and 70 per cent of the year, the low income risk doubled between 1980 and 1995. The annual entry and exit rates to and from a state of low income did not correspond with the profile in aggregate unemployment during the period. There was a consistent gender difference in the transition rates, with higher exit rates and lower entry rates to low income for men compared with women. Both rates fell for the period as a whole. Consequently, the near stationarity in the aggregate low income share results from declines in both the exit and the entry rates to a low income state.

In the multivariate analyses, children in the family were consistently found to increase the low income risk while being married or cohabiting consistently reduced the risk. Unemployment tended to increase the risk more for women than for men, and this was more pronounced in the 1990s than in the 1980s. Education tended to reduce the risk, both in annual cross sections and in estimations of the risk of long term economic poverty. The impact from education was generally more pronounced among women than among men.

Age dependent differences in the low income risk were generally more pronounced among people outside the labour force. Among participants in the core age group, age-dependent differences were less clear, but overall they pointed to the lowest risk for men in the 36-45 year old group. For non-participants, the overall age dependence was clear, with a higher risk for people younger than 26 and a lower risk for those older than 34. Regarding the risk of long-term low income, women older than 64 had a higher risk than men of the same age, presumably reflecting gender differences in eligibility for and coverage by supplementary pension schemes. On the other hand, being a woman in itself tended to reduce the risk of long-term economic poverty in the non-participants group. Overall, 4 per cent of our observations fell in the group with a long-term low income status.

Finally, we should emphasise the restrictions of the present analysis. A number of income categories, rent support and individual discretionary social assistance, both in cash and in kind, are not included due to data limitations. The excluded income categories are typically targeted toward the low income group and, consequently, the exclusion results in our estimates of low income shares being upwardly biased. Another restriction is the exclusion of people older than 75. They are, however, mainly provided for by the same types of pensions as the included 66-75 year old group. The coverage by supplementary private or labour market related pensions may, however, be higher among the youngest group of mainly retired people. This would tend to produce a downward bias in our estimates. Our conjecture is that the first exclusion regarding income components tends to dominate, with the net result that our estimates of the low income share tend to have an upward bias.

2.10 Appendix

Table 2.A.1 Alternative low income/poverty lines. Annual amounts (DKK)

	Relative low income line[1]	Absolute low income line[2]	Basic National Old Age Pension for Single Pensioner	Permanent Social Welfare Benefit for a Single Person[3]
1980	25.578	26.328	24.666	24.666
1981	27.516	29.499	27.180	24.462
1982	31.298	32.517	30.318	27.286
1983	32.827	34.714	32.574	37.626
1984	34.874	36.929	34.830	39.090
1985	37.071	38.537	36.708	39.996
1986	39.164	39.636	38.214	40.716
1987	42.031	41.459	39.342	27.594
1988	44.000	43.101	40.464	28.380
1989	46.000	44.953	42.672	28.800
1990	48.000	46.171		
1991	48.000	47.303		
1992	48.906	48.176		
1993	49.000	48.651		
1994	52.963	49.138		
1995	55.588	50.163		

1. 50 per cent of the median of disposable income, individual average adjusted for household size by use of equivalence scale.
2. Calculated from the numbers in the first column. First, the numbers in the first column are deflated by the consumer price index (CPI). Next, the average over the period of the deflated low income lines is calculated. Finally, the numbers in the second column are calculated by inflating this average with the CPI.
3. The amounts indicate the upper limit for welfare benefits of indefinite duration. From 1980 to 1983 this was set at 90 per cent of the base amount of the national old age pension. From 1983, specific scales were introduced for social assistance. The amounts shown do not include the possibility of additional rent and child support. From 1987 the cash benefits were scaled down, as the rent was paid fully for the people in question.

Table 2.A.2 Annual sample means of disposable incomes, 1980-1995. DDK[1]

Year	Number of observations	Variable	Mean	Standard deviation	Maximum
1980	11.618	Household[2]	89.476	59.425	578.320
		Individual[3]	54.787	29.029	340.188
1981	11.630	Household	97.389	71.107	844.000
		Individual	60.044	36.105	590.527
1982	11.598	Household	110.186	80.071	1.192.799
		Individual	67.898	40.412	876.000
1983	11.751	Household	115.026	83.707	1.113.401
		Individual	71.381	41.990	911.917
1984	11.960	Household	121.131	89.197	1.538.408
		Individual	75.481	43.114	569.781
1985	12.059	Household	128.910	95.699	1.593.622
		Individual	80.601	46.625	919.250
1986	12.001	Household	135.980	107.475	1.801.886
		Individual	85.735	53.202	1.059.933
1987	12.048	Household	144.621	109.392	1.532.000
		Individual	91.719	54.806	1.002.000
1988	12.156	Household	151.209	115.218	1.478.000
		Individual	95.874	56.364	777.000
1989	12.184	Household	157.825	119.774	1.599.000
		Individual	100.393	59.557	1.000.000
1990	13.636	Household	168.574	126.080	2.145.000
		Individual	104.769	63.481	1.261.765
1991	14.035	Household	162.036	129.589	1.592.800
		Individual	106.795	67.841	1.024.000
1992	14.297	Household	166.667	133.574	1.641.000
		Individual	109.580	69.957	892.500
1993	14.457	Household	168.031	134.690	1.317.000
		Individual	110.698	71.680	1.017.000
1994	14.473	Household	177.969	135.537	1.999.250
		Individual	117.857	71.343	939.250
1995	14.483	Household	184.811	139.415	1.805.900
		Individual	122.615	73.264	1.014.900

1. All disposable incomes are censured below 0, i.e. the minimum in all years is 0. Until 1981 incomes were, for discretion, censured above at 1,000,000 DKK.
2. Disposable income of the household.
3. Disposable income per individual in the household using the equivalence scale.

References

Abrahamson, P. (1992., Poverty and welfare in Denmark, *Scandinavian Journal of Social Welfare*, 1992:1, pp. 20-27.

Barr, N. (1993). The Economics of the Welfare State. *Oxford University Press.*

European Commission (1994). *Employment in Europe*, Bruxelles.

Forsikringsoplysningen (1976-90). *Sociale ydelser - hvem, hvad og hvornår*, København.

Foster, J., Greer, J. and Thorbecke, E. (1984), A Class of Decomposable Poverty Measures, *Econometrica*, pp 761-766.

Friis, H. (1981). Nederst ved bordet. Rapport om fattigdom og fattigdomspolitik i Danmark, *Socialforskningsinstituttet, publikation* 108, København.

Gustafsson, B. and Lindblom, M. (1993). Poverty Lines in Seven European Countries, Australia, Canada and the USA, *Journal of European Social Policy*, 3(1), pp 21-38.

Gustafsson, B. (1995). Assessing Poverty - Some Reflections on the Literature, *Journal of Population Economics*: 361-381.

Halleröd, B., Heikkilä, M., Mäntysaari, M., Ritakallio, V. and Nyman, C. (1996). Poverty Research in the Nordic Countries, *Mimeo.*

Hansen, E.J. (1986). Danskernes levekår 1986 sammenlignet med 1976, *Hans Reitzel*, København.

Hansen, E.J. (1989), Fattigdom, Begreber og metoder i forskning og politik, *Socialforskningsinstituttet, Rapport* 89:5, København.

Hansen, F.K. (1990). Materielle og sociale afsavn i befolkningen, *SFI Rapport* 90:4, Socialforskningsinstituttet, København.

Ingerslev, O. (1990). Forløbsanalyser af indkomstudvikling og indkomstfordeling, *Samfundsøkonomen, nr. 6: 17-22.*

Jorgenson, D.W. (1998). Did We Lose the War on Poverty? *The Journal of Economic Perspectives*, Vol. 12, No. 1: 79-96.

Kangas, O. and Ritakallio, V.M. (1995). Different methods - different results? Approaches to multidimensional poverty, *Conference Paper*, ISA RC 19 Conference on 'Comparative Research on Welfare State Reforms', University of Pavia, Sept. 1995.

Pedersen, P.J. and Pedersen, S. (1998). Arbejdsmarkedspolitik, arbejdsløshed og beskæftigelsesopsving, in N. Smith (ed.), *Arbejde, incitamenter og ledighed*, Aarhus University Press.

Økonomiministeriet (Ministry of Economic Affairs) (1993). *Lovmodel*, København.

3 Income Poverty in Finland 1971-1995

MARKUS JÄNTTI AND VELI-MATTI RITAKALLIO

3.1 Introduction

We study trends in income poverty in Finland from 1971 to 1995. This period is characterized by wide variation in economic performance, ranging from frequent cycles in the 1970s through steady growth in the 1980s to a sharp contraction in the 1990s. During these two and a half decades, the Finnish welfare-state institutions underwent substantial changes. Both economic performance and welfare-state institutions likely affect poverty and this period would appear to present ample opportunities for poverty to vary.

Our starting point, 1971, is given by the availability of reliable and comparable microdata on income, the Household Budget Survey (HBS) in 1971.[1] We measure poverty roughly every five years until 1990, after which we have annual data from Income Distribution Surveys (IDS). The ending point, 1995, is the last year IDS microdata are available to us.

We start the paper by reviewing macroeconomic and institutional developments over the period. Given the depth of the recession of the 1990s, our macroeconomic review lays much of its emphasis on this period. We then review previous literature on income poverty in Finland and briefly describe the data sets on which our empirical analyses are based.

In our analysis, we examine the evolution of both relative poverty – defined in terms of having income below a fraction of the contemporaneous median - and a poverty line that is fixed in real income – taking as our poverty standard a fraction of the median in 1985. We use standard methods to summarize poverty in each year and examine the robustness of the resulting trends to our choices of other methods, such as the fraction of median and the equivalence scales that were chosen. We then break down

---

[1] The first modern HBS was conducted in 1966. We are less comfortable with the comparability of those data, though. Also, the 1966 data was extensively studied by Uusitalo (1989) (inequality) and Gustafsson and Uusitalo (1990) (poverty).

the population in each year by observable characteristics of the household (reference person) to gain insight in both the variation in poverty risks and in the composition of the poverty population. A summary concludes the chapter.

3.2 Economic and Social Developments in Finland 1971-1995

Compared to other European nations, the economic structure of Finland was long that of a backwards agrarian society. More than half of the economically active population worked in primary production after World War II, while e.g. Sweden had passed that stage in 1920. A rapid transformation into a service economy through an industrial phase began in the 1950s. In three decades, Finland went through changes that in most European countries had taken place earlier and more slowly. By the late 1980s, less than ten per cent of the economically active population worked in primary production, while their share was 36 per cent in 1960. From a poverty perspective, it was particularly important that small farms (less than 10 hectares), at very high risk of poverty, substantially declined in number and as a share of all farms (Uusitalo 1989). Manufacturing's share was relatively stable. Services grew rapidly: in 1990 the service sector's share of the labour force was 53 per cent.

The delay in as well as the rapid pace of Finland's industrialization are explained by its peripheral position in the international economy. When it became integrated into European markets, it had the 'advantage of backwardness', i.e. the option to apply the latest technology. The effects of this rapid economic and structural transformation have been felt throughout society (Alestalo and Uusitalo 1986, 250-253).

Table 3.1   Real GDP (in 1985 PPP dollars) per capita in the Nordic countries

Year	Denmark	Finland	Iceland	Norway	Sweden
1950	5,263	3,506	3,808	4,358	5,807
1960	6,760	5,291	4,964	5,610	7,592
1970	9,670	8,108	6,772	8,034	10,766
1980	11,342	10,851	11,566	12,141	12,456
1990	13,909	14,059	13,362	14,902	14,762

Note: The PWT series does not extend beyond 1992.
Source: Penn World Tables, 5.6.

The 1970s and 1980s were a period of rapidly rising living standards, institutional development and progress optimism. Gross Domestic Product (GDP), measured in constant prices, increased by 43 per cent in both decades. Thus, real GDP was more than twice as high in 1990 compared to 1970. Finnish GDP per capita had by the 1980s risen close to and by 1990 to around the Nordic average (see Table 3.1).

Partly as a consequence of being late in industrializing, economic growth in Finland has been quite rapid. As we show in Table 3.2, for instance, real GDP per capita growth was during the post World War II era comparatively high in all periods (except the early 1990s). In the 1980s, for instance, annual average GDP growth was 3.3 per cent, compared to around 2 per cent per year in the other Nordic countries and 1.5 in the United States. Several factors are important in accounting for differences in growth rates. 'Catching up' is quite likely a contributing factor to the high Finnish growth rate.

Table 3.2   Annual average real GDP growth in selected countries 1950-1992

Country	1950-59	1960-69	1970-79	1980-1989	1990-92
Denmark	2.2	4.3	1.8	1.8	1.0
Finland	3.7	4.4	3.4	3.3	-5.4
Iceland	3.2	2.3	5.9	2.2	-2.1
Norway	2.5	3.9	4.0	2.3	2.0
Sweden	2.7	3.5	1.7	1.8	-1.6
United Kingdom	2.2	2.4	2.3	2.4	-1.3
United States	1.3	2.8	1.9	1.5	-0.3

Note: The PWT series does not extend beyond 1992.
Source: Penn World Tables, 5.6.

Modern infrastructure was built in Finland in the 1960-80 period. Modernization was accompanied by urbanization and internal migration to the south of Finland (Alapuro 1980). The demographic structure has, from a poverty perspective, developed favorably. The baby boomers were in their early twenties in 1970 and in their forties in 1990. Fertility was much lower than in the 1950s, so that families with many children, who are at high risk of poverty, became quite rare. The share of the elderly did increase but, as we shall see, their poverty risk was reduced and thus they did not contribute to an increased poverty population.

Welfare institution in Finland came to be modelled largely after those in Sweden (see Esping-Andersen and Korpi 1987). In 1960, there were very few welfare state institutions to talk of. Most of the modern welfare state institutions came into being in the 1960s and 1970s. For instance, the compulsory work-related pensions in the private sector were introduced in the 1960s. Social expenditures in 1970 were around 51 million 1995 FIM. By 1990, social expenditures had tripled, compared to the doubling of real GDP per capita. The increase in social expenditures in the 1990s is associated only with increases in unemployment-related transfers and expenditures.

Public services also expanded considerably during the period we examine. The fact that 29 per cent of the work force was employed in the public sector, mainly at the municipality level in 1996 gives some idea of the scope of public services. Public sector employment has in particular expanded female employment, which is both historically and currently at high international levels (77 per cent of the working age female population in 1990). Female employment is also mainly in full-time jobs and the dominant family type has two earners (Kangas and Ritakallio 1999).

The period from 1970 to 1990 can be characterized as one in which both the economy and welfare state institutions developed favourably. The 1990s, by contrast, witnessed the largest peace-time contraction of the economy. As we shall see, however, the welfare-state institutions survived more or less intact.

3.2.1 Macroeconomic conditions

The early 1970s was characterized by rapid business cycle movements. The decade started with a short boom and there was a short recession in 1971 where-after followed a period of high economic growth, up to 7 per cent per annum. A longer recession lasted from 1974 to 1979 – economic growth was at a stand still during 1975-77. The unemployment rate rose, for the first time, to above 5 per cent with a peak in 1978 of 7 per cent. Compared to other countries, however, Finland suffered lightly from the first oil shock. The unemployment rate in many countries rose to a persistently high level of around 10 per cent and growth was negative. The Finnish situation was in part alleviated by the bilateral trade arrangement with Russia, from which Finland imported among other goods also crude oil. Oil price increases were thus met with increased Finnish exports.

The 1980s, by contrast, were a period of fairly stable growth, except for the brief slowdown in growth in 1981. Average GDP growth was 3.7 per cent and the unemployment rate was quite low varying between 3 and 5 per cent. In 1990, the economy plunged and the rate of growth was deep in the red for three years. After 1994, growth has resumed but unemployment is still a major concern.

Thus, Finland entered during 1990 its deepest peace-time recession, as measured by the fall in production. Following a period of sustained economic growth, increasing employment and low unemployment rates, the economy plummeted. Several circumstances, each of which on its own had likely caused but a small decline in economic activity, were active at the same time. There was a small international recession starting around that time, which, coupled with an over-valued currency decreased export demand. Following the liberalization of financial markets, the real estate and stock markets had overheated, and prices came tumbling down. Trade with the Soviet Union came to halt upon its disintegration.[2]

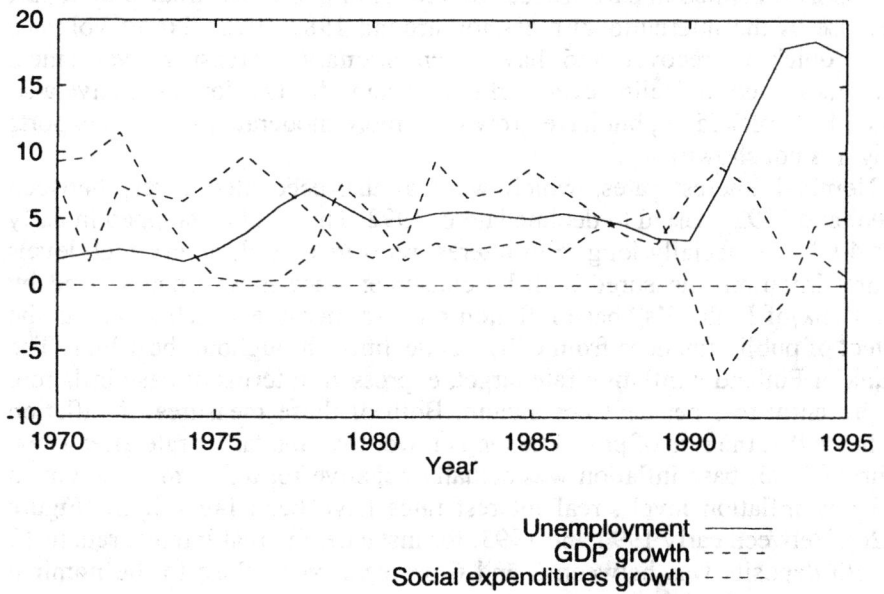

Figure 3.1 Percentage changes in GDP and social expenditure and the unemployment rate in Finland, 1970-95

The economic downturn that started in 1990 is, measured in terms of the decline of output, the most severe of peace-time recessions in Finland this century. The cumulative decline in GDP was around 15 per cent. The

---

[2] See Bordes et al. (1993) or Honkapohja et al. (1993) for a discussion of the causes of the economic crisis.

volume of economic output was below its 1990 level for six years, reaching its 1990 level only in 1996. Output declined from more than three consecutive years, reaching its low point in early 1993 at less then 90 per cent of the 1990 level. GNP growth was negative from late 1990 to late 1993, a three year decline. With the exception of a dip in early 1996, growth has been fairly strong since then (see Figure 3.2(a)).

Industrial output, as measured by volume (Figure 3.2(b)) reached its minimum in mid 1991. Since then, two key export sectors, metal and manufacturing, have expanded beyond pre-recession levels. "Other" manufacturing, however, has only barely reached its 1990 volume. Investments started to increase in 1994 after having declined since the early 1990s.

Exports declined in part because of very strong terms of trade and in part because of the international recession around 1989-1990. Export volumes were quick to recover and have been strongly increasing ever since. Imports started to decline even earlier and came further down but have also since 1993 picked up, but have grown at a more moderate pace than exports (Figures not shown).

Nominal interest rates, which were at unprecedented levels between 1990 and 1992, started to decline late in 1992. This decline stopped in early 1994 when especially long-term interest rates increased to very high levels again. Inflation, measured both by consumer price index changes and by the Bank of Finland's "base inflation rate" (a measure which subtracts the effect of public finances from CPI) has declined throughout the 1990s. The Bank of Finland's inflation rate target, expressed in terms of base inflation, is presently two per cent per annum. Both of these measures of inflation indicate that the rate of price change is lower than the target rate after 1994. During 1995, base inflation was actually negative for a few months. Given the low inflation levels, real interest rates have been fairly high (Figure 3.2c). Between early 1994 and 1995, for instance, the real interest rate in 12 month deposits was between 5 and 6 per cent, very close to the nominal rate.

With the onset of the recession, both real estate and stock prices collapsed. The stock market reached a low point in late 1992 after which stock prices have risen strongly. Housing prices, arguably a type of asset the price fluctuation of which affects a far larger proportion of the population than the prices of stocks and shares, came down more slowly, reaching a low point in early 1993, but have remained depressed to at least early 1996.

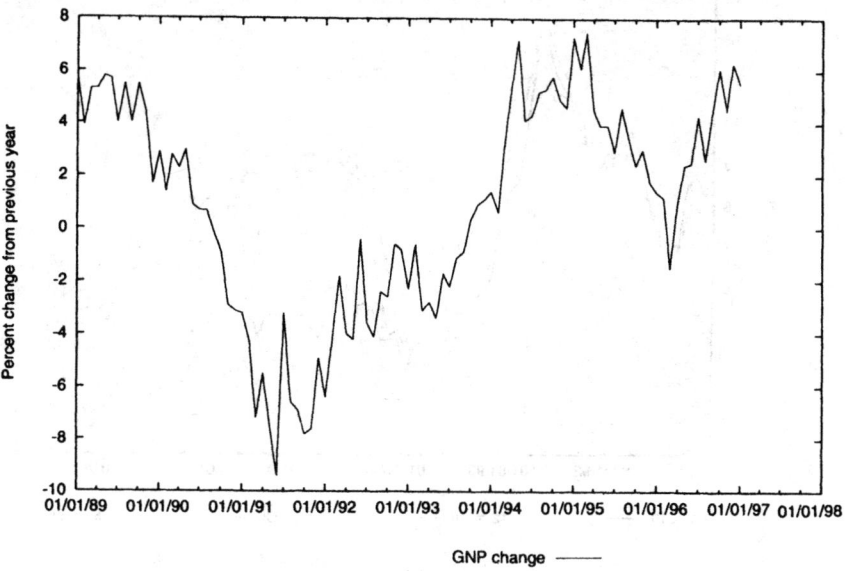

Figure 3.2a GNP growth

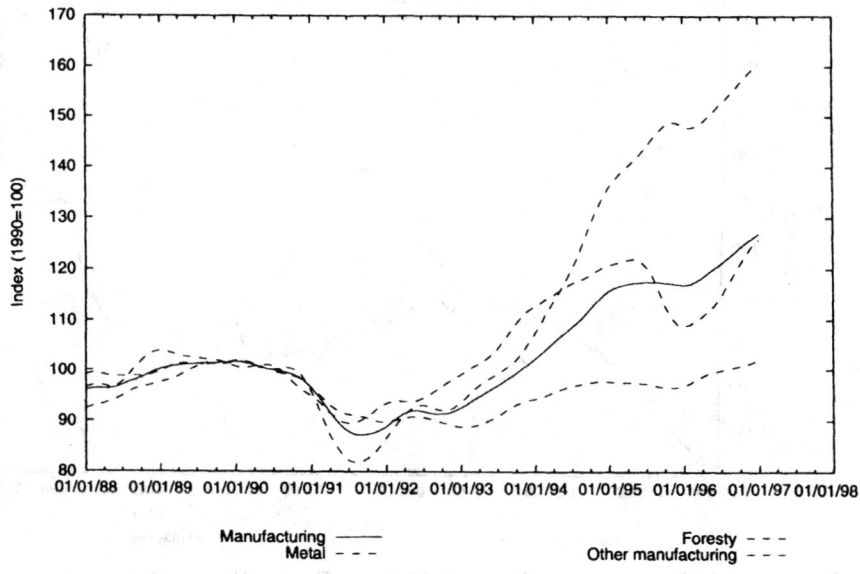

Figure 3.2b Industrial output

70 *Poverty and Low Income in the Nordic Countries*

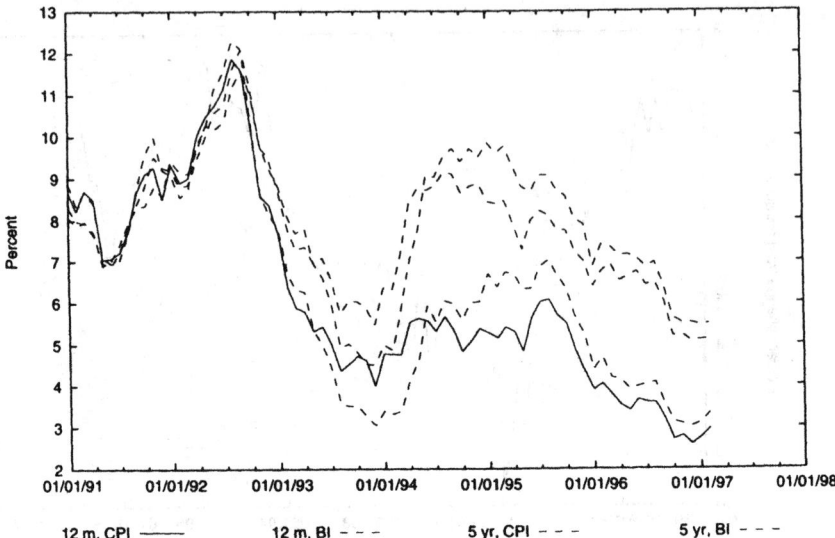

Figure 3.2c Real interest rates (Differing by period, (12 months, respectively 5 years) and price index, being the consumer price index (CPI) and an index published by the Bank of Finland, excluding certain components of CPI.

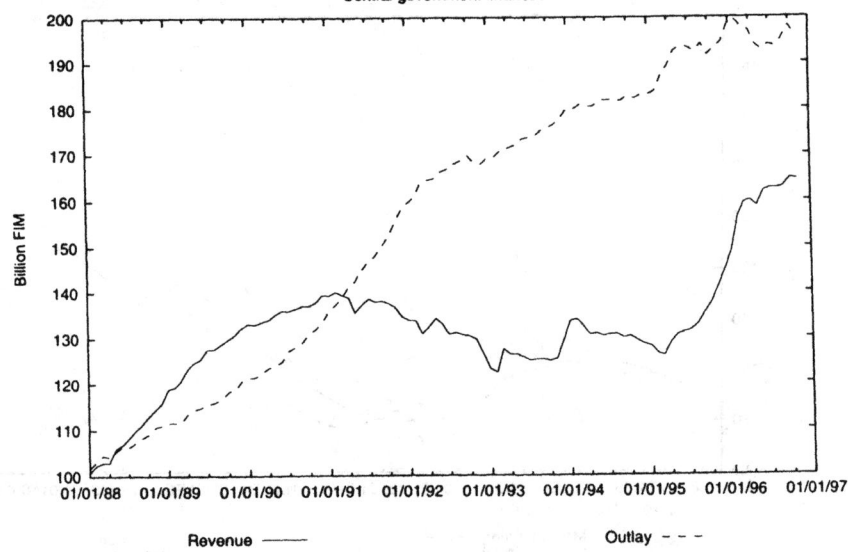

Figure 3.2d Government finances (Source: Bank of Finland)

The adverse business conditions that have prevailed in Finland during the early 1990s, in particular with respect to domestic demand, are quite likely to have led to large scale failure of businesses. The bankruptcy rate did indeed increase sharply in 1991 – it more than doubled from 2.6 in 1990 to 5.5 in 1992.

The unemployment rate, closely connected to GDP growth, increased explosively in the early 1990s. Unemployment increased from 3.4 per cent in 1990 to a high of 18.4 per cent in 1994. In 1995, 17.2 per cent of the work force was still unemployed. As labour force participation also declined, the rate at which employment declined was even greater than just the change in unemployment rates indicates. Long-term unemployment, virtually nil prior to 1991, is now a major part of the unemployment problem.

Long-term unemployment – defined here as an unemployment spell that has lasted over 12 months – increased as a share of overall unemployment from 3.8 per cent to 30.1 per cent in 1995 (see Table 3.3). This means that the share of long-term unemployed of the overall labour force, shown in the fourth column, has increased from 0.1 to 4.9 per cent during the same time. Thus, there are more long-term unemployed in the labour force now than there were unemployed in 1990.

Table 3.3 Unemployment and long-term (12 months) unemployment in Finland (per cent)

Year	Overall	Long-term/ all-	Long-term/ labour force
1988	4.6	10.1	0.5
1989	3.5	6.0	0.2
1990	3.4	3.8	0.1
1991	7.6	2.1	0.2
1992	13.1	7.6	1.0
1993	17.9	17.4	3.1
1994	18.4	27.1	5.0
1995	17.2	30.1	5.2
1996	16.3	30.1	4.9

Note: U is the number of unemployed, U12 is the number of those who have been unemployed longer than 12 months and LF is the size of the labour force.

Source: Ministry of Labour

The unemployment rate decreased in the late 1980s as the number of vacancies increased, consistently with the general over-heating of the economy.[3] Vacancies reached their peak as unemployment reached its trough, and although there has been some inching up in 1996, vacancies have since remained very low. Changes in employment and unemployment show that, although unemployment is slowly declining, variations in the rate of change in employment are in part responsible for the very slow decline in the rate of unemployment.

The economic downturn considerably reduced government revenue and increased outlays, resulting in a large budget deficit (Figure 3.2d). The deficit has been financed by first foreign and later domestic government borrowing, which has resulted, predictably, in a rapidly growing public debt to GNP ratio. Since the central government budget was on average balanced during the preceding two decades and was in surplus in the years immediately before the recession, public debt was initially very small. Thus, even after more than six years of deficit spending the debt to GNP ratio is only slightly above 70 per cent, an internationally not very alarming figure. The large increase in public debt has however strengthened pressures to reduce the public sector's share of the economy and roll back the welfare state.

3.2.2 Social policy and other institutional developments

One of the most important institutional changes in advanced democracies has been the expansion of the welfare state. Different countries have chosen different types of welfare systems. The development of social expenditures, welfare institutions and social rights in Finland has been extensively analyzed in several cross-national studies. The common result has been that Finland is a late comer to what Esping-Andersen (1990) calls the group of social democratic or Nordic welfare states (see Alestalo and Uusitalo 1986, 1992, Kangas, 1994).

The construction of the Finnish welfare state institutions took place during the 1960s to 1980s, a relatively short period of fairly large changes. During those three decades, Finland put in place a system of income transfers and a net of publicly provided welfare services, both of which are in scope, coverage and structure comparable to the more well-known Swedish system. Typically for the Nordic countries, an aim for the Finnish welfare state institutions is to enable also the economically inactive parts of

---

[3] See e.g. Ministry of Labour (1997) for data on vacancies, unemployment and real wages.

the population to benefit from economic growth. The working-age population, however, was supposed to support itself by (heavily taxed) earnings. Extensive public involvement in the industrial relations system was an important means to achieve this goal.

Social policy in Finland is closely connected with "income policy", the governments part of the collective bargaining arrangements. In order to facilitate moderate or otherwise macro-economically sound collective bargains, the government has offered the labor market organizations substantial social policy packages. A long list of those reforms that came as part of the bargains in the 1960s and 1970s can be found in Alestalo and Uusitalo (1986, p. 260). This practice led many critics to claim that social policy was conducted by extra-parliamentary methods.

Income policy has been closely connected with Social Democratic governments. In 1991, Social Democrats lost the elections and became part of the opposition for the first time since 1968. During the following parliamentary session, there was limited support for centralized bargaining. Social Democrats came back into the office in 1996 and since then there has been a return to the traditional income policy model. However, now the theme has been agreeing on cutbacks instead of introducing new policies. Concerning wage differences, the first income policy agreements in the late 1960s and early 1970s tended to lower wage differences. Agreements were based on the idea of "solidary wage policy". Pay raises were expressed in equal absolute magnitudes. Later, when the unions of white-collar employees gained a stronger foothold, the pay raises became increasingly proportional (Uusitalo 1989, 88-89).

A development that was important for poverty alleviation was the system of legislated work-related pensions. In the 1960s, when only the national pension – consisting of a flat-rate basic part and a income-tested supplement – covered all the elderly, the legislated old-age pensions equaled no more than 35 per cent of the average annual earnings. In the 1970s, this replacement rate had risen to 50 per cent. In the 1980s, wages grew more rapidly than basic pensions with a resulting decline in the replacement rate from 49 per cent in 1980 to 38 per cent in 1990. The national pension had by the 1980s acquired a much diminished role as the income source of the elderly, as the work-related pension scheme, legislated in 1962, grew in importance. By 1990, the national pension was the sole source of income for less than 2 per cent of the elderly. Those 2 per cent are also the least well-off part of the elderly population (Jäntti et al. 1996).

The implementation of earnings-related legislated pensions made Finland part of the Nordic model of an institutional or broad-based model of social policy. Pension rights in Finland were until the 1960s the least generous of all OECD countries. The maturing of the earnings-related pension system has moved Finland to above average OECD generosity, but Finland still lags behind the most generous pension providers. Overall, the 1970s was a time of gradual maturing of the pension systems and a period when central welfare services (municipal children's day care, comprehensive school system and municipal health centers) were organized. The completion of the welfare state was carried out in the early 1980s, unlike in several other western countries, once the depression of the late 1970s had passed. The areas of the welfare system which went through major improvements were at that stage sickness insurance and maternity leave policies, unemployment insurance and the last-resort income support system. Common to all these changes was a substantial increase in the generosity of the benefits.

In the 1970s, a largely anglo-saxon discussion, in both public policy and public policy research, began on the crisis of the welfare state. Partly because of the economic instability that began with the first oil crisis, the welfare state became to be viewed as bloated and in need of reforms. The neoconservative electoral victories of Ronald Reagan in the United States and of Margaret Thatcher in the United Kingdom offered a chance to those who favoured a diminished welfare state to act out their plans.

In Finland, this discussion did not enter the public debate. All political coalitions appeared interested in continuing to construct the welfare state along Nordic lines. The political climate was radically transformed with the economic crisis of the 1990s. The Finnish public sector had no tradition of running deficits. In the early 1990s, because of the increased cost of unemployment and large drops in revenue, large deficits appeared which in turn soon led to rapid growth in public debt. These developments, boosted by increased neoliberal rhetoric, led to substantial cuts in income transfers and in particular in public services.

One measure of the evolution of the welfare state is the size of social expenditures. During the period we study, social expenditures grew faster than GDP in all years except 1979-80 and 1994-95 (see Figure 3.1). Both exceptions are in years immediately following recessions. The expansion of social expenditures in both the 1970s and 1980s was quite rapid. Between 1970 and 1978, the growth rate was 8.3 per cent while the average GDP growth rate was 3.4 per cent. In the 1980s, the growth rates were 6.5 and 3.3. The decline at the end of the 1980s suggests the period of most rapid expansion was ending even before the 1990s depression. The large increase in social expenditure in the depression is due mostly to the increase in unemployment benefits. These increases in expenditure were triggered automatically, as a consequence of past legislation and do not reflect an active effort at poverty alleviation.

Measured in terms of social expenditure's share of GDP, Finland reached the average of the Nordic countries and EU-12 (25 per cent) in 1986. Sweden, whose share was 33 per cent in the mid-1980s, was still, however, well ahead of Finland. The GDP share of social expenditures peaked in 1993 at 37 per cent. Even if social expenditures underwent substantial increases in the beginning of 1990s, the truth is that in the same time social rights were cut remarkably. According to the calculations made by the Ministry of Social Affairs, the cutbacks between 1992-96 reduced annual social expenditures by 18.5 billion FIM (8.5 per cent) to the year 2000. Kosunen (1997) shows that cuts were carried out across the board. All the major sectors of social transfers have undergone cutbacks (the so-called cheese paring technique). The largest cuts were in sickness-insurance and unemployment insurance. Her conclusion is that changes have not been radical in that the goals of the systems have largely been preserved. According to the opinion surveys, general support for the welfare state has remained strong and is against major cutbacks (Forma 1998).

However, public expenditure increased as a share of GNP between 1990 and 1992 but has since remained fairly stable (see Statistics Finland 1996). The share of such welfare-relevant items as social welfare, health and education remained by and large quite stable while transfers to households increased rapidly, reflecting the increased unemployment insurance and benefits payments. Although expenditures on welfare and health care and on education declined quite little in terms of GNP shares, the level of spending on these items declined as GNP plummeted.

3.3 Previous Research on Poverty in Finland

Until the mid 1980s, Finnish research on income poverty was almost non-existent. However, signs of a new wave of poverty research then became discernible. The driving force behind the development was the expansion of social assistance dependence, increasing consciousness about social exclusion and marginalization and a totally new interest in investigating the variations in the extent and risk of experiencing economic poverty. Socio-political researchers presented in several forums the inexplicable lack of poverty study. The social administration launched a large project, which dealt with poverty-related issues. It is interesting to note that the rediscovery took place in the mid-1980s, when economic growth and extra investments in welfare policies were still going on (see Ritakallio 1986). Later, it has also been shown that the 1980s was a period of decreasing poverty in Finland, in the sense of traditional low income poverty (see

Gustafsson and Uusitalo 1990, Ritakallio 1994a).

In Finland, the most important contributions of the extent of economic poverty have been studies by Uusitalo (1989), Heikkilä (1990) and Ritakallio (1994c,b,a). Heikkilä used the cross-sectional data from the 1986 living conditions survey; the others employed the cross-sectional data of six household budget surveys carried out between 1966 and 1990. The criterion for poverty used in these studies has been disposable income, and the equivalence scales were of the OECD type. They also used several poverty lines. The most common poverty lines have been the level of the current minimum pension and 50 per cent of median equivalent disposable income per person. Thus, all the studies mentioned analyzed relative poverty.

Heikkilä (1990) and Ritakallio (1994b) adapted several operational definitions simultaneously, and Ritakallio also conducted sensitivity analyses within the relative income method. Ritakallio's and Uusitalo's work analyzed the shift of the income poverty rate over the years using time series data. Ritakallio also compared the trend in poverty rates and poverty gaps between seven OECD countries. Both last-mentioned authors also assessed the impact of the welfare state on poverty by differentiating the push and pull effects of income transfers in terms of poverty rate and poverty gap.

It is worth mentioning that Gustafsson and Uusitalo (1990) and Ritakallio (1994b) have clearly demonstrated the achievements of the welfare state in terms of poverty reduction in Finland. According to Ritakallio, long-term economic poverty almost disappeared until 1990 mainly because of redistributive policies, even though the factor income poverty increased over the period analyzed. On the other hand, studies by Heikkilä (1990) and Kangas and Ritakallio (1998) have reinforced the view that poverty is such a complex phenomenon that identifying it by means of a single indicator may lead to biased results on the severity of poverty. "Traditional poverty" characterized by continuous subsistence on low income seems to have been replaced by new modes of poverty distinguished by unstable labour force position. Furthermore, it has meant that poverty researched indirectly through annual incomes has become more problematic than previously. Given a situation with unstable income, short periods with acceptable income may raise the annual income over the poverty line even though income during the larger part of the year falls below the poverty line.

Gustafsson and Uusitalo (1990) tell of poverty a very similar story as that for inequality. Poverty dropped from quite high levels in 1966 to a very much lower levels in 1976. Taking 50 per cent of median income as the poverty line, poverty dropped from around 13 per cent in 1966 to less than

5 per cent in 1976. Between 1976 to 1985, the poverty rate dropped further to 3.5 per cent. Thus, the large drop in poverty occurred in the late 1960s and the first half of the 1970s, with some further reduction going to the 1980s.

The present study extends previous Finnish literature in several different ways. We use data up until 1995 to measure poverty. We examine the robustness of the measured trends in poverty by looking at two different ways of setting the poverty line, by using several equivalence scales and using poverty indices that are sensitive to the distribution of income among the poor. We also examine the incidence of poverty among subpopulations and the composition of the poverty population using consistent population breakdowns over the whole period.

3.4 Data

We use data from two sources to cover the period 1971 to 1995. For the years 1971 to 1990, we use income data from the Household Budget Surveys (HBS), collected by the Central Bureau of Statistics in 1971, 1976, 1981, 1985 and 1990. The sample sizes after non-response are 2986, 3348, 7368, 8200 and 8258, with non-response rates of about 25 to 30 per cent. The income variables were collected from tax and various other registers, augmented with interview data, and are generally considered to be of fairly high quality.

From 1991 to 1995, we use the annually collected Income Distribution Surveys (IDS). The IDS is a so-called rotating half-panel, that is, each person in the sample is interviewed in two consecutive years and in every year, half the sample is in its first and the other half in its second year. We do not make use of this two year panel in this study.[4] The IDS sample size is around 10000 (12086, 10417, 9176, 8964 and 9262) households in every year. Non-response rates were around 25-28 per cent.

The IDS concept of disposable income is the same as that in HBS. As with the HBS, most income information in the IDS stems from registers. We subtract from disposable income imputed rent from owner-occupied housing (which is included in the domestic concept of disposable income). This renders our concept of disposable incomer very similar to that used in, say, the Luxembourg Income Study. We assign the equivalent household disposable or factor income to each individual in the household and use sampling weights, corrected for non-response, to estimate population level

---

[4] In fact, we ignore the correlation of two consecutive samples in our calculations of the standard errors. Observations more than a year apart are uncorrelated.

statistics.

We define a "base case", a collection consisting of a specific equivalence scale and choice of poverty standard. In the base case, we use the OECD equivalence scale in which the first adult has the unit weight, all other adults are weighted by .7 and all children by .5. We also use two other scales, from the family

$$y = \frac{y^*}{s^k}, \qquad (1)$$

where y and y^* are adjusted and unadjusted income, s denotes household size and k is the size elasticity, which we define to be either .25 or .75.

As our base-case poverty line z, we choose 50 per cent of the current adjusted disposable median income. We vary this choice in two ways. Firstly, we also examine a line that is fixed in real prices, by taking the appropriately deflated median adjusted disposable income in 1985 as the basis of a poverty line. Secondly, for each of the bases (one relative and one "real") we use 40, 50 and 60 per cent of the base as a line.

To summarize the extent of poverty, we use the so-called Foster et al. (1984) family,

$$F_\alpha = \frac{1}{N} \sum_{i=1}^{n} w_i \, I(y_i < z) \left[\frac{z - y_i}{z}\right]^\alpha \qquad (2)$$

where y_i is adjusted income, z the poverty line, N and n are the population and sample size and w_i is the sample weight. The parameter α ranges from 0 to 2, giving us the head count ratio, the relative poverty gap and a distribution-corrected index (F_0, F_1, and F_2). Using two bases for poverty lines, at three different fractions for three equivalence scale then used to estimate three indices applied to multiple years yields a very large number of poverty estimates. In our presentation, we necessarily need to be selective. To reiterate, our base case consists of the three FGT indices estimated using 50 per cent of current OECD adjusted disposable median income.

The HBS available to us only has household level data. We are therefore unable to produce breakdowns by individual characteristics for the whole period and so omit such altogether. All breakdowns are by the characteristics of the household's reference person ("household head").[5] We disaggregate by age (10 year intervals), area (the North, Central and South of Finland as well as the Helsinki region), socioeconomic positions (farmer, entrepreneur, white-collar, blue-collar worker, other) and by household

---

[5] Geographic location, of course, is a characteristic of the household itself.

type (lone parent, two parent, childless couple, elderly, single non-elderly, other).

3.5 Trends in the Distribution and Incidence of Poverty

3.5.1 Overall developments

We start by examining the evolution over time of the Foster et al. (1984) indices ($\alpha=0,1,2$), using the OECD equivalence scale, setting the poverty line at 50 per cent of the current and of the 1985 median (see Table 3.4). Focusing first on the current median, the pattern of poverty in the 1970s and 1980s is by now fairly familiar. The proportion of the population that was poor declined from 1971 to 1990 (albeit with a small increase between 1976 and 1981), increased by just less than a percentage point between 1990 and 1991. From 1992 onwards it has moved, perhaps somewhat erratically, between 2.5 and 3.4 per cent. Thus, in 1995, 3 per cent of the population was poor.

Taking a closer look at the poverty indices that are sensitive to the depth of poverty, as well as its distribution (F_1 and F_2), the overall pattern looks fairly similar to that of the head-count ratio. Thus, with the exception of 1976-1981, poverty declined to 1990, increased to 1991 and has since 1993 declined a little. One difference between the picture derived from looking at these indices as opposed to the head count is that, using the head count, poverty increased by half a percentage point between 1994 and 1995, whereas it remained unchanged (F_1) or even declined (F_2). These changes are unlikely to be statistically significant. They are, however, suggestive of the fact that poverty indices that take account of further aspects of poverty than only its incidence may move differently than just the share of the poor.

We now turn to poverty as measured against a line that is fixed in real terms, namely 50 per cent of the 1985 median, deflated using the cost-of-living index. There was a large decline in poverty using this standard between 1971 and 1976, when the proportion of the poor declined from 30 per cent to 11. The proportion of the population with incomes below this fixed poverty line further declined to just 1.2 per cent in 1990. In the early 1990s, this declining trend stopped and the proportion poor is in 1995 1.8 per cent. An examination of the higher order poverty indices does not in this case reveal any additional information, at least not in the sense that the direction of change between two particular years would be reversed.

Table 3.4 Overall trends in poverty incidence, severity and distribution – Finland, 1971-1995

Year	Current median			1985 median			n
	F_0	F_1	F_2	F_0	F_1	F_2	
71	8.8	2.4	1.1	30.1	8.3	3.5	2986
76	5.1	1.1	0.4	10.5	2.0	0.7	3348
81	5.8	1.5	0.7	7.4	1.8	0.8	7368
85	3.5	0.9	0.4	3.5	0.9	0.4	8200
90	2.7	0.6	0.3	1.2	0.3	0.2	8253
91	3.6	0.8	0.3	1.5	0.4	0.2	12086
92	3.4	0.8	0.3	1.9	0.5	0.2	10417
93	3.2	0.8	0.4	2.0	0.6	0.3	9176
94	2.5	0.6	0.3	1.8	0.4	0.2	8964
95	3.0	0.6	0.2	1.8	0.4	0.2	9262

Note: Numbers given are values of index using the OECD equivalence scale and setting the poverty line at 50 per cent of the reference median. H, HI and HI(1-C^2) are the head count ratio, or F_0, the average poverty gap in the overall population, or F_1 and F_2, where F_α is the so-called Foster et al. (1984) poverty index.

Source: Authors' calculations from HBS (1971-1990) and IDS (1991-95) microdata.

Next, we ask if the changes observed in the 1990s are statistically significant. With these sample sizes, a "naive" estimate of the standard errors of the headcount ratio estimators suggests that a difference exceeding half a percentage point tends to be significant in that sense that the asymptotic t-ratio exceeds 2 (see Table 3.5).[6]

---

[6] The naive standard errors were estimated using $se(P) = \sqrt{n^{-1} P (1-P)}$, where P is the (weighted) estimate of the head-count ratio and n is the (unweighted) sample size.

Table 3.5   Naive t-tests for change in the proportion of poor – Finland 1971-95

	71	76	81	85	90	91	92	93	94
76	-3.6 (-5.7)								
81	-2.9 (-5.0)	0.7 (1.5)							
85	-5.2 (-9.4)	-1.6 (-3.7)	-2.3 (-6.7)						
90	-6.0 (-11.0)	-2.4 (-5.7)	-3.1 (-9.4)	-0.8 (-3.0)					
91	-5.2 (-9.5)	-1.6 (-3.7)	-2.3 (-7.0)	0.0 (0.1)	0.8 (3.4)				
92	-5.4 (-9.9)	-1.8 (-4.2)	-2.5 (-7.5)	-0.2 (-0.6)	0.6 (2.5)	-0.2 (-0.8)			
93	-5.6 (-10.1)	-1.9 (-4.6)	-2.6 (-8.0)	-0.4 (-1.3)	0.5 (1.8)	-0.4 (-1.5)	-0.2 (-0.7)		
94	-6.3 (-11.6)	-2.7 (-6.4)	-3.4 (-10.6)	-1.1 (-4.1)	-0.3 (-1.1)	-1.1 (-4.7)	-0.9 (-3.8)	-0.7 (-2.9)	
95	-5.8 -(10.5)	-2.1 (-5.0)	-2.8 (-8.6)	-0.5 (-2.0)	0.3 (1.1)	-0.6 (-2.3)	-0.4 (-1.5)	-0.2 (-0.7)	0.5 (2.2)

Note: The naive standard errors were estimated using $se(\hat{P}) = \sqrt{n^{-1}\hat{P}(1-\hat{P})}$, where $\hat{P}$ is the (weighted) estimate of the head-count ratio and n is the (unweighted) sample size. *Source*: Authors' calculations from HBS (1971-1990) and IDS (1991-95) microdata.

The data are drawn, however, from complex sampling designs and the estimators are subject to two different sources of sampling error. We have also estimated so-called bootstrap standard errors (not shown here) for these statistics in the 1990s.[7] The bootstrap standard errors, which take into account also the randomness of the median, tend to be somewhat larger and

---

[7] The bootstrap samples were drawn by resampling with replacement from the data a sample of size n, from which a bootstrap estimate of poverty P was calculated. This was repeated K=1000 times and the standard deviation of the bootstrap estimates was taken as an estimate of the standard error of P.

suggest that, given the sample sizes and sample estimates of the poverty statistics, a difference that is larger than .6 percentage points tends to be statistically significant. Thus, not unexpectedly, the naive t-tests tend to over-reject the null that poverty is the same in two years.

An obvious limitation of the approach chosen above is that the position of the poverty line may, in itself, affect the rankings of years. Jenkins and Lambert (1997) suggest methods that allow for rankings that are robust, in the sense that if two years are ranked according to poverty at the (not necessarily same) poverty lines chosen, the ranking holds also for all lines that are lower than those chosen.

Table 3.6 Poverty incidence at 40, 50 and 60 per cent of reference median – Finland 1971-1990

Year	Current median			1985 median		
	40 per cent	50 per cent	60 per cent	40 per cent	50 per cent	60 per cent
71	4.5	8.8	14.4	17.1	30.1	45.4
76	2.0	5.1	11.7	4.0	10.5	20.5
81	2.7	5.8	11.3	3.4	7.4	14.7
85	1.7	3.5	7.9	1.7	3.5	7.9
90	1.1	2.7	7.4	0.6	1.2	2.4
91	1.5	3.6	8.7	0.8	1.5	2.9
92	1.5	3.4	7.4	1.0	1.9	3.9
93	1.5	3.2	7.0	1.2	2.0	4.2
94	1.1	2.5	6.4	0.8	1.8	3.8
95	1.2	3.0	7.9	0.7	1.8	3.9

Note: Numbers given are the head count ratio using the OECD equivalence scale and setting the poverty line at 40, 50 and 60 per cent of the reference median.

Source: Authors' calculations from HBS (1971-1990) and IDS (1991-95) microdata.

While we could in principle implement their approach, it would in practice be quite cumbersome, because of the large number of pairwise comparisons involved. Instead, we examine in Table 3.6 poverty incidence at 40, 50 and 60 per cent of the two reference lines. This provides a rough check of the ordering – indeed, Atkinson (1987) calls an approach much like this an examination of restricted dominance.

An examination of the trends in poverty evaluated at 40, 50 and 60 per cent of the current median are informative in at least two ways (see Table 3.6). Note first that the increase in poverty between 1976 and 1981, shown in Table 3.4, is not associated with "restricted dominance" over the range of lines. At 40 and 50 per cent of the current median, there are fewer poor in 1976 than in 1981 but this is reversed at 60 per cent the line. Thus, the increase between 1976 and 1981 does not appear to be robust. The other differences in the proportion of the poor, however, do tend to be in the same direction at all three points. If poverty increased (decreased) at 50 per cent of the current median, it did so also at 40 and 60 per cent. While this does not suggest overall head count dominance, the finding does suggest a degree of robustness to the trend as measured by a single poverty line point estimate of poverty.

A similar conclusion can be reached by examining the head count ratios using 40, 50 and 60 per cent of the 1985 median, shown in the last three columns of Table 3.6. An exception to an otherwise identical trend at each of the three poverty lines is the last one, the difference in poverty between 1994 and 1995. The differences for these are very small, one tenth of a percentage point, and the point estimate at 50 per cent of the median is the same (1.8 per cent). Thus, since the lines cross, one can not conclude dominance either way.

We next examine whether or not the choice of equivalence scale greatly affects the poverty estimates (see Table 3.7). Our base case, the OECD scale, and the parametric equivalence scale with the "size elasticity of needs" taken to be .75 yield fairly similar trends. Assuming much greater economies of scale, as we do in setting the size elasticity at .25, changes the picture dramatically. The increase in poverty between 1976 and 1981, for instance, is with this less generous scale almost a doubling – from 5.8 to 10.3 per cent. Moreover, poverty is in 1995 higher than it was in 1971, although it is lower than in 1981. The reasons for this quite dramatic reversal of trends needs to be examined more closely. We return to this by looking at the evolution of poverty incidence by household type.

Using the poverty standard that is fixed in real income, the changes over time look less dissimilar for different equivalence scales (shown in the last three columns of Table 3.7). Poverty using the least generous scale is higher in all but the first year, and the difference between poverty estimated using different scales tends to increase over time. The general pattern of poverty change, however, is much the same. This much higher level of poverty found using the elasticity of .25 is likely connected to an increase in the prevalence of single person households along with an increase in the poverty risk of this group. We return to this issue below.

Table 3.7 Poverty incidence using different equivalence scales – Finland 1971-95

Year	Current median			1985 median		
	$s^*=s^{.25}$	OECD	$s^*=s^{.75}$	$s^*=s^{.25}$	OECD	$s^*=s^{.75}$
71	8.8	8.8	8.2	24.4	30.1	30.2
76	5.8	5.1	5.2	11.0	10.5	10.2
81	10.3	5.8	5.7	13.0	7.4	7.3
85	9.8	3.5	3.5	9.8	3.5	3.5
90	8.8	2.7	2.8	6.1	1.2	1.2
91	9.5	3.6	3.8	6.3	1.5	1.5
92	9.6	3.4	3.6	7.5	1.9	2.0
93	9.0	3.2	3.4	7.9	2.0	2.2
94	9.0	2.5	2.6	8.4	1.8	1.7
95	9.5	3.0	3.2	8.3	1.8	1.9

Note: numbers given are the head count ratio setting the poverty line at 50 per cent of the reference median and using the equivalent number of adults $s^*=(a+c)^{.25}$, $s^*=1+.7(a+1)+.5c$ (the OECD scale) and $s^*=(a+c)^{.75}$, where a and c are the number of adults and children.

Source: Authors' calculations from HBS (1971-1990) and IDS (1991-95) microdata.

Finally, we examine the role of the public sector over time by looking at the difference between the share of poor prior to taxes and transfers and after such are paid.[8] This provides a crude way of assessing the importance of the public sector in moving from market to disposable income poverty. We ignore the order in which this transformation occurs. In principle, public transfers should be divided into those that are taxable (such as unemployment insurance payments and other work-related transfers) and those that are not (such as housing benefits and child allowances). The correct sequence would then be to examine market income + taxable transfers − taxes + non-taxable transfers = disposable income. Doing so

---

[8] Note that we use the same poverty line, i.e., a fraction of the current or 1985 median adjusted *disposable* income in measuring the incidence of poverty prior to taxes and transfers. General practice in these pre- post comparisons differs - many analysts also change the poverty line between these two income concepts – but we think the interpretation of the results simpler using our chosen method.

would be quite cumbersome, because there is some variation in the taxability of a transfer from year to year and it would entail looking at four rather than three poverty indices. Moreover, in some years some transfer programs have been partly administered as tax reductions (e.g., the presence of children used to give tax deductions). Arguably, it is the role of net transfers (transfers less taxes) that is more interesting, and this is what we examine.

Table 3.8 The proportion of poor measured in equivalent factor and disposable income – Finland 1971-90

Year	Current median Poverty measured in			1985 median Poverty measured in		
	Factor income	Disposable income	Difference	Factor income	Disposable income	Difference
71	20.0	8.8	11.3	34.2	30.1	4.1
76	18.9	5.1	13.7	22.2	10.5	11.7
81	21.4	5.8	15.5	22.7	7.4	15.3
85	21.7	3.5	18.2	21.7	3.5	18.2
90	24.9	2.7	22.2	22.1	1.2	21.0
91	26.3	3.6	22.7	22.7	1.5	21.2
92	30.4	3.4	27.0	27.7	1.9	25.8
93	34.7	3.2	31.5	32.4	2.0	30.3
94	35.2	2.5	32.7	33.5	1.8	31.8
95	34.1	3.0	31.1	31.9	1.8	30.1

The results are quite striking, although arguably not entirely unexpected. The proportion of the population with factor income below the current median poverty line was fairly stable at around 20 per cent until 1985, whereafter it increased to around 25 per cent in 1990. As a consequence, most likely, of the 1990s depression, more than a third of the population has income below this poverty line in 1995. The relatively stable relative poverty rate since 1985 has been accompanied by an increasing gap between factor and disposable incomes. The pattern for the line that is fixed in real terms is quite similar.

3.6 Poverty Risks in Selected Population Groups

In order to gain an understanding of the nature of poverty in Finland over the sample period, we now turn to an examination of the structure of poverty by population subgroups. We examine breakdowns of the population by age of the household reference person, household type, location and the socio-economic status of the reference person. For each breakdown, we show the poverty rate of each group with respect to our base case with the relative poverty line, as well as the sample size of each group.

We also show the distribution of the poverty population among the population decompositions. In parentheses below each population groups' share of the population of poor persons, we display that group's share of the overall population. Thus, if a group's poverty population share exceeds its share of the overall population, it is overrepresented among the poor.

3.6.1 Age of household reference person

We have, for completeness, calculated the poverty rates for each ten-year age intervals starting with "below 20". This first group is very small (for instance, in 1992 there were only 54 households in this group in the sample; see Table 3.9). For those groups that are relatively large, the age profile of poverty is highest for the young (20-29), fairly constant for the prime-aged (30-59) and, by the 1990s, lowest for the oldest groups. The two oldest groups of households, those between 60-69 and 70+, have experienced a decline in their poverty risks while the youngest (20-29) have seen it increase.

Jäntti et al. (1996) examine poverty (and inequality) among the elderly against the institutional shift from flat-rate national to legislated work-related pensions as the pension regime. Their results, which do not extend beyond 1990, suggest that the maturing of the work-related pensions has played a major role in reducing poverty among the elderly. Our results suggest that this process has continued. In fact, it may even have been strengthened by the increase in poverty among younger age groups brought on by income losses that in turn were brought about by increased unemployment. A small increase among the oldest age group after 1993 may have been brought about by the introduction for fiscal reasons of income testing of also the flat-rate part of the national pension.

Table 3.9   Poverty incidence by age of reference person – Finland 1971-95

Year	\-19	20-29	30-39	40-49	50-59	60-69	70-
71	0.0 (15)	4.9 (427)	5.0 (573)	8.9 (707)	12.6 (609)	11.9 (472)	15.0 (183)
76	9.6 (16)	4.0 (569)	3.9 (690)	3.5 (668)	7.6 (619)	7.2 (512)	9.3 (274)
81	23.1 (42)	6.7 (1053)	4.4 (1658)	5.1 (1638)	5.7 (1545)	7.6 (857)	8.9 (575)
85	25.4 (28)	5.7 (1077)	2.7 (2502)	2.5 (1936)	3.0 (1291)	4.5 (802)	5.5 (564)
90	6.9 (49)	3.9 (1142)	2.5 (1780)	1.9 (2093)	1.8 (1353)	3.5 (993)	5.1 (843)
91	25.0 (40)	7.1 (1595)	1.7 (2506)	3.5 (3229)	2.5 (2198)	3.5 (1530)	5.0 (988)
92	43.5 (54)	6.5 (1384)	2.3 (2213)	2.9 (2812)	2.7 (1874)	2.2 (1256)	3.4 (824)
93	44.6 (48)	6.3 (1242)	3.0 (1996)	2.8 (2556)	3.0 (1597)	1.6 (1033)	0.8 (704)
94	51.9 (48)	4.7 (1157)	2.4 (1929)	2.1 (2505)	1.8 (1579)	1.2 (995)	1.1 (751)
95	48.4 (42)	7.7 (1156)	2.3 (2021)	2.3 (2527)	2.4 (1684)	1.2 (1051)	1.7 (781)

Note: numbers given are the head count ratio for OECD equivalence scale at 50 per cent of the reference median. Numbers in parentheses are the sample sizes of each group.

Source: Authors' calculations from HBS (1971-1990) and IDS (1991-95) microdata.

Persons living in young households were in 1971 underrepresented among the poor almost by a factor of one half (see Table 3.10). In the 1990s, by contrast, they are overrepresented among the low income population, by a factor of at least two. In 1995, almost one in three of all poor persons lived in a household whose reference person was between 20 and 29 years old. The over-representation of the elderly among the poor has by the 1990s turned into an underrepresentation. An age group whose presence in the poverty population has also been subject to some change, consists of those persons living in households whose reference person is in the age group 50-59. These were also over-represented in the 1970s and have since formed a smaller share of the poverty population than of the overall.

Table 3.10 Composition of the poor by age of reference person – Finland 1971-95

	Age of reference person						
Year	-19	20-29	30-39	40-49	50-59	60-69	70-
71	0.0	7.6	13.7	26.7	25.7	17.4	9.0
	(0.3)	(13.6)	(23.8)	(26.5)	(17.8)	(12.7)	(5.3)
76	0.6	12.3	19.5	16.9	25.5	16.5	8.9
	(0.3)	(15.6)	(25.4)	(24.8)	(17.3)	(11.7)	(4.9)
81	2.1	17.1	22.0	19.5	17.3	12.1	9.9
	(0.5)	(14.8)	(29.0)	(22.1)	(17.8)	(9.3)	(6.5)
85	2.5	21.1	22.5	16.1	13.7	12.8	11.3
	(0.3)	(13.0)	(29.8)	(23.4)	(16.0)	(10.1)	(7.3)
90	1.0	18.3	25.5	17.8	9.0	12.5	15.9
	(0.4)	(13.0)	(28.5)	(26.4)	(13.6)	(9.7)	(8.5)
91	2.3	29.1	13.1	25.9	9.4	9.0	11.3
	(0.3)	(14.6)	(27.8)	(26.6)	(13.3)	(9.3)	(8.1)
92	5.7	27.2	19.3	22.6	10.7	6.1	8.3
	(0.4)	(14.1)	(28.1)	(26.7)	(13.2)	(9.1)	(8.3)
93	5.6	25.8	24.3	24.3	12.9	4.9	2.3
	(0.4)	(13.1)	(26.3)	(28.1)	(13.6)	(9.7)	(8.8)
94	7.1	25.0	24.3	24.8	10.3	4.4	4.1
	(0.3)	(13.3)	(25.4)	(28.6)	(13.8)	(9.4)	(9.1)
95	5.6	32.4	20.4	21.3	11.3	3.6	5.4
	(0.3)	(12.8)	(26.3)	(27.6)	(14.3)	(9.4)	(9.3)

Note: numbers given are the head count ratio of the group relative to the overall head count ratio for OECD equivalence scale at 50 per cent of the reference median. Numbers in parentheses are the population proportion of each group.
Source: Authors' calculations from HBS (1971-1990) and IDS (1991-95) microdata.

The decreased poverty risk of the elderly households is, as discussed above, a consequence of the change in pension regime. The increase in the poverty of youth households is most likely associated with both an increase in the proportion of youths in school and with the rise in youth unemployment rates after 1990. In 1990, the poverty rate of the population who was between 20-29 year old was 18 per cent. A year later, it was 29 and has since varied between 25 and 32 per cent. The increase after 1990 can likely be attributed mainly to increased unemployment along with increased labour force withdrawal.

3.6.2 Household type

Poverty incidence among different types of households is, in part, similar to that found for the breakdown by age (see Table 3.11). First, elderly households have seen their poverty rate reduced from 14.2 in 1971 to 1.1 per cent in 1995. Lone-parent households, while not very frequent in the early years we have data for, appear to have quite low poverty risks in the 1990s. Two-parent families as well as childless couples are, likewise, at low risk of being in poverty.

The low rate of lone-parent poverty is quite remarkable, as this group is traditionally at very high risk of poverty. However, they are also a group whose higher poverty risk is well known and it is subject to many transfer programs, such as child allowances, housing assistance and either unemployment benefits or (calculated in terms of equivalent adults) relatively generous social welfare payments. Thus, although lone parents are relatively disadvantaged, many transfer programs are designed to alleviate their more acute monetary shortages. A recent comparison of children in lone-mother families Bradbury and Jäntti (1998) appears to corroborate this finding. The Nordic countries – except Iceland, which is not in the Luxembourg Income Study database – had the lowest lone-mother poverty rates.

One group has a poverty risk in 1995 almost identical to that in 1971, namely single (non-elderly) adults. Roughly 9 per cent of single non-elderly adults were poor in both of those years. However, this group has doubled its share of all persons. This increase in the share of non-aged single persons has led to an increase in the likelihood that the average person is poor.

Again, the share of poor persons living in each of the household types mirrors the evolution of their poverty risks. Lone parents, the elderly and other households start off by being overrepresented among the poor. Persons in lone-parent households are about as frequent among the poor as in the population at large, and elderly and other households are, along with two-parent households and childless couples underrepresented among the poor. Single persons, on the other hand, who in 1971 were as frequent among the poor as among the whole population, populate more than one-third of the "poverty slots" when one in ten of the whole population lives in such a household.

In examining aggregate poverty using different equivalence scales above (see Table 3.7), we found that assigning the largest economies of scale, the trend was very different than that found using more generous scales. One possible explanation for that finding lies in the evolution of the relative poverty rates of single person households and their share of all persons.

Table 3.11   Poverty incidence by household type – Finland 1971-95

	Household type					
Year	Single parent	Two parent	Elderly	Childless couple	Single person	Other
71	24.9 (70)	6.5 (838)	14.2 (205)	7.2 (546)	9.2 (301)	9.6 (1026)
76	5.6 (68)	4.5 (1003)	7.7 (355)	3.8 (523)	7.9 (427)	5.4 (972)
81	10.2 (137)	5.2 (2141)	8.1 (669)	3.6 (1214)	11.0 (708)	5.0 (2499)
85	3.4 (220)	3.0 (3195)	4.8 (669)	2.0 (1116)	9.2 (655)	2.6 (2345)
90	1.9 (170)	2.4 (2171)	4.0 (1058)	1.3 (1492)	7.0 (1000)	2.1 (2362)
91	3.9 (749)	2.2 (1763)	4.1 (1463)	2.3 (2578)	10.5 (1636)	2.5 (3897)
92	6.4 (678)	2.2 (1617)	2.6 (1199)	2.4 (2202)	9.2 (1414)	2.3 (3307)
93	5.7 (595)	2.7 (1454)	0.4 (991)	2.6 (1913)	8.2 (1290)	2.6 (2933)
94	2.4 (628)	1.4 (1377)	0.5 (1033)	2.9 (1803)	6.4 (1261)	2.3 (2862)
95	2.7 (616)	2.7 (1408)	1.1 (1102)	2.7 (1967)	9.4 (1346)	2.1 (2823)

Note: numbers given are the head count ratio for OECD equivalence scale at 50 per cent of the reference median. Numbers in parentheses are the sample sizes of each group.
Source: Authors' calculations from HBS (1971-1990) and IDS (1991-95) microdata.

It turns out that the fact that overall poverty does not decline over the period studied using the scale that is not very generous to large households, i.e., that assumes very little increase in needs for each additional person (size elasticity .25), is driven by the high poverty rates found for single-person and elderly households. The poverty risk of single persons using this equivalence scale was 23.1 per cent in 1971 and 40.1 in 1995, compared to 9.2 and 9.4 using the OECD scale (table not shown). A constant poverty rate using the OECD scale occurs while we find, using another scale, for the same subgroup a steep increase in poverty. The development is similar but less pronounced for elderly households.

Table 3.12 Composition of the poor by household type – Finland 1971-95

Year	Household type					
	Single parent	Two parent	Elderly	Childless couple	Single person	Other
71	7.4 (2.6)	27.8 (37.5)	8.9 (5.5)	10.1 (12.2)	5.2 (5.0)	40.6 (37.2)
76	2.1 (1.9)	35.2 (39.9)	8.4 (5.6)	8.0 (10.8)	7.6 (4.9)	38.8 (36.9)
81	4.6 (2.6)	34.7 (38.6)	10.7 (7.7)	7.9 (12.8)	17.3 (9.2)	24.8 (29.0)
85	2.6 (2.7)	31.4 (36.9)	12.1 (8.9)	7.6 (13.3)	25.8 (10.0)	20.5 (28.3)
90	2.2 (3.2)	32.7 (37.2)	15.5 (10.7)	7.1 (15.0)	23.3 (9.1)	19.3 (24.9)
91	8.3 (7.5)	11.6 (18.5)	12.6 (11.0)	10.1 (15.7)	32.4 (11.0)	25.0 (36.3)
92	15.1 (8.0)	12.2 (19.1)	8.6 (11.2)	11.1 (15.6)	28.9 (10.6)	24.1 (35.5)
93	14.0 (7.8)	15.5 (18.5)	1.6 (11.5)	13.0 (16.1)	27.1 (10.6)	28.8 (35.4)
94	8.0 (8.2)	10.5 (18.1)	2.4 (11.7)	19.4 (16.4)	27.5 (10.6)	32.1 (35.0)
95	7.1 (7.9)	15.6 (17.5)	4.4 (12.0)	15.0 (17.1)	34.1 (10.9)	23.7 (34.5)

Note: numbers given are the head count ratio of the group relative to the overall head count ratio for OECD equivalence scale at 50 per cent of the reference median. Numbers in parentheses are the population proportion of each group.

Source: Authors' calculations from HBS (1971-1990) and IDS (1991-95) microdata.

The explanation for this finding lies in the favorable developments for multiperson households (or, conversely, the lack of favorable developments for singleperson households). Using less generous equivalence scales pushes multi-person households up in the distribution of equivalent income, which seems to be pushing also the adjusted median up, leaving, so to speak, single-person households behind. Apparently this gap has grown over time, as multi-person households have become comparatively better off.

3.6.3 Region

Poverty rates by region, shown in Table 3.13, reveal a substantial convergence in level-of-living differences by region taken over the whole period from 1971 to 1995. The differences in the poverty rates in the central and northern regions compared to the Helsinki region were 8 and 12 percentage points in 1971. The difference in 1995 is only 1.2 and 1.5 points. The central and northern regions have alternated as the region with the highest poverty rate. In the beginning of the period, the central had a higher rate and by 1995, the north topped the regional ranking. In the 1990s, it would appear that the differences may have increased a little.

Table 3.13   Poverty incidence by area – Finland 1971-95

Year	Region			
	Helsinki	South	Central	North
71	3.0 (370)	5.1 (1224)	15.4 (1001)	11.6 (391)
76	1.4 (479)	4.1 (1479)	6.8 (986)	9.9 (404)
81	2.3 (979)	5.8 (3295)	7.1 (2211)	7.9 (883)
85	1.1 (909)	3.3 (3224)	5.0 (2861)	4.7 (1206)
90	1.2 (1170)	2.3 (3317)	4.2 (2661)	3.5 (1105)
91	1.8 (1821)	3.6 (7135)	4.7 (2386)	4.1 (744)
92	1.8 (1670)	3.3 (4496)	4.9 (2922)	2.7 (1329)
93	1.9 (2027)	3.2 (3634)	4.0 (2470)	3.1 (1045)

Table 3.13 (continued)

94	1.9	2.4	2.7	3.2
	(1348)	(3982)	(2559)	(1075)
95	2.0	2.9	3.2	4.5
	(1483)	(4056)	(2617)	(1106)

Note: Numbers given are the head count ratio for OECD equivalence scale at 50 per cent of the reference median. Numbers in parentheses are the sample sizes of each group.

Source: Authors calculations from HBS (1971-1990) and IDS (1991-95) microdata.

There is, however, not much variation in the regional poverty rates in the 1990s. For this period no firm conclusions appear warranted about the direction of change in the regional differences and regional poverty rankings because of their volatility.

Internal migration, at the level on which we are measuring regions, has mainly been from the central regions of Finland to the south – see Table 3.14. Because the dispersion of poverty risks by region has decreased quite dramatically, so has that of each region's share of the poor. More than every second poor person lived in central Finland in 1971, while less than one in twenty lived in Helsinki. By now, a little more than a quarter live in central Finland while just over one in ten live in Helsinki. Regions other than Helsinki have over-representation of the poor – more than two fifths of the poor live in the south of Finland (excluding the Helsinki region).

The regional breakdown we use is quite standard in Finland and has been used by others to examine regional differences in various socio-economic phenomena, including mortality (see, e.g., Martikainen and Valkonen 1995) and inequality (Jäntti and Ritakallio 1997). However, much of the internal Finnish migration has been within the regions. In particular, we understate the movement into largish cities within each region. Given the nature of our data, however, more detailed breakdown e.g. by cities in the regions are not very practical.

3.6.4 Socio-economic status

The breakdown of the population by the socio-economic status of the reference person is fairly unsurprising. First, the groups with a strong (wage) labour force connection – white- and blue collar workers – are always at lowest risk of poverty. Even in 1971, their poverty rates were less than 3 per cent, and throughout the 1990s they were one per cent or lower. Farmers and entrepreneurs, who in 1971 had poverty rates of 20 and 16 per cent were, compared to the other groups, still in 1995 at high risk of having low income, with 6 and 9 per cent of such households having disposable income below the poverty line.

Table 3.14 Composition of the poor by area – Finland 1971-95

	Region			
Year	Helsinki	South	Central	North
71	4.8 (14.1)	25.0 (42.8)	53.7 (30.6)	16.5 (12.5)
76	4.1 (15.1)	35.3 (44.6)	36.6 (27.8)	23.9 (12.5)
81	6.2 (16.0)	43.1 (43.7)	33.3 (27.5)	17.4 (12.8)
85	5.0 (16.6)	40.0 (43.5)	38.2 (27.1)	16.8 (12.7)
90	7.8 (17.1)	36.0 (43.8)	39.9 (26.4)	16.4 (12.8)
91	8.1 (15.9)	58.9 (58.2)	25.3 (19.2)	7.8 (6.7)
92	8.6 (16.3)	42.0 (43.5)	38.6 (26.8)	10.9 (13.4)
93	9.9 (17.1)	43.9 (43.3)	33.3 (26.5)	12.8 (13.1)
94	13.7 (17.5)	41.7 (43.6)	28.3 (26.1)	16.3 (12.8)
95	11.4 (17.5)	43.3 (44.4)	27.3 (25.9)	18.0 (12.2)

Note: numbers given are the head count ratio of the group relative to the overall head count ratio for OECD equivalence scale at 50 per cent of the reference median. Numbers in parentheses are the population share of each group.

Source: Authors' calculations from HBS (1971-1990) and IDS (1991-95) microdata.

It should be noted, however, that the incomes of these groups are likely the least accurately measured. In particular, it is commonly believed that substantial underreporting of income occurs within these groups. However, in the absence of a convincing case to the contrary, it would appear that over time the position of these groups has improved.

Finally, the residual category "other", consisting of pensioners, students and others who are not economically active, have experienced a large decline in poverty risk. More than a fifth in 1971 and one in ten in 1976 of

Table 3.15 Poverty incidence by socio-economic status – Finland 1971-95

Year	Socio-economic status				
	Farmer	Entrepreneur	White-collar worker	Blue-collar worker	Other
71	19.7 (844)	15.9 (93)	2.3 (616)	2.6 (960)	21.1 (473)
76	14.7 (350)	12.0 (121)	0.7 (922)	2.2 (1162)	11.1 (793)
81	14.3 (794)	8.8 (349)	1.2 (2123)	2.9 (2511)	14.0 (1591)
85	7.8 (795)	10.3 (520)	0.4 (2609)	1.4 (2764)	8.7 (1512)
90	6.1 (547)	8.9 (509)	0.4 (2762)	0.9 (2267)	6.3 (2168)
91	11.2 (844)	8.3 (1245)	0.4 (4087)	1.0 (2787)	8.5 (3123)
92	8.9 (700)	9.4 (1060)	0.4 (3501)	1.0 (2159)	6.9 (2997)
93	8.8 (619)	12.6 (881)	0.4 (3109)	0.6 (1756)	5.3 (2811)
94	5.6 (701)	9.1 (698)	0.2 (2872)	0.5 (1780)	4.3 (2913)
95	6.4 (716)	9.4 (695)	0.5 (3100)	0.7 (1911)	5.7 (2840)

Note: numbers given are the head count ratio for OECD equivalence scale at 50 per cent of the reference median. Numbers in parentheses are the sample sizes of each group.

Source: Authors' calculations from HBS (1971-1990) and IDS (1991-95) microdata.

such households had income below the poverty line. While their poverty rate has fluctuated somewhat in the early 1990s, by 1995 no more than 6 per cent of those households had income below the poverty line.

In 1971, two in five poor persons lived in farm households, and a little more than a third in households whose reference person was not economically active ("other"). In 1995, by contrast, "other households" accounted for 60 per cent of the poverty population, while the share in farm

Table 3.16 Composition of the poor by socio-economic status – Finland 1971-95

Year	Socio-economic status				
	Farmer	Entrepreneur	White-collar worker	Blue-collar worker	Other
71	39.0 (17.3)	8.6 (4.7)	6.1 (23.3)	11.7 (40.3)	34.6 (14.4)
76	34.2 (12.0)	10.1 (4.3)	3.8 (29.8)	16.2 (37.5)	35.6 (16.4)
81	24.4 (10.0)	7.2 (4.8)	6.3 (31.6)	17.5 (35.1)	44.6 (18.5)
85	18.5 (8.4)	17.9 (6.2)	3.9 (32.9)	13.2 (33.5)	46.4 (19.0)
90	13.7 (6.1)	22.4 (6.9)	4.8 (36.0)	9.3 (29.3)	49.8 (21.7)
91	15.3 (4.9)	17.2 (7.4)	3.9 (36.4)	8.2 (28.0)	55.4 (23.3)
92	13.0 (4.9)	19.2 (6.9)	3.7 (35.5)	7.4 (25.0)	56.7 (27.6)
93	13.2 (4.8)	26.0 (6.6)	4.0 (34.8)	4.1 (22.3)	52.7 (31.5)
94	11.0 (4.9)	23.5 (6.4)	3.0 (33.5)	4.6 (22.2)	57.9 (33.0)
95	9.8 (4.6)	20.1 (6.5)	5.7 (34.1)	5.3 (23.3)	59.1 (31.5)

Note: numbers given are the head count ratio of the group relative to the overall head count ratio for OECD equivalence scale at 50 per cent of the reference median. Numbers in parentheses are the population share of each group.

Source: Authors calculations from HBS (1971-1990) and IDS (1991-95) microdata.

households was one in ten. Households headed by entrepreneurs now account for one fifth of the poverty population, as opposed to 9 per cent in 1971. Blue- and white-collar workers, by contrast, account for far fewer among the poor than their population share would suggest, were poverty risks more evenly distributed across the population.

3.7 Concluding Comments

We have examined the trends in low income poverty in Finland using both relative and fixed-price poverty lines. We find that, using most summary approaches, poverty has declined over the 1971-1990 period and stayed fairly constant in the 1990s. The decline in poverty prior to 1990 was to be expected, because during this period unemployment was low, economic growth fairly stable and high and many welfare-state institutions were expanded. The stability of poverty in the 1990s is somewhat more remarkable. A large decline in GDP and dramatically increased unemployment did not lead to increases in poverty.

The poverty risks of selected demographic groups, who have traditionally been at high risk of poverty, such as the elderly and lone parents, has declined substantially during the period and are lower than that of the average. This development can be contrasted with that of non-aged (mostly young) single persons, whose poverty rate has, depending on the equivalence scale used, either stayed constant or increased over time. Thus, in 1995, the typical poor Finn was a young single adult.

This insulation of the low income population from large adverse effects of the economic depression is a sign that at least in part, welfare-state institutions did (part of) what they were supposed to, namely to protect people against adverse economic developments. There are reasons to be cautious with respect to the future evolution of income poverty. High public debt and the budgetary restrictions that follow from membership in the European Monetary Union, due to start in January 1999, together with increasing market-oriented rhetoric in public debate, has lead to pressure against the present scope and coverage of welfare state institutions. The gap between market income and disposable income poverty has increased substantially during the 1990s. Future decreases in income transfers are therefore likely to lead to increased income poverty.

References

Alapuro, R. (1980). *An interface periphery*, Research Reports 25, Research Group for Comparative Sociology, University of Helsinki, Helsinki.

Alestalo, M. and Uusitalo, H. (1986). "Finland", in P. Flora, ed., *Growth to limits. The western European welfare states since World War II*, Vol. 1, De Gruyter and Aldine and Mouton, Berlin, pp. 198-292.

Alestalo, M. and Kuhnle, S. (1986). The Scandinavian Route: Economic, Social and Political Developments in Denmark, Finland, Norway and Sweden. In R. Eriksson, E. J. Hansen, S. Ringen and H. Uusitalo eds. *The Scandinavian Model. Welfare States and Welfare Research*, M. E. Sharpe, Inc., Armonk, pp. 3-38.

Alestalo, M. and Uusitalo, H. (1992). Social expenditure: A decompositional approach, in J. E. Kolberg, ed., *The study of welfare state regimes*, M.E. Sharpe Inc., Armonk, pp. 37-68.

Atkinson, A. B. (1987). On the measurement of poverty, *Econometrica* 55, 749-764.

Bordes, C., Currie, D. and Söderström, H. T. (1993). Three assessments of Finland's economic crisis and economic policy, *Suomen Pankin Julkaisuja, Sarja C*, Bank of Finland, Helsinki.

Bradbury, B. and Jäntti, M. (1998). *Child poverty across industrialized countries*, Occasional paper, UNICEF, International Child Development Centre, Florence.

Esping-Andersen, G. (1990). *The three worlds of welfare capitalism*, Princeton University Press, Princeton.

Esping-Andersen, G. and Korpi, W. (1987). From poor relief to institutional welfare states: the development of Scandinavian social policy, in R. Eriksson, E. J. Hansen, S. Ringen and H. Uusitalo, eds, *The Scandinavian Model. Welfare States and Welfare Research*, M. E. Sharpe, Inc., Armonk, pp. 39-74.

Forma, P. (1998). *Mielipiteiden muutos ja pysyvyys: Suomalaisten mielipiteet hyvinvointivaltiosta, sosiaaliturvasta ja hyvinvointipalveluista vuosina 1992 ja 1996*, (Stability and Instability of the Opinions. Finnish Attitudes to Welfare State, Social Security and Social Service, in 1992 and 1996). Raportteja 222, STAKES, Helsinki.

Foster, J., Greer, J. and Thorbecke, E. (1984). A class of decomposable poverty measures, *Econometrica* 52, 761-766.

Gustafsson, B. and Uusitalo, H. (1990). The welfare state and poverty in Finland and Sweden from the mid-1960s to the mid-1980s, *Review of Income and Wealth* 36(3), 249-266.

Heikkilä, M. (1990). *Köyhyys ja huono-osaisuus hyvinvointivaltiossa*, Publications 8/90, National Board of Social Welfare, Helsinki. (English title: Poverty and deprivation in a welfare state).

Honkapohja, S., Koskela, E. and Paunio, J. (1993). *The crisis of the Finnish economy*, Discussion Papers 351, Department of Economics, University of Helsinki, Helsinki.

Jenkins, S. P. and Lambert, P. J. (1997). Three 'i's of poverty curves, with an analysis of U.K. poverty trends., *Oxford Economic Papers* 49(3), 317-327.

Jäntti, M., Kangas, O. and Ritakallio, V.-M. (1996). From marginalism to institutionalism: distributional consequences of the transformation of the Finnish pension regime, *Review of Income and Wealth* 42(4), 473-491.

Jäntti, M. and Ritakallio, V.-M. (1997). Income distribution and poverty in Finland in the 1980s, in P. Gottschalk, B. Gustafsson and E. Palmer, eds, *The distribution of economic welfare in the 1980s*, Cambridge University Press, Cambridge.

Kangas, O. (1994). The merging of welfare state models?, *Journal of European Social Policy* 4(2), 79-94.

Kangas, O. and Ritakallio, V.-M. (1998). Different methods – different results? Approaches to multidimensional poverty, in H. J. Andress, ed., *Empirical Poverty Research in a Comparative Perspective*, Avebury, Aldershot.

Kangas, O. and Ritakallio, V.-M. (1999). Social policy or structure? Income transfers, socio-demographic factors and poverty in the Nordic countries and in France, in B. Palier and D. Boguet, eds, *Comparing Social Welfare Systems in Europe*, Vol. 3, MIRE, Paris. Forthcoming.

Kosunen, V. (1997). The recession and changes in social security in the 1990s, in M. Heikkilä and H. Uusitalo, eds, *The Cost of Cuts. Studies in cutbacks of social security and their effects in the Finland of the 1990s*, National Research and Development Centre for Welfare and Health, Helsinki, Finland, pp. 41-68.

Martikainen, P. and Valkonen, T. (1995). Lama ja enneaikainen kuolleisuus (Recesion and Early Mortality), Vol. 11 of *Väestö, Tilastokeskus (Statistics Finland)*, Helsinki, Finland.

Ministry of Labour (1997). *Finnish Labour Review*, number 1-2, Planning Secreteriat.

Ritakallio, V.-M. (1986). *Kartoitus suomalaisesta köyhyystutkimuksesta ja arviot tutkimustarpeista* (Survey of the Finnish Poverty Research and an Assessment of the Future Needs of Research), Publications 16/86, National Board of Social Welfare.

Ritakallio, V.-M. (1994a). *Finnish poverty: A cross-national comparison*, Working Paper 119, Luxembourg Income Study.

Ritakallio, V.-M. (1994b). *Köyhyys Suomessa 1981-1990: Tutkimus tulonsiirtojen köyhyyttä poistavista vaikutuksista* (Poverty in Finland 1981-1990: A Study of effects of income transfers), *STAKES*, Helsinki.

Ritakallio, V.-M. (1994c). Köyhyyden muuttunut kuva suomessa 1966-90 (Changed Pictures of Poverty in Finland between 1966-90), in M. Heikkilä and K. Vähätalo, eds, *'Huono-osaisuus ja hyvinvointivaltion muutos'*, Gaudeamus Kirja, Tammer-Paino, Tampere, pp. 169-190.

Statistics Finland (1996). *Statistical of Yearbook Finland*, Statistics Finland, Helsinki.

Uusitalo, H. (1989). *Income Distribution in Finland*, Studies No. 148, Central Statistical Office of Finland, Helsinki.

4 Poverty in Iceland

STEFÁN ÓLAFSSON AND KARL SIGURÐSSON

4.1 Introduction: General Background and Previous Research

There has been little research into poverty in modern Iceland. The history of Iceland up to the present century has been, however, to a great extent marked by poverty. After the completion of the settlement of Iceland and the passing of the Early Republic by the 13th century, a prolonged period of stagnation set in with all the characteristics of poverty in a primitive agricultural subsistence economy. The population fluctuated greatly with the environmental conditions, and was at its highest around a level of 50,000, which is the estimated maximum number of inhabitants during the Early Republic (from 10th to 13th centuries). In addition to the vagaries of fragile subsistence based on agriculture in a cold climate, volcanic eruptions, isolation and various plagues took their toll repeatedly and checked the population. The subsistence was supplemented by some inshore fishing where possible and other meagre means, but on the whole this situation lasted until the 19th century. It was only after the middle of that century that the population at last exceeded the 50,000 level and continued to grow steadily (Guðmundur Hálfdanarson (1993)). The social historian Gísli Ágúst Gunnlaugsson (1978 and 1986) has estimated that during the period from 1700 to 1900 the "natural" maximum rate for poverty in Iceland may have approached 40 per cent, but in good years when the population was also at a relatively low level it may have been closer to 20 per cent. Taking an example from two bad years, 1703 and 1880, he has specified the nature and extent of poverty. For the year 1703 he estimates that about 14 per cent of the population were in absolute need of assistance in order to survive, whilst another 18 per cent of adults were too poor to be able to marry (Gísli Ágúst Gunnlaugsson (1986), p. 13-14). In 1880 he estimates the comparable figures to have been 10 per cent and 25 per cent respectively.

By the last quarter of the 19th century, the modernisation of the fishing industry was well under way, bringing with it the concomitant patterns of change, such as urbanisation, mechanisation and industrialisation; state-building and growing pressure for independence from Denmark; increased economic growth, and even a gradually improved standard of living (Stefán Ólafsson, 1993, pp. 195-216).

Nonetheless, it has been estimated that by the turn of the century

Iceland was amongst the poorest regions in Europe (Magnús S. Magnússon og Gísli Gunnarsson (1987)). Development during the 20th century has however been very rapid, as evidenced by the fact that by the 1960s Iceland was already on a level with the neighbouring countries regarding GNP per capita and nowadays generally ranks amongst the top 10 to 15 most affluent nations (Stefán Ólafsson (1990)).

The twentieth century has thus been a period of extremely rapid development in Iceland. As regards the development of the welfare state it appears that Iceland introduced modernist legislation, such as that regarding pensions, accident insurance and sickness, quite early compared to other countries. During the 1930s comprehensive legislation on social security was introduced, aiming at organisational co-ordination as well as consolidation of rights and means of financing. At the end of the Second World War a new major piece of legislation was introduced, with the stated goal of establishing as comprehensive and as advanced a system of social security as any known in the world at the time (Stefán Ólafsson, 1993a, p. 67 and 1993b, pp. 399-430). By 1950 Iceland thus enjoyed a welfare system broadly comparable to that of the Scandinavian systems at the time, and social expenditure as a proportion of GNP was also comparable. However, during the Sixties and Seventies, Iceland lagged somewhat behind in extending rights and increasing the generosity of the programs, compared to the major Scandinavian states. Nowadays the situation is that the Icelandic welfare state is to a large extent based on the Scandinavian model, but is a relative laggard within that group.

In the modern period the most significant attempt to estimate the poverty level in Iceland was carried out in 1986 by Sigurður Snævarr, an economist at the National Economic Institute.[1] He used tax data for 1984 and an absolute definition of the poverty line, based amongst other things on the amount of minimal pay and the value of some social benefits. In working out his definitions and calculations (for example the family equivalence ratios), he followed the guidelines used by OECD.[2] The figures were based on gross earnings and their limitations were duly explained by the author. The findings were that about 23 per cent of taxpayers were under the

---

[1] See also the other contributions to a conference on poverty in Iceland, held by the Association of Local Governments (Samband íslenskra sveitarfélaga) in 1986, in an unpublished collection titled "Fátækt á Íslandi", available at the Social Sciences Research Institute, University of Iceland.

[2] The OECD recommendations give a couple the weight of 1.7 and each child 0.5. The other method the author used, which produced lower poverty rates, gave couples the factor of 1.5 and each child 0.25.

poverty line when a stricter version of equivalence ratios were used, but this fell to about 17 per cent when the weightings for children and extra adults were lowered. Looking specifically at employees, the figures ranged between 14.5 and 19.7 per cent, while pensioners scored in the range of 30 to 35 per cent and the self-employed varied from 24 to 37 per cent. The latter group was generally assumed to be exaggerated due to an expected higher level of tax evasion than is common amongst other groups of tax payers. These results were generally badly received in Iceland, and considered by many commentators to be unbelievably high. An economist at the Wage Investigation Committee (*Kjararannsóknarnefnd*), Ari Skúlason (1986), attempted an estimate of the poverty level amongst the members of the Federation of Labour (ASÍ) at the same time, on the basis of payroll data and using a considerably lower absolute poverty line. His conclusion was that the poverty population ranged between 8 and 17 per cent, depending on definitions. These estimates pointed in particular to the groups of single parents and pensioners as being particularly prone to falling into poverty, along with the lowest paid on the labour market.

On the whole, the outcomes of previous research are thus rather inconclusive, especially with regard to definitions of the most meaningful poverty line. The approach of using relative measures of poverty levels, basing the poverty line on, for example, 50 per cent of the median family earnings has not previously been used systematically.

4.2 Poverty in Perspective: The Level of Living Environment in Contemporary Iceland

In order to understand poverty in Iceland it is necessary to explain, if only briefly, the major characteristics of the level of living in Iceland. It is also useful to assess changes in the socio-economic environment during the last 10 to 15 years, since that may have specifically affected the situation of the poor.

On the whole, one can say that the level of living environment in Iceland is different from that prevailing in the Scandinavian countries. This is primarily due to the large role of the fishing industry in the economy. The fishing sector (fishing and fish processing) is the biggest export industry of the country, even though it directly employs only about 10-11 per cent of the labour force. In comparison to manufacturing, fishing is subject to greater fluctuations in fortune, since it is not only sensitive to market fluctuations but also to natural or climatic fluctuations. This means that the GNP of Iceland fluctuates more than is common amongst the OECD countries. This has in some ways affected the level of living, since these fluctuations have generally vibrated throughout the whole economy. A recession in the fishing sector thus tends to a large extent to become a recession for the whole economy. Governments have also been prone to shape their economic policy disproportionately on the needs of the fishing sector.

On the basis of a level of living survey done in 1988 in Iceland, and a comparison to similar Scandinavian surveys done during 1986-1988, one can characterise the main features of the living standard of the Icelanders (Stefán Ólafsson (1990) and Joachim Vogel (1990)). Pay levels are lower in Iceland than in Denmark, Finland, Norway and Sweden. Employment participation is amongst the highest in Iceland, unemployment the lowest, working hours the longest, dual-earner households are more common in Iceland and the holding of a second job is also the most common there. So the Icelanders start off from a position of lower living standards, even though the GNP per capita is similar to the average for the Nordic countries as a whole. When the high volume of work in Iceland is taken into consideration, along with the considerably lower levels of taxation, one can safely say that the situation becomes much more equal to the other Nordic countries in terms of total disposable earnings (see Stefán Ólafsson (1990), pp. 39-42 and National Economic Institute, (1995), p. 11). This corresponds with the fact that private consumption levels are relatively high in Iceland, despite the lower basic pay levels described above. The high level of private consumption is reflected in a higher level of home ownership than in the other countries, a higher standard and larger size of housing, extensive car ownership and also a high level of ownership of various durable consumer items. A direct and targeted comparison of the private consumption levels of the manual working classes in the Nordic countries indicates, for example, that the Icelandic working class has an above average position within the Nordic group in respect of the level of living items examined (Stefán Ólafsson (1990), pp. 90-94).

But it still is evident that the Icelanders have to strive harder for their high level of living. Extra earnings (for overtime, extra jobs and the work of a spouse) constitute a larger proportion of the total family earnings in Iceland than in the other countries. This means that the level of living in Iceland is more precarious. It is particularly vulnerable in the face of a tighter labour market for employees, and it is also vulnerable in the face of a forced temporary absence from the labour market due to health problems, maternity leave and similar, since the generosity of the Icelandic welfare state is more limited than that of the other countries. It is also vulnerable because the Icelanders in general are great materialists and aim high in their private consumption, and perhaps do not always exercise caution in building up debt. This is, for example, reflected in the fact that Icelanders complain more than their Nordic neighbours about not managing to make ends meet in their daily life while at the same time enjoying an above average level of private consumption. On the whole, Icelanders have built their high level of living on an overheated economy during the post-war period, where ample opportunities for extra work have been available, along with considerable opportunities for short-term windfall earnings, for example for unskilled workers on the fishing fleet, especially on the trawlers. All of this has, however, changed somewhat in the last decade, with a prolonged recession in the fishing sector and rising unemployment. The following account describes the changes in the level of living environment which have affected the poor specifically during the last 10 to 15 years.

Firstly, we look at the general distribution of earnings in Iceland from 1986 to 1994.[3] On the whole, figures 4.1 and 4.2 indicate that the income distribution in the country has become slightly more unequal during this period. This at least applies to the part of the population which, according to tax records, has some earnings from employment.

Since the concept of employment earnings only covers those who report employment earnings, the most significant groups which are excluded are pensioners and the self-employed. If those were included, the main effect on the distribution would be to increase the share of the pensioner population, i.e. in the upper reaches of the age groups.[4]

---

[3] The data comes from the National Economic Institute, Tekjur, eignir og dreifing þeirra árin 1993 og 1994 (November 1995).
[4] National Economic Institute (1995), p. 7.

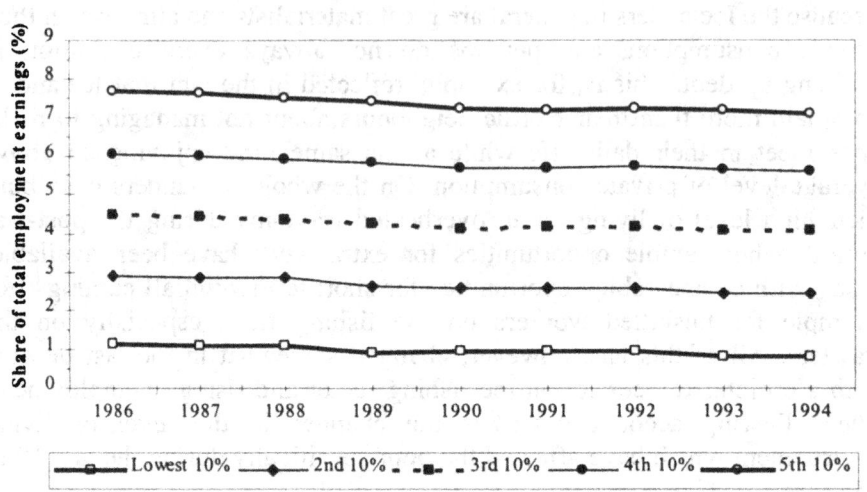

Figure 4.1 Income shares of the lowest 5 deciles, 1986-1994[5]

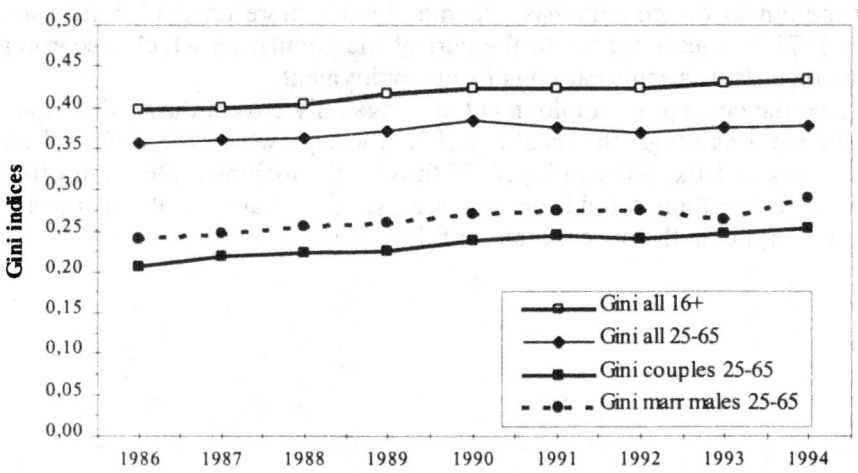

Figure 4.2 Inequality of employment earnings

Note: The top line shows the Gini indices for all individuals 16 years of age and over, the second line shows the indices for all in the age bracket 25-65, the third refers to couples 25-65 and the last only refers to married males 25-65 years of age. All the figures are tax data from National Economic Institute.

---

[5] The figures are based on employment earnings of tax payers aged 16 and over.

In addition one would ideally want to have better representatives from the group of the unemployed as well as from those that are not active on the labour market. These figures are nonetheless important as indicators about what has been happening to the distribution of earnings on the labour market during the period. Changes in the overall distribution of incomes are likely to have affected the probability that people in the lower rungs of the distribution might drop below the poverty level. On the whole, one would expect that an increase in inequality might increase the size of the poverty population, at least when measured in relative terms.

The Gini indices show a creeping trend towards increased inequality in the distribution of employment earnings. The figures are highest for all taxpayers 16 years of age and above, slightly lower when the age bracket is narrowed to 25-65 and the inequality is further reduced when one only considers couples or only married males between 25 and 65 years of age.

The next figure (Figure 4.3) shows some of the effects of the large fluctuations of the gross national income in Iceland, as well as the developments in wages and salaries during recent years.

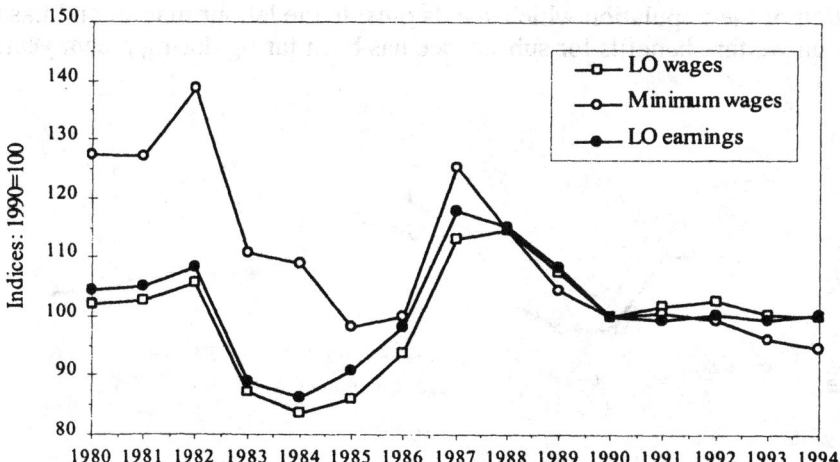

Figure 4.3 Purchasing power of LO (ASÍ) wages, minimum wages and monthly earnings of LO members, between 1980 and 1994

In 1983-4 there was a major recession in the fishing sector which was met with a drastic reduction of real pay levels. Unemployment increased slightly at the same time. This recession was, however, a short term one, as usual, and the following upswing was quite powerful. The year 1987 was the peak year both in terms of GNP and real pay levels. The period from 1988 to 1994 can perhaps best be described as a period of stagnation which nonetheless shows some significant signs of revival from 1994. On the whole, pay reductions tend to be slightly more drastic than reductions of earnings during periods of recession, and this is quite clear from the figure above. What is particularly interesting from the figure is the development of the minimum wage, which has lagged slightly behind in the last years. The purchasing power of the minimum wage has, however, been better maintained than appears from the graph due to a few supplementary payments to low wage earners, which have resulted from collective bargaining in the labour market since 1988. When those payments are taken into account, the drop in the real minimum wage rate in the last two years disappears and a more stable pattern emerges. On the whole then, the development of minimum wages is not likely to have caused any significant equalising effects in the income hierarchy, as indeed was indicated in Figures 4.1 and 4.2.

Figure 4.4 shows the developments of some major social security benefits from 1980 to 1994. This is an important indicator of how the section of the population which stands outside the labour market and has to rely on welfare benefits for subsistence has been faring during recent years.

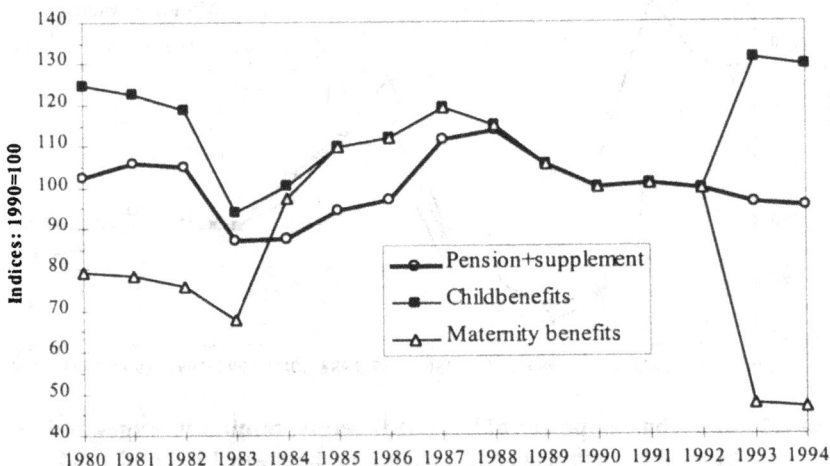

Figure 4.4   Purchasing power of major social security benefits 1980-1994

The most important benefit is obviously the pension, including the income supplement (i.e. the major benefit for old age and invalidity, which is also comparable to the benefits for the unemployed). The child and maternity benefits are, however, important for families, especially single-parent families. In general, the reduction of the real benefits was milder than that of the wages during the recession of 1993-4. But on the whole, the development of the purchasing power of pensions since 1987 is quite similar to that of the LO-wages and earnings, with a significant reduction to 1990 and a relative stability, or a slight decrease, since then. The system of child and maternity benefits was changed in 1992-3 with the former being increased in value while the latter was lowered. In addition, some steps have been taken towards means-testing of pensions and child benefits during recent years, i.e. giving reduced benefits to the higher income classes. On the whole, however, there have not been any such developments in the values of the major social security benefits during recent years which are likely to have greatly improved the earnings position of pensioners, nor others relying on benefits for survival, such as the unemployed.

Lastly, we examine the major features of the employment developments which are likely to have affected the situation of the poorer sections of the population, e.g. the employment level.[6]

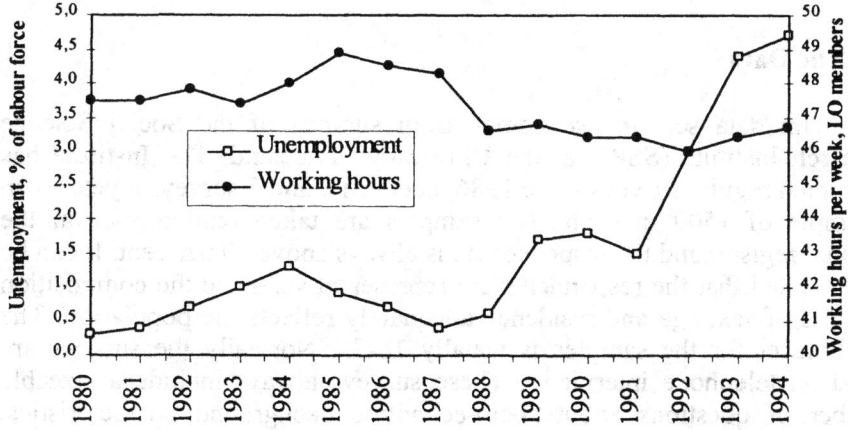

Figure 4.5 Unemployment levels and weekly working hours, 1980-1994

Figure 4.5 shows how unemployment has risen drastically during the stagnation period from 1988. The high peak at the top of the serious recession in 1984 kept unemployment below 1.5 per cent of the labour force, which reflects the generally low level of unemployment in Iceland in

---

[6] The data for Figures 4.4 and 4.5 comes from Kjararannsóknarnefnd and the Ministry of Social Affairs.

the post-war period. Most of the time unemployment has remained close to or below the 1 per cent level. The steep climb up to the present level of 4-5 per cent is thus a historically significant development in Iceland, and for the most part a new experience for the population and government alike. In an economy such as the Icelandic one, where high volumes of work have constituted such a significant part of the level of living, this is indeed a very significant development (Stefán Ólafsson, (1992)). It has simultaneously reduced work-participation and cut overtime work. On the whole, one would expect this change to have affected the chances of falling into poverty significantly, and in the absence of sufficiently countervailing trends one would in effect expect an increase in the size of the poverty population during recent years.

Now we come to our own analysis of poverty in Iceland during the last 10 years. Firstly, we describe the data used in our study and then present the results from our measurements of relative poverty rates in Iceland. Finally, we show how poverty rates differ between major socio-economic groups, both on the basis of gross family earnings and disposable family earnings.

4.3 The Data

The main data set we use comes from surveys of the Social Science Research Institute (SSRI) at the University of Iceland. The Institute has conducted regular surveys since 1986, between 2 and 5 surveys a year, with a sample of 1500 in each. The samples are taken randomly from the national register and the response rate is always above 70 per cent. It can be safely stated that the respondents are representative, since the composition in terms of sex, age and residence adequately reflects the population. The age bracket for the samples is usually 18-75. Normally the surveys are based on telephone interviews. These surveys always include a sizeable number of questions about socio-economic background characteristics. Amongst those are questions on total earnings of respondents and total earnings of the family (the respondent and the spouse). In addition there are questions on work participation, working hours, occupational class, industry and employment sector, employment status, reasons for non-participation in the labour market, marital status and education. In some of the surveys we have included questions on the number of dependent children in the household.

In each year since 1986 there has been at least two surveys, one in the spring and one in the autumn. In fact, in most of the years we have access to more surveys than that, i.e. up to as many as 5. For our analysis we have, however, only relied on those surveys in which we have the data on the number of dependent children in the household. This is because we need information on family income per equivalent adult for our analysis of poverty rates. According to the standard procedure we assign a weight to the family members as follows: respondent=1, spouse=0.7, each child living in the household=0.5. For a household consisting of a couple and two children we then divide the family earnings by 2.7 to obtain the family earnings per equivalent individual. In some households there are likely to be additional family members who in some cases may share the family income, for example elderly or sick relatives and adult offspring. This could also apply to individuals in the age group 18-25/30 who live at their parents' home, unless they themselves are the respondents. In most cases, such additional members are, however, likely to bring some earnings or benefits into the family budget. Their exclusion from our analysis may not seriously affect the overall outcome since their earnings or benefits are also excluded in our measurement of family earnings.

The measure of family earnings is based on a question worded as follows: "How large, approximately, were the total family earnings last month, i.e. before tax?". The instructions to the interviewers stated that this should include an addition of everything: all employment earnings for both respondent and spouse, earnings from extra jobs and overtime, overtime, study loans for students, social security benefits and similar. There was also a separate question on the total earnings of the respondent himself, in case he was not married or cohabiting. That question, however, only refers to employment earnings but, on the basis of a comparison of employment earnings and total earnings to which we have access, we have adjusted it to make it comparable to the base of the family earnings. This required an increase in the reported earnings of single respondents by an average of 10 per cent.

The question on family earnings is well tried and tested in the SSRI's surveys since it has remained unchanged during the whole period. It generally has a good response, with the refusals and the 'don't knows' usually remaining below 10 per cent of respondents. The main drawback of this sort of data is that respondents remember their own earnings inaccurately, and even more so for the earnings of a spouse, so the reply is bound to be approximate, as indeed is called for in the question. The indication is, though, that the deviations may cancel out and thereby avoid a systematic bias. A comparison of outcomes from this source with figures of payroll data for employees within the Federation of Labour (ASÍ) gives a satisfactory correspondence, with the reservation that our figures are generally higher.[7] That, however, is logical, since our figures include more earnings components than the other data, which is based solely on earnings from the main job. This data source, i.e. the survey material, is, however, different from the tax data that Sigurður Snævarr used in his study of poverty and it is only logical that our outcomes should be different. Tax evasion and underreporting of benefits and other earnings, as well as different sources for information on family members, contribute to that difference.

In addition to the regular half-yearly surveys of the Social Sciences Research Institute, we have also made use of the Level of Living Survey of 1988. That was a survey amongst 2000 individuals of 16-75 years of age, based on interviews in the homes of the respondents. This survey was modelled on the Scandinavian level of living surveys undertaken in 1986-7. This survey included a more detailed breakdown of earnings components for both the respondent and the spouse, as well as earned benefits, and also more detailed information on family composition. The main value of that survey is that it included a large array of questions on various levels of living components, and even included some subjective attitudes to the level of living, such as satisfaction with life, the financial situation of the family, and difficulties experienced in making ends meet in the day-to-day running of the home. It also included a question of received financial assistance from local authorities due to family hardship. This material will be used to reflect further on the situation of the poor in Iceland in our ensuing analysis.

On the whole, we feel confident that our data can give a valid measure of the poverty level and the composition of the poverty population in Iceland. There still remains the uncertainty of establishing whether the 20-30 per cent of our survey sample members whom we do not manage to reach are different as regards level of living. Since telephone ownership is nearly universal in Iceland, and the basic demographic and regional composition of our respondents reflects the population adequately in all our surveys, we can only assume that this is a minimal risk factor.

The array of surveys at hand which have the necessary data is such that we should also be able to give a reasonable assessment of developments in the poverty level from 1986 to 1997. The surveys we use for the trend analysis are from 1986 (2 surveys added, sample 3,000), 1988 (3 surveys, sample 5,000), 1989 (3 surveys, sample 4,500), 1991 (1 survey, sample

---

[7] See the report "Kjör Íslendinga í árslok 1988: Könnun á atvinnu og tekjum í nóvember 1988 með samanburði við kannanir frá maí 1988 og nóvember 1987" (SSRI, February, 1989) and comparison to *Fráttabréf Kjararannsóknarnefndar*.

1,500), 1992 (1 survey, sample 1,500), 1993 (1 survey, sample 1,500), 1995 (2 surveys, sample 3,000), 1996 (2 surveys, sample 3,000) and 1997 (2 surveys, sample 3,000). For the year 1995 we have also estimated the disposable earnings, on the basis of tax data on taxation and transfer levels by income brackets. This gives us the possibility of comparing the gross and net poverty level for that year, which on the whole gives more comparable data to that used in the studies from the other Nordic countries.

4.4 The Total Poverty Level

The poverty criteria we use follow the practice of the other participants in the project of poverty in the Nordic countries, i.e. the poverty line is drawn at 50 per cent of the median equivalent family earnings. This is the standard procedure for the approach based on assessing relative poverty rather than absolute poverty.[8] We also look at the sensitivity of this line by calculating the proportion of the population falling 25 per cent below and 25 per cent above the poverty line.

Our data set offers the possibility of estimating the proportion of *individuals* who have less than 50 per cent of the median employment earnings. For the period as a whole this proportion fluctuates between 14 and 16 per cent of the respondent population. This is, however, not in any way a good measure of real poverty, since it takes no note of family earnings, number of dependants nor the effects of taxation and transfers, but it is useful to bear it in mind for purposes of comparison and verification.

---

[8] See the present contributions of Björn Gustafsson and Peder J Pedersen and Nina Smith. See also Ringens (1988) pp. 351-365.

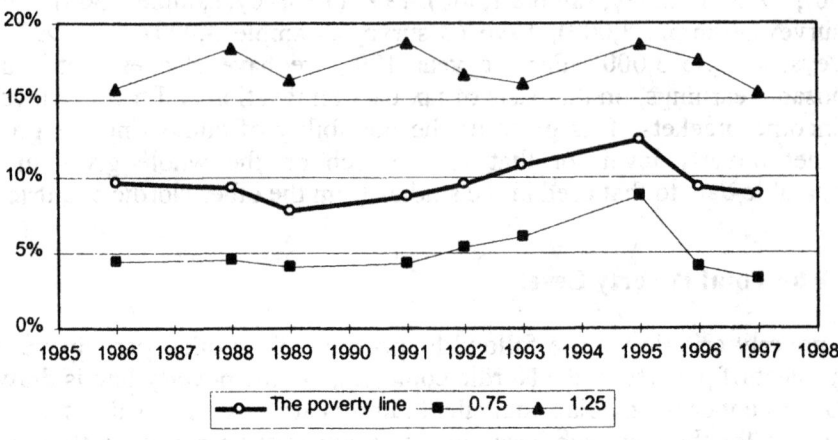

Figure 4.6 The poverty population and its sensitivity (+/- 25 per cent)

A more direct measure of poverty levels is presented in figure 4.6. There we have *family earnings* per family member on the basis of the equivalence ratios, based on our sub-sample of 13 surveys described in the section on the data above. The line in the middle is the defined poverty line for 50 per cent of the median equivalent family earnings, and the lower line shows the proportion falling under the line placed 25 per cent below the poverty line, while the upper line shows the proportion for those placed 25 per cent above the poverty line.[9] This is a realistic measure of gross poverty levels, i.e. before one considers the effects of taxes and direct transfers on the distribution. The main poverty rate (50 per cent of the median equivalent family earnings per head) is close to 10 per cent in 1986, drops significantly in 1989 to about 8 per cent, and gradually climbs from then on all the way up to 1995, where it ends at about 12.5 per cent. This trend is, however, reversed in 1996-7. The lower line showing the proportion falling below 25 per cent of the median earnings shows the same pattern, and the increase in the size of the poverty population towards the latter part of the period is particularly marked. The upper line fluctuates more irregularly, with deviant peaks in 1988 and 1991 along with the peak in 1995. The firm indication is, however, that the extent of poverty increased in Iceland during the first half of the Nineties, but it decreased again in 1996-7 with the general upswing in the Icelandic economy after 1995.

---

[9] The actual poverty lines are documented in Appendix I, both in nominal and real terms.

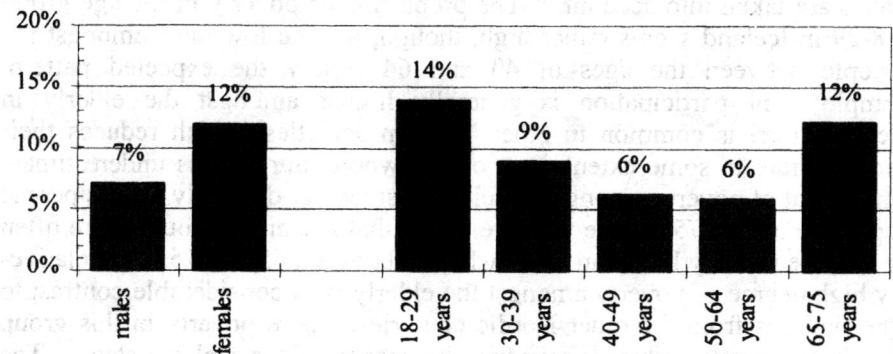

Figure 4.7   Poverty ratios by age and sex (averages 1986-1995)

In figures 4.7 to 4.9 we show the incidence of poverty by socio-economic groups during the whole period, by adding together the thirteen samples used in figure 4.6.[10] This gives an "average" or static picture of the poverty population, but in Appendix 4.I we report briefly on changes for each group during the period.

Figure 4.7 shows that poverty was more common amongst females than males and in the lower age groups as well as in the highest.[11] Therefore, on the whole, there are thus traces of a Rowntree poverty cycle in Iceland, such as found in his early studies in Britain.[12] Rowntree pointed to three periods during the life-cycle as particularly vulnerable to poverty, i.e. early childhood, the childbearing years for families and lastly old age. Thus the burden of having children restrains the finances of the family, nowadays most often by reducing the employment participation of mothers, and in old age reduced activity on the labour market and failing health are often associated with poverty. Traces of Rowntree's poverty cycle are generally found to be present in modern societies, especially when one looks at factor earnings (employment earnings and capital income for the self-employed and propertied) but less so when the redistributive effects of transfers and

---

[10] The results from the 13 combined samples give 8,132 respondents, 4,270 males and 3,862 females. The weakest groups in terms of reliability, due to small number of respondents, are the unemployed, farmers, students and single parents. See Appendix I for a more detailed documentation of the number of respondents by category and years.

[11] Age here refers to the age of the respondents, who in the great majority of cases is one of the two heads of the household, the husband or the wife.

[12] See Erikson and Fritzell (1988).

taxes are taken into account.[13] The proportion of poverty in the age group 18-29 in Iceland seems rather high, though, but the low rates amongst the people between the ages of 40 and 64 follow the expected pattern. Employment participation is generally higher amongst the elderly in Iceland than is common in other Western societies, which reduces their poverty rate to some extent. But, on the whole, our figures underestimate the extent of poverty amongst the elderly, since our data only covers people up to the age of 75. Those who are above that age are no doubt more often under the poverty line than those who are between 65 and 75. The relatively high degree of poverty amongst the elderly is in considerable contrast to the findings from the other Nordic countries, where poverty in this group has been greatly reduced, primarily by means of the welfare state.[14] The welfare state in Iceland is admittedly smaller than those of the large Scandinavian nations, for example as regards expenditure and transfers (Stefán Ólafsson 1993a and 1993b). The persistently rather high poverty rate for the elderly in Iceland, compared to that of the neighbouring Nordic countries, seems to be one of the consequences of the smaller welfare state in Iceland.

The higher poverty rate amongst females is partly explained by the fact that women live longer than males and therefore make up a larger proportion of the elderly poor, but, in addition, the position of women as single parents also significantly contributes to this outcome.

Figure 4.8 shows that the poverty rate is nearly twice as high in the provincial areas as in the Reykjavík area, where about 60 per cent of the national population reside. This is somewhat surprising, since earnings have often been higher in some of the provinces, especially in thriving fishing villages, and in addition, the Reykjavík area is generally believed to house a disproportionately high number of the elderly and the infirm. The main reason for this is, therefore, likely to be due to high poverty rates amongst farmers, and perhaps also amongst female workers in the fish processing industry.

---

[13] Hedström and Ringen (1987), pp. 227-239, and Smeeding, O'Higgins and Rainwater (1990).

[14] See Erikson and Fritzell (1988) as well as Hedström and Ringen (1987).

Poverty in Iceland 117

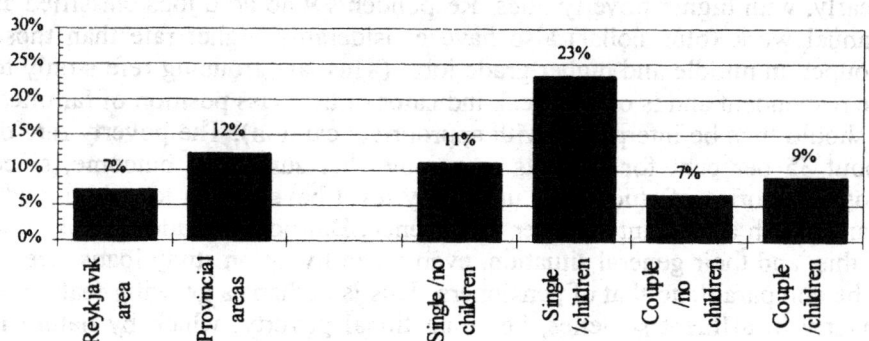

Figure 4.8 **Poverty ratios by region and marital status (averages 1986-1995)**

Looking at family status, it emerges that single parents are the most exposed to poverty, as expected, but their rate is only just above the 20 per cent mark. Single individuals without children of their own come next, and couples with children have a slightly higher rate than couples without dependent children.

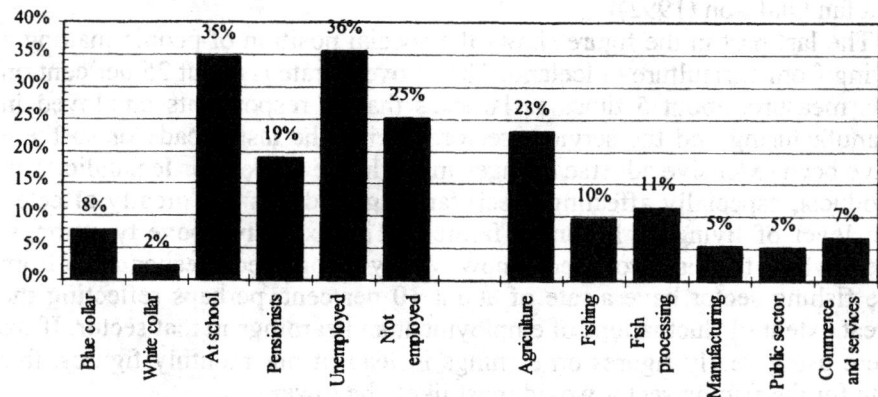

Figure 4.9 **Poverty ratios by class and industry (averages 1986-1995)**

The third figure in this series (Figure 4.9) demonstrates the importance of the link to the labour market for exposure to poverty.[15] The unemployed, students, pensioners and others who are not in active employment stand out

---

[15] In all cases the categories in the figures refer to the respondent's status, not to a single household head.

clearly, with higher poverty rates. Respondents who hold jobs classified as manual work (blue collar) also have considerably higher rate than those grouped in middle and higher grade jobs. (This last grouping refers only to the respondent and is only a weak indicator of the class position of families. It should thus be interpreted with appropriate caution). The poverty rate of about 35 per cent for students is a somewhat surprising outcome, since most categories of students at university level have access to public study loans which are meant to cover subsistence. But not all students make use of this, and their general situation, even when living on study loans, seems to be comparable to that of pensioners. This is perhaps a growing feature of poverty in affluent societies, i.e. educational poverty, which by nature is short term and in most cases only a prologue to a life above the average living standard of the society, since most students generally proceed to jobs which give earnings above the average. This sort of poverty is clearly of a different nature to the poverty of the elderly, the employed poor, the long-term unemployed and single parents. Lastly, the high proportion of poverty amongst respondents who are not active on the labour market (household workers) demonstrates the importance of double incomes for families, especially families with dependent children, in high-work societies such as Iceland, and indeed this seems to apply to the other Nordic societies as well (Stefán Ólafsson (1992)).

The last part in the figure shows the special position of people making a living from agriculture in Iceland. Their poverty rate is about 25 per cent on this measure, about 5 times as large as that of respondents employed in manufacturing and the services sector. During the last decade or so there have been extensive adverse changes in the home market for Icelandic farm products, especially affecting sheep farming, and this has greatly affected the level of living of Icelandic farmers. The extensive poverty amongst them which this has produced is now widely recognised. Respondents from the fishing sector have a rate of about 10 per cent, perhaps reflecting the great extent of fluctuations of employment and earnings in that sector. If we were using yearly figures on earnings instead of our monthly figures, this rate for the fishing sector would most likely be lower.

The indication from the data on changes in poverty ratios by socio-economic groups from 1986 to 1995, reported in Appendix 4.I, is that the rate for single parents, singles without children, females and for those residing outside the Reykjavík area have risen most during the period. That analysis is, however, unreliable due to the small numbers of respondents from some of the categories.

4.5 The Net Poverty Level 1995:
Total and disposable family earnings compared

Up to now, we have analysed the total poverty rates by using figures on gross equivalent family earnings. In this last section we have corrected the total poverty level for the year 1995, from Figure 4.6, by taking into account the effects of taxes and transfers on the distribution of earnings. This is based on figures from the National Economic Institute which show direct tax and transfer effects at differing family earnings levels for 1994. We have applied those figures to our own data for 1995 since we do not have adequate data on family composition in 1994 in our data.[16] In Figure 4.10 we show the total poverty level, based on gross family earnings, as well as our estimated net poverty level, based on net disposable earnings.

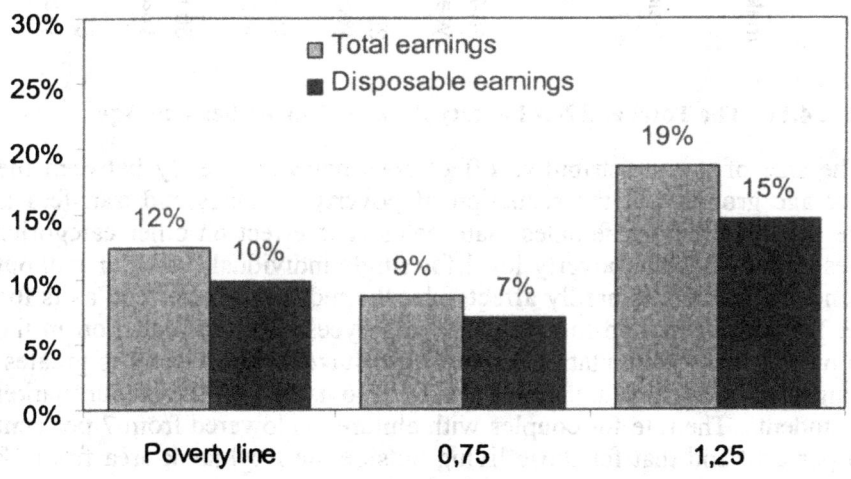

Figure 4.10   The Total and Net Poverty Level in 1995

As the figure shows the redistributive effect of taxes and transfers reduced the overall poverty rate in 1995 from about 12.5 per cent to just under 10 per cent. The size of the effect is similar when looking at the group which falls under the line drawn at 75 per cent of the poverty line, but the effect is larger for the group which is covered by the margin 25 per cent above the poverty line. This is the most realistic measure of relative

---

[16] There have been no significant changes in the effects of taxes and transfers between 1994 and 1995, so the one-year discrepancy of the data should not give cause for concern.

poverty in Iceland which we can produce on the basis of our data, using net disposable family earnings per equivalent family member.

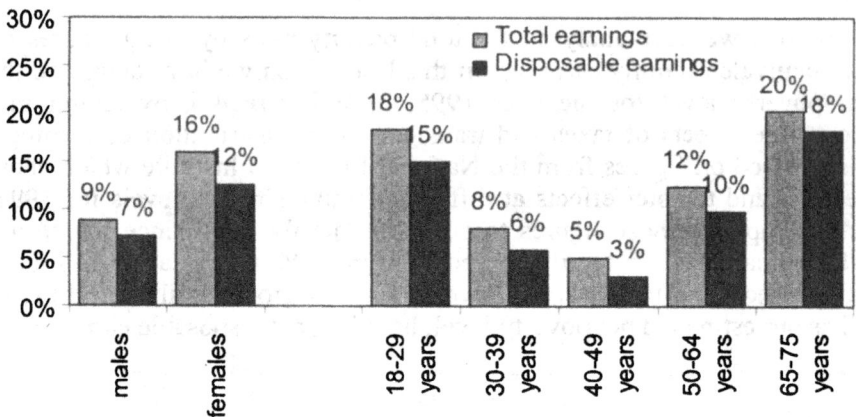

Figure 4.11   The Total and Net Poverty Rate in 1995, by Sex and Age

The size of the redistributive effect does not vary greatly between the major age groups, but the reduction of poverty by taxes and transfers is more marked amongst females than males. The effect on other categories varies more. Thus the poverty level for single individuals, with or without dependent children, is hardly affected by the redistributive effect, as is the level for pensioners and middle class employees. But the reduction in the size of the poverty population as a result of taxes and transfers is greatest amongst the unemployed, the non-pensioned outsiders on the labour market and students. The rate for couples with children is lowered from 7 per cent to 4 per cent and that for those living outside the Reykjavik area from 18 per cent to 14 per cent.

While the Icelandic welfare state is admittedly smaller than that of the other Nordic welfare states, as already mentioned, the comparison of total and disposable earnings in this section exaggerates the smallness of the effects of the welfare state in reducing poverty in Iceland, since, for example, old-age pensions and unemployment benefits are already included in our concept of total family earnings. The adjustment by means of taxes and direct transfers (which only covers child benefits and housing subsidies) in this section only measures a part of the total effect of the welfare state in reducing poverty. The conclusion is, however, valid, that the estimate of the poverty rate by means of net *disposable* equivalent family earnings, reported in this section, is the most realistic measure of the overall extent of poverty in Iceland.

4.6 Conclusions

This study of poverty in Iceland is based on data from the regular surveys of the SSRI at the University of Iceland from 1986 to 1997, as well as the Scandinavian Level of Living Survey from 1988, also undertaken by the SSRI. The method for assessing the size and development of the poverty population derives from recent contributions to the study of relative poverty levels. The baseline for poverty is defined as 50 per cent of median family earnings. This calculation is further adjusted by dividing the family earnings by the number of family members sharing the total income, whereby the share of the respondent is 1.0, that of the spouse is 0.7 and that of each child or other additional member is 0.5. This equivalence scaling is frequently used in contemporary comparative studies of poverty rates.

Previous research into poverty in Iceland has obtained varying results, due to varying definitions of poverty lines, as well as differing equivalence scaling and data sources. The best estimate of poverty on the basis of tax data put the size of the poverty population in the range of 17-23 per cent of the tax paying population, while estimates of poverty amongst members of the Federation of Labour suggested a poverty rate as low as 8 per cent, albeit with a considerably lower poverty line and less restrictive equivalence scaling.

Our estimate of the size of the poverty population, on the basis of total family earnings per equivalent family member, indicates that just under 10 per cent of the population fell under the poverty line (50 per cent of median equivalent family earnings) in 1986. The proportion declined slightly, to about 8 per cent in 1989, but from then on it increased persistently, ending at about 12.5 per cent in 1995, and then declined again in 1996-7, at the same time as the unemployment rate declined from about 5.5 per cent to about 3.5 per cent. When the redistributive effects of taxation and direct transfers (child benefits and housing subsidies) are taken into account, the net poverty rate for 1995 is lowered from 12.5 per cent to about 10 per cent. This is the best estimate of the overall size of the poverty population in Iceland we can produce from the data at hand.

Poverty is, according to our measures, most marked amongst the unemployed, individuals of 18-29 years of age who are still at school or university, farmers, pensioners, single parents and in households with only one breadwinner. The rate for single parents and other single individuals has increased most markedly during the last years.

The general increase in poverty rates in the 1990s is closely connected to an unprecedented increase in unemployment in Iceland and a less tight labour market. This has simultaneously reduced overtime work for males and lowered the work participation rate amongst females. In an economy where high participation in work and long working hours contribute a relatively large part of the total family earnings, and are thus a particularly important basis of the level of living, this is bound to hit hard. Amongst the unemployed, those who were self-employed prior to becoming unemployed have been particularly badly hit, since their unemployment benefit rights are more restricted than is common amongst employees.[17] The trend towards higher poverty levels corresponds to a significant increase in the number of individuals receiving financial assistance from the Reykjavík Social Services Institute (Félagsmálastofnun) in 1993 and 1995. [18]

Poverty in Iceland is more extensive amongst females than males, mainly due to the higher representation of females in the group of single parents and in the population of pensioners due to the greater longevity of females. Poverty is also more marked in the provincial areas than in the Reykjavík area. That is primarily the effect of relatively high poverty rates amongst farmers and the high vulnerability of the fish processing industry to fluctuations.

Even though couples with children do not have a particularly high poverty rate compared to the highly vulnerable groups of the unemployed, students, farmers, single parents and pensioners, they comprise about 55 per cent of the poverty population, as they are a large proportion of the overall population (see Appendix 4.II). They are thus the single largest marital status group amongst the poor. Evidently it is difficult to establish a family in Iceland, as has indeed emerged before, i.e. from the results of the Level of Living Survey (Ólafsson (1990)).

The increase in the rate of poverty in Iceland during the Nineties corresponds to an increased inequality in the distribution of employment earnings as well as increased unemployment. The adverse development of the labour market is probably the most important explanation of the increased inequality and the higher poverty level in the first half of the 1990s, and the decline in unemployment since 1996 also correlates with a reversal of the trend towards increased poverty during 1996-1997.

---

[17] Guðbjörg Andrea Jónsdóttir and Stefán Ólafsson, *Atvinnulausir á Íslandi (1993)*, pp. 50-60.
[18] The number had, however, declined in 1992 after having been stable in 1990 and 1991. See Ársskýrsla Félagsmálastofnunar (1994), p. 82, and also for 1995.

4.7 Appendix
Trends in Poverty Ratios by Socio-Economic Groups, 1986-1995

In the figures reported in this Appendix the trend in poverty rates is examined with a breakdown by socio-economic groups. Firstly by sex, then age, region, family status, connection to the labour market and lastly by industry. The data is unreliable due to the small number of responses in some of the categories and should therefore only be taken as a rough indication of trends.

The first figure in this series indicates that the poverty rate has risen slightly more for females than males during the 1990s.[19] Looking at poverty rates by age groups, the main feature is an increased poverty level for the elderly as well as the 18-29 group. Both groups, however, have high spots, in 1988 and 1986 respectively. In case of the elderly this is probably an error fluctuation due to the small numbers of respondents group (the 65-75 years of age) in our samples. The peak for the youngest cohort in 1986 is more difficult to explain at this stage. The only other age group which has a significant rise during the latter part of the period is the 50-64 group, with a particularly steep rise between 1991-3 and 1995. Poverty rates by regions show a firm rise both for the Reykjavík area and the provinces, with the increase slightly more pronounced outside the Reykjavík area.

Now we come to family status. Here we see a rise for single parents from about 20 per cent to about 30 per cent, and an even more drastic increase in a shorter time for the single respondents who have no children (students, the young and unemployed etc.), from about 5 per cent to 30 per cent. For couples there is no significant change during the period.

Looking at the attachments to the labour market, it emerges that poverty amongst the student population rises towards the end of the period, but they were also relatively high before 1990, which makes it difficult to say whether this is a random fluctuation or a reflection of a changed position. The other groups: pensioners, home workers and those active on the labour market remain around the same level throughout the period. Lastly, the breakdown by industry reveals on the whole only minor changes over time, for example for the farming population. The only persistent rise is for those employed in fish processing, a predominantly female occupation, which has been subject to increasing unemployment in recent years.[20]

---

[19] The figures for 1992 are based on an addition of the single surveys from 1991, 1992 and 1993. This was done in order to strengthen the set since the breakdown by socio-economic groups strains the reliability of the rather small samples that we have when relying on one sample of 1,500.

[20] Guðbjörg Andrea Jónsdóttir and Stefán Ólafsson (1993). *Atvinnulausir á Íslandi*.

124 *Poverty and Low Income in the Nordic Countries*

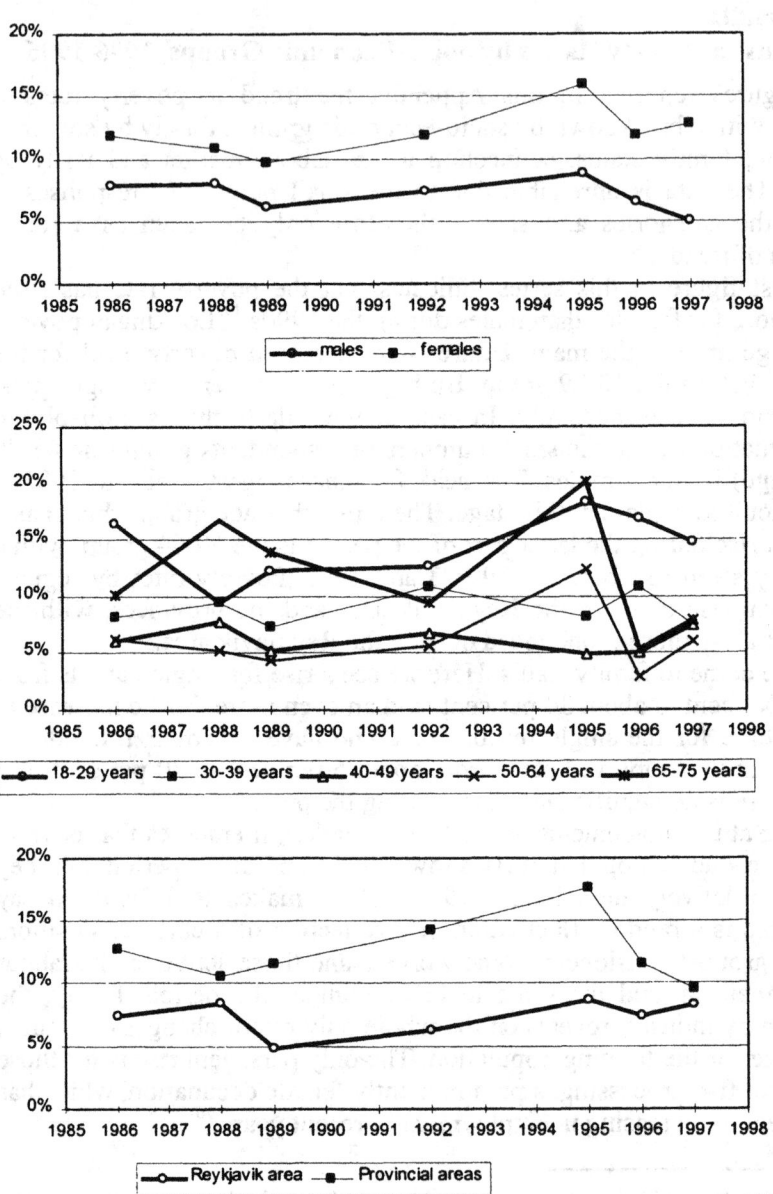

Figures 4.A.1 – 4.A.2 – 4.A.3

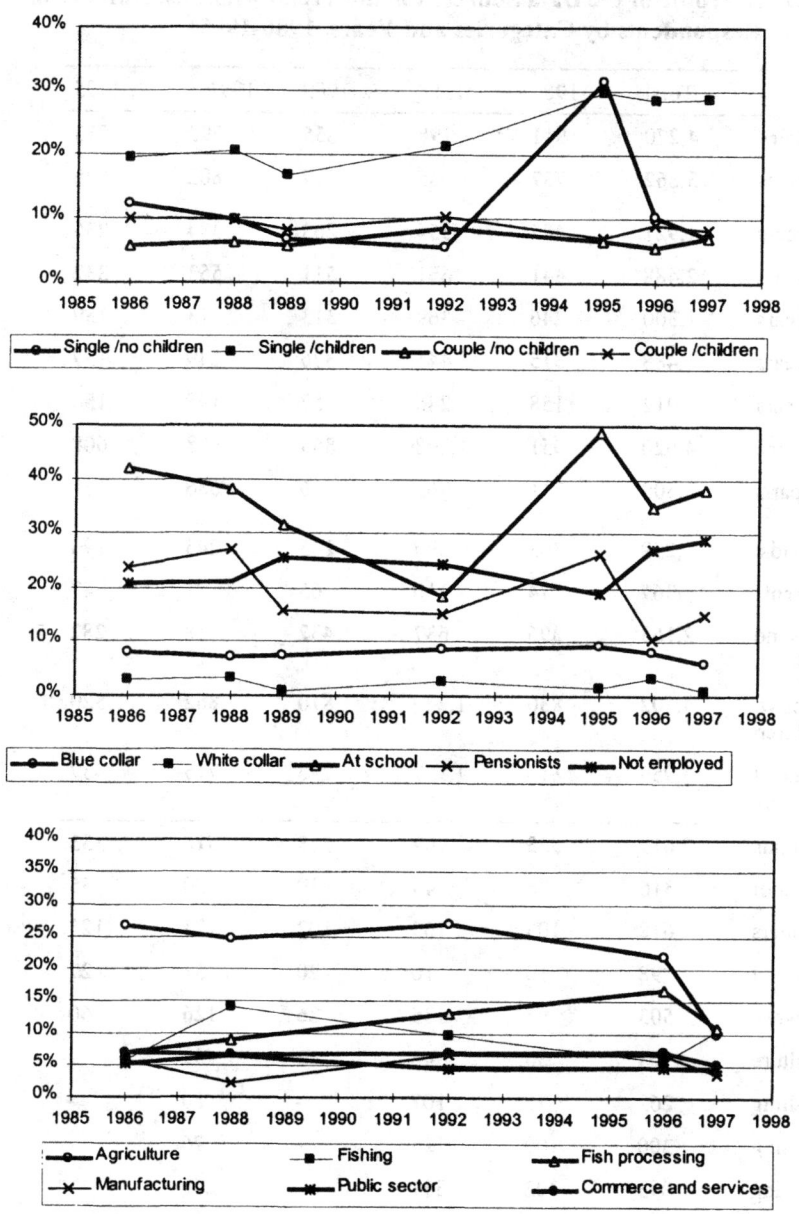

Figures 4.A.4 - 4.A.5 - 4.A.6

Table 4.A.1 A Profile of the Data Sources for the Trend Analysis. Number of Respondents by Categories and Years, 1986-1995

	Total	1986	1988	1989	1991-3	1995
Males	4,270	911	1,198	855	793	513
Females	3,862	752	1,065	717	802	526
18-29 years	1,921	485	554	263	384	235
30-39 years	2,488	441	651	511	553	332
40-49 years	1,300	246	369	313	213	159
50-64 years	1,488	315	441	326	249	157
65-75 years	912	158	246	157	195	156
Reykjavik area	4,620	951	1,298	855	908	608
Other parts	3,509	711	965	716	686	431
Single individs.	1,299	363	296	205	245	190
Single parents	367	74	110	65	71	47
Couples, no children	2,165	396	637	432	418	282
Couples w. children	4,302	830	1,220	870	862	520
Manual workers	3,959	814	1,197	796	715	437
Non-manuals	2,619	533	707	528	518	333
At school	316	98	44	39	80	55
Pensioners	618	105	165	102	121	125
Unemployed	98	10	10	20	31	27
Homework	503	96	135	86	126	60
Agriculture	163	56	48	-	59	-
Fishing	262	75	107	-	80	-
Fish processing	300	100	124	-	76	-
Manufacturing	893	302	351	-	240	-
Public sector	1,441	449	577	-	415	-
Commerce and services	1,774	458	793	-	523	-

Table 4.A.2 Poverty lines used

	Nominal kr.	Real kr.
1986	15032	35057
1988	28585	46012
1989	29877	40641
1991/3	37268	39353
1995	38973	38973

128 *Poverty and Low Income in the Nordic Countries*

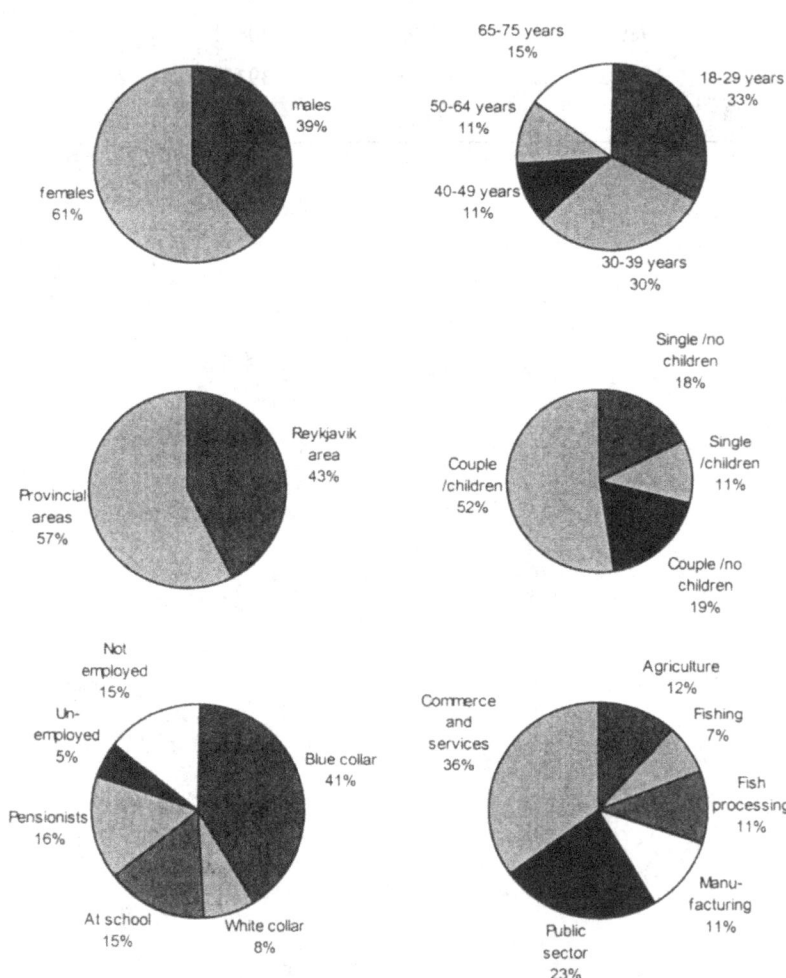

Figure 4.A.7 The Composition of the Total Poverty Population
Averages 1986-1995

References

Ársskýrsla Félagsmálastofnunar Reykjavíkur 1994 (The Reykjavík Council's Social Services' Yearly Report).

Björnsson, Jón og Guðbrandsson, Bragi (eds). *Fátækt á Íslandi*. Reykjavík: Samband íslenskra sveitarfélaga (unpublished mimeo, available at the SSRI, University of Iceland).

Erikson, R. and Fritzell, J. (1988). The Effects of the Social Welfare System in Sweden on the Well-Being of Children and the Elderly, in J. L. Palmer, T. Smeeding and B. B. Torrey (eds), *The Vulnerable*. Washington D.C.: The Urban Institute Press.

Gunnlaugsson, Gísli Ágúst (1986). *Fátækt á Íslandi fyrr á tímum*, in Jón Björnsson og Bragi Guðbrandsson (eds).

Gunnlaugsson, Gísli Ágúst (1978). Milliþinganefnd í fátæktarmálum 1902-1905. róun fátækramála 1870-1907, in *Saga* 1978.

Gunnlaugsson, Gísli Ágúst (1993). Fólksfjölda- og byggðaþróun 1880-1990, in Guðmundur Hálfdanarson and Svanur Kristjánsson (eds), *Íslensk þjóðfélagsþróun 1880-1990*. Ritgerðir.

Hálfdanarson, Guðmundur (1993). Íslensk þjóðfélagsþróun á 19. öld, in Guðmundur Hálfdanarson and Svanur Kristjánsson (eds), *Íslensk þjóðfélagsþróun 1880-1990*. Ritgerðir.

Hálfdanarson, Guðmundur and Kristjánsson, Svanur (eds), *Íslensk þjóðfélagsþróun 1880-1990*. Ritgerðir. Reykjavík: Félagsvísindastofnun and Sagnfræðistofnun

Hedström, P. and Ringen, S. (1987). Age and Income in Contemporary Society: A Research Note, *Journal of Social Policy*, vol. 16, pt. 2, April, pp. 227-239.

Jónsdóttir, Guðbjörg Andrea and Ólafsson, Stefán (1993). *Atvinnulausir á Íslandi 1993*. Reykjavík: Ministry of Social Affairs and Social Sciences Research Institute, University of Iceland.

Kjararannsóknarnefnd *(Wage Investigation Committee, various years)*, Fréttabréf. Reykjavík: Kjararannsóknarnefnd.

Magnússon, Magnús S. and Gunnarsson, Gísli (1987). Levnadsstandarden på Island 1750-1914, ín Gunnar Karlsson (ed.), *Levestandarden i Norden 1750-1914*. Reykjavík: Sagnfræðistofnun.

National Economic Institute (jóðhagsstofnun, 1995). *Tekjur, eignir og dreifing þeirra árin 1993 og 1994*. Reykjavík: jóðhagsstofnun, Fréttabréf.

Ólafsson, Stefán (1990). *Lífskjör og lífshættir á Norðurlöndum. Samanburður á þjóðfélagi Dana, Finna, Íslendinga, Norðmanna og Svía*. Reykjavík: Iðunn.

Ólafsson, Stefán (1992). The Rise or Decline of Work in the Welfare State: Equality and Efficiency Revisited, in J. E. Kolberg (ed), *Between Work and Social Citizenship*, pp. 36-76. New York: M. E. Sharpe.

Ólafsson, Stefán (1993a). Variations Within the Scandinavian Model: Iceland in a Scandinavian Comparison", in E. J. Hansen et. al. (eds), *Welfare Trends in the Scandinavian Countries*. New York: M. E. Sharpe.

Ólafsson, Stefán (1993b). Firóun velferðarríkisins, in Guðmundur Hálfdanarson and Svanur Kristjánsson (eds), *Íslensk þjóðfélagsþróun 1880-1990*. Ritgerðir.

Ólafsson, Stefán (1993c). Innreið nútímaþjóðfélags á Íslandi, in Magnús Snædal and Turið Sigurðardóttir (eds.), *Frændafundur*. Reykjavík: Háskólaútgáfan.

Ringen, Stein (1988). Direct and Indirect Measures of Poverty, *Journal of Social Policy*, vol. 17, pt. 3, 1988, pp. 351-365.

Skúlason, Ari (1986). *Leitin að láglaunamanninum. Niðurstöður launakönnunar 1983*, in Jón Björnsson og Bragi Guðbrandsson (eds).

Smeeding, T., O'Higgins, M. and Rainwater, L. (1990) (eds), *Poverty, Inequality and Income Distribution in Comparative Perspective*. Hemel Hempstead: Harwester Wheatshealt.

Snævarr, Sigurður (1986). *Tekjujöfnun á Íslandi. Úttekt á opinberum aðgerðum*, in Jón Björnsson og Bragi Guðbrandsson (eds).

Snævarr, Sigurður (1987). Fátækt í velferðarríkinu?, in the journal *Mannlíf*, vol. 5, August 1986.

Snævarr, Sigurður (1987). *Att undersöka fattigdom*, contribution to Seminariet om att mäta och simulera fördelningen av ekonimiska resurser, Hanaholmen, Finland, May 25-27.

SSRI (1989), *Kjör Íslendinga í árslok 1988: Könnun á atvinnu og tekjum í nóvember 1988 með samanburði við kannanir frá maí 1988 og nóvember 1987*. Reykjavík: SSRI.

Vogel, Joachim (1990), *Leva i Norden: Levnadsnivå och ojämlighet vid slutet av 80-talet*. Köbenhavn: Nordisk Statistisk Skriftserie.

5 Extent, Level and Distribution of Low Income in Norway 1979-1995

ROLF AABERGE, ARNE S. ANDERSEN AND
TOM WENNEMO[1]

5.1 Introduction

The purpose of studying the extent and structure of poverty is based on the following types of questions: Has poverty increased or diminished over time? Are there regional or demographic differences? What effect do specific welfare schemes have on poverty?

Poverty is a concept Norwegians generally reserve for other parts of the world or the distant past. Still, the concept has increasingly surfaced in the media and public debate, directing attention at people or groups of people who have financial problems. There are probably many reasons for this.

The period of rapid growth in the mid-1980s, with huge and seemingly easy profits, helped focus attention on economic inequality. This was reinforced by rapidly rising unemployment, and by the so-called 'debt crisis' from 1989. The combination created a climate that led not only to economic disparity, but also to increasing talk of poverty as a social problem. The debt crisis was a result of several coinciding factors. The period 1984-1987 was characterised by risk-taking players with large loans, first and foremost for financing housing in a market with rising prices and high interest levels. The turning point came in 1988 when a sharp decline in housing prices coincided with a contracting job market.

The increase in the number of recipients of social assistance probably helped focus attention on the problem of poverty. This, however, was hardly a decisive factor. The increase in the number of social assistance clients had also been considerable during the economic boom from 1983 to 1987. It was probably rising unemployment and the debt crisis that legitimised the introduction of poverty as a possible social problem.

---

[1] We would like to thank Tone Veiby for her writing and editing work, Liv Hansen for her work on the figures and Björn Gustafsson and Peder J. Pedersen for their comments.

The definition of poverty has, however, changed over time and has gradually been used as a relative concept; i.e. the poverty line depends on the general standard of living in society. This meaning is in sharp contrast to the original absolute definition of poverty. According to this definition, people were classified as poor if their combined financial resources were inadequate to cover the costs of a minimum quantity of basic goods such as food, clothing and shelter. The transition from the absolute to relative concept makes the definition of poverty more diffuse and provides room for ideas varying from absolute need to an unacceptably low standard of living. The concept of what is an unacceptably low standard of living will naturally depend on the general standard of living in society. As such the term 'low income' provides a more relevant association to what is meant by relative 'poverty' than the traditional definition of poverty. This is also the reason why we have used low income instead of poverty in the title of this work. The term poverty is, however, so well established in international literature that we nevertheless will use this term below instead of low income. We will return to the definition, operationalisation and measurement of poverty in sections 5.2, 5.4 and 5.5.

Quantifying the number of those poverty-stricken will depend on a number of conditions that are subject to debatable choices. The most important are the definitions of

- population
- income and accounting period
- scale for comparability (equivalence scale)
- poverty line

The basic population in this analysis will be all people living in Norway; i.e. it also includes all children even though children do not have an income of their own. We will also use two different income definitions and three different poverty lines. As expected, the results given in sections 5.6-5.8 show that the change in the selection of income definition and poverty line has significance for the level and scope of poverty. However, the pattern in the development over time is basically unaffected by the aforementioned changes in definition. With respect to choice of equivalence scale we have exclusively based our discussion on the OECD scale. This choice is guided by the desire for comparability with the results in the other Nordic countries. Since the selection of equivalence scale affects the form of the distribution of income (equivalent income), this choice will also affect the level and scope of poverty. To avoid drowning readers by numbers, we have, however, chosen not to vary the equivalence scale. Instead this should be a topic for future studies. The choice of one year as the accounting period is governed both by tradition and availability of data, but naturally provides no information as to whether poverty is chronic or not. To shed light on this question, in section 5.9 we have used data on individual income histories based on repeated observations of annual incomes for the years 1986 to 1995.

5.2 Measuring Poverty

"Poverty" can be said to exist if there are residents in a society who have material assets under a reasonable minimum level according to social standards. This assertion is, however, vague and requires precise definition on several points in order for it to have an analytical content. We have to take a position on what is meant by

(i) individual material assets,
(ii) what level of assets is reasonable and should thus be used as a borderline for poverty,
(iii) summary measures of poverty.

The treatment of the first two points corresponds to developing criteria for identification of the poor, while point (iii) gives us measures/indices intended to provide information about the extent and degree of poverty.

As pointed out above, in this work we will only touch on the economic aspects of the definition of poverty. But even with such a limitation, it is not self-evident how one should define and operationalise the concept of poverty. If one chooses to regard poverty as an absolute concept, it could be argued that poverty does not exist in Norway today, e.g. if the low income or poverty line is determined by given historical minimum standards for nutrition and other necessities. Another extreme is to regard poverty as a strictly relative concept and thus independent of the country's general level of prosperity, i.e. the low income or poverty line is not historically determined, but is adjusted in relation to the income trend and other changes in society. Townsend (1979) says that the relative approach reflects how the requirements for participating in society change, and that one's ability and opportunity to participate in social life is therefore the decisive aspect of poverty. In its pure form the relative approach will in practice exclude society's ability to end poverty and consequently many anti-poverty programmes will only have limited success. Relative poverty is therefore about income disparities with special emphasis on the lower end of the distribution of income.

We will return to the definition of income in sections 5.4 and 5.5. But even with a relevant definition of income we encounter the problems of determining and comparing poverty lines for people who belong to households of different sizes and composition. In most applied studies, the problem of interpersonal comparison of economic welfare is handled in a pragmatic way with the use of one or another form of normalisation, called an equivalence scale. This study uses the OECD scale. This scale gives single adults a weight of 1 while each extra adult person in the household is weighted 0.7, and each child under 16 is weighted 0.5. It should be noted that this scale does not have a more convincing professional basis than other proposed scales in the economic literature. The household members' normalised income (equivalent income) is obtained by dividing the household income by the household's equivalent weight. The equivalent income (also called income per consumption unit) can therefore be interpreted as the income household members would have to have as single persons to achieve the same standard of living as the one they enjoy as members of a larger household.

For a given poverty line it is natural to characterise poverty in society by the percentage of the population that has an equivalent income below this line. This measure has, however, limited information value because it does not distinguish between a situation in which the average income of the poor is near the poverty line and a situation in which the average income is considerably lower.

In order to take into account how poor the poor are, one can use the relative deviation between the poverty line and the average income of the poor (poverty gap) multiplied by the poverty rate as a measure of poverty. The question is now whether this measure together with the poverty rate provides a complete description of poverty? The answer is *no* because none of these measures is affected by how income is distributed between the poor, and thus neither by a transfer of income from one poor person to one that is less poor. Most people will agree that such a transfer will increase the degree of poverty. Consequently, we also need a measure that captures the differences among the poor. In this study we will use the sum of the relative quadratic deviations from the poverty line as a supplementary measure to capture the relative income differences among the poor.

We will now give a formal definition of the measures of poverty mentioned above. Let F be the distribution of income and let z be the poverty line. To measure the incidence and extent of poverty we will use three measures that belong to the so-called FGT family of poverty measures, see Foster et al. (1984). The FGT family $\{P(a)\}$ is defined as

(1) $\quad P_a = \int_0^z \left(1 - \frac{x}{z}\right)^a dF(x).$

For a = 0 we have

(2) $\quad P_0 = F(z)$,

i.e. P_0 is the poverty rate.

For a = 1 we have

(3) $\quad P_1 = P_0 \cdot I$,

in which $I = 1 - \dfrac{\mu(z)}{z}$ is the poverty gap and $\mu(z)$ is the average income of the poor.

Ravallion (1992) has pointed out that P_1 can be interpreted as an indicator of the potential to eliminate poverty by objective-oriented transfers to the poor. If the population consists of n persons, it follows directly from the definition of P_1 (P_0 and I) that nzP_1 is the minimum cost of raising all the poor up to the poverty line. If on the other hand we cannot identify the poor, we would have to give z to all persons in the population to eliminate poverty. This will cost nz. Consequently, P_1 is equal to the relationship between the minimum and maximum cost of eliminating poverty.

For a = 2 we obtain

(4) $\quad P_2 = \int_0^z \left(1 - \dfrac{x}{z}\right)^2 dF(x)$

which is a poverty measure that is dependent on the poverty rate, the poverty gap and the difference between the poor.

As mentioned, we will use P_0, P_1 and P_2 in this study. The variances of the non-parametric estimators of P_0, P_1 and P_2 are given in Appendix 5.II.

5.3 Previous Research in Norway

There is little tradition of poverty research in Norway. Nor has the government shown any particular interest in general in the problems of poverty. Norway does not have an official poverty line. There is precious little Norwegian research grouped under the designation poverty research.

In addition to specific poverty research we will also refer to research concerning problems associated with low income. The fairly extensive research on, for instance, social assistance recipients and the general research on living conditions will not be touched upon.

In the 1970s research was concentrated around problems associated with low income. How should the low income group be delimited? Who are they? How do they live? As part of the government-initiated survey of living conditions Rødseth analysed the distribution of income in Norway, Rødseth (1977). Rødseth based his analysis exclusively on income. One of the conclusions was that in the 1960s no dramatic changes took place in the percentage of people with low income. Rødseth's analysis also contains one of the few early analyses of chronic poverty based on the Occupational History Survey. He shows that between one third and one half of the people who are poor for one year belong to the group he defines as chronicly poor. Another early analysis of low income households showed *inter alia* that there was little correlation between income and consumption for households with low income, see Statistics Norway (1972). The interest in the situation of low income households also resulted in an analysis that compared the living conditions of low income households and other households, see Andersen et al. (1980).

Stjernø (1985) introduced the concept of modern poverty or neo-poverty. Stjernø critically reviews a number of definitions of poverty and tries to estimate the extent of poverty based upon them. He looks at households with incomes under the amount they would have received in basic pension for their type of family, households that receive social assistance, households that have an income per member of under 50 per cent of the average income, households that lack specific goods and households that define themselves as poor. With the exception of the latter (subjective poverty), where the poverty rate is 2 per cent, the estimates vary from around 5 per cent to nearly double that. In particular, definitions based on a lack of normal goods can produce high estimates. Stjernø is particularly concerned that definitions of poverty solely based on income are insufficient. He does not, however, try to define, much less operationalise, modern poverty on the basis of a more comprehensive set of criteria.

The so-called 'debt crisis' in the late 1980s gave rise to discussions about poverty as a result of the development of household debt obligations and the development of the labour and housing markets, see Lunde and Poppe (1991) and Gulbrandsen (1991). Lunde and Poppe analyse what they call neo-poverty, using Townsend's definition of poverty. Neo-poverty is not characterised by households that do not have the most important life necessities, but that they have too little to "ensure participation in normal work and social activities and a minimum of reasonable consumption". The analysis of the preconditions of neo-poverty is not based on income limitations, but on data on financial problems experienced.

Certain recent analyses examine limitations of the poor on the basis of income limits much used in the EU (50 per cent of average or median income). An analysis of the panel for the Income Distribution Survey conducted by Statistics Norway showed only a small percentage of households that were poor for one year were poor in each of the subsequent four years, (see Epland and Korbøl (1992)). This analysis shows, however, that there are relatively few of those who are poor for one year that have incomes over the average in subsequent years.

In another analysis various demarcations of the poor are evaluated, based on various definitions and demarcations of income that take certain expenses into consideration, and various other economic measures (subjectively experienced financial problems, material need, receipt of social assistance, housing situation) are compared for the poor and non-poor, (see Andersen et al. (1995)). The estimates of the percentage of poor households vary from barely 5 per cent to nearly 10 per cent. The analysis also shows that the connection between objective poverty measures, based on income, assets and expenses, and various measures of financial problems, both objective (social assistance) and subjective, is not strong. The connection is the weakest for poverty measures that only base themselves on income and assets. It is strengthened somewhat when expenses are included. The same applies to the connection between poverty and access to material goods such as housing, second homes and cars.

5.4 Data

The population consists of all people living in Norway on 1 January in the individual relevant years. The sample is drawn as a household sample. A household means all people living in the same house sharing the same food. This study is based on data from Statistics Norway's Income Distribution Surveys, which are based on samples of individual tax returns for the years 1979, 1982 and 1984-1995 and data on household composition.

The number of people in the samples varies between 6,500 and 24,500. The sample in 1991 contains a large special sample of the self-employed, relatively few of whom are in the group of poor people. The increase in the sample from around 7,000 in 79/85 to around 25,000 in 1991 therefore increases the precision of the estimates only modestly.

In this study we have used two income definitions: income after tax and disposable income. The reason for this is given in section 5.5.

Income after tax = Earnings (wage income)
+ Net income from self-employment before allocations for reserves and depreciation
+ Gross capital income
+ Transfers
− Tax

and

Disposable income = Income after tax
− Capital expenditure (debt interest)

Net income from self-employment before allocations for reserves and depreciation = Income from agriculture, forestry, fishing and other industries
+ Income from handicrafts etc. made in the home
+ Allocations for reserves
+ Ordinary depreciation
− Losses from self-unemployment and real property

Any employee can claim a deduction for any deficit or loss that occurred that same year, regardless of whether or not it occurred in trading. The loss must be due to deductible expenses.

While an income earner may have a loss in one trade, he/she may still have net income from self-employment because of revenues from other trades.

Gross capital income = Income from residence, cabin and country home
+ Interest income
+ Dividends from shares
+ Other investment earnings

Transfers = Benefits from National Insurance Scheme
+ Occupational pension, annuities, etc.
+ Other benefits and allowances
+ Family allowance
+ Housing benefit
+ Grant
+ Tax allowance for dependants

For a more detailed definition of what is included in the individual entries, see the explanatory booklet that accompanies the Norwegian tax return.

The available data makes it possible to show how the individual income components contribute to the result from the distribution of income after tax and disposable income. Earnings, which for most people forms the most important of the income components, are fixed for many employees as the product of hourly pay and working hours. We cannot, however, say anything about how the variation in hourly wages and working hours respectively contributes to the observed income disparity. Data on individual hourly wages and hours are not available in the Income Distribution Surveys. Therefore we do not comment on the changes in poverty resulting from possible changes in hourly wages and working hours and the connection between these two variables.

5.5 Definition of Low Income/Poverty Lines

The definition of poverty, both as a relative and an absolute concept, lays down several requirements that must be complied with in order for a given individual to be viewed as poor: the person must have a consumption or a standard of living far under the norm; the person must have very few material resources, *and* the lack of material resources must be the *reason* for the low consumption or the low standard of living. It is seldom that one has all the data. Very often we only have information about material resources. In other cases, we only have information about consumption. Consequently, it is often necessary to emphasise only one of the conditions which, in combination, must be fulfilled in order to say that a person is poor.

Researchers often emphasise the lack of material resources and use low income and perhaps assets as measures of poverty. Other measures of poverty place an emphasis on consumption instead, and use low consumption expenditure as a measure of poverty.

Both approaches have their advantages and drawbacks. If one emphasises consumption, those with low consumption, but not necessarily low incomes, will be regarded as poor. But is it true to say that people who do not indulge themselves in the same way as most people and instead place an exaggerated emphasis on saving, are really poor?

If one emphasises income and assets, it can be claimed that people in various phases of life can have different needs and thus do not achieve the same level of prosperity with the same income. For example, it is normal to borrow money to buy a home at a young age, pay back the loan over a certain number of years and then live debt free in a home which has been paid for towards the end of one's life. A person in the establishment phase will therefore need a higher cash flow than a debt free pensioner in order to enjoy the same standard of living.

We may agree with Townsend and say that the poor are those who do not satisfy certain fundamental needs or needs that most people perceive as necessary to participate fully in society.

In the determination of and reference to the poverty line we will therefore use the term income in the context of equivalent income (income per unit of consumption). This study makes use of three different poverty lines. One is strictly relative and is defined as half the median income. The other is defined as the average of the year-specific median-related (price adjusted) poverty lines. This poverty line must therefore be expected to show a diminishing poverty rate in a society with economic growth. The third type of line varies by type of family and is determined by the annual basic pension and family allowance payments. These lines are meant to reflect politicians' evaluations. We acknowledge, however, that neither the basic pension nor family allowance is intended as a poverty line. These poverty lines reflect both relative and absolute aspects of poverty.

In referring to the low income/poverty lines we have not defined precisely what is meant by income. Traditionally, income is defined as the maximum consumption one can allow oneself without depleting one's net wealth. Because of a lack of data we can, however, only approximate this definition. We have therefore chosen to use two alternative definitions of income. The one designates disposable income and is in accordance with standard practice in official statistics in letting capital income be calculated as net income (less debt interest). This income definition may, however, cover significant differences in consumption opportunities. The most important reason for this is that the tax rules in the 1970s and '80s allowed unlimited deductions for debt interest in determining net taxable income. With very high marginal taxes, the benefit of using deductions for debt interest was considerably greater for people with high incomes than for people with low incomes. In extreme cases people with high incomes could thus be non-taxpayers with an apparently extremely small disposable income. This problem was amplified by the fact that the value of services from housing and second homes was substantially underestimated in connection with the taxation of these goods. For these reasons it will be important to use an alternative definition of income. This will be distinguished from disposable income in that we include capital income gross and therefore without deduction for debt interest. This definition, which we describe as income after tax, was previously used by Aaberge and Wennemo (1988) and Strøm et al (1993) in studies of income inequality in Norway. See also section 5.4.

Table 5.1 Alternative poverty lines. NOK in current and fixed prices

	Basic-pension for singles	Disposable income				Income after tax			
		50 per cent of the year's median income		50 per cent of the median average		50 per cent of the year's median income		50 per cent of the median-average	
	1995 prices	Current prices	1995 prices	Current prices	1995 prices	Current prices	1995 prices	Current prices	1995 prices
1979	56628	16987	44165	18675	48555	18100	47059	21625	56224
1982	57871	23959	44399	26201	48555	26241	48628	30339	56224
1984	58750	28076	45173	30179	48555	31703	51007	34945	56224
1985	59702	30336	46179	31897	48555	34938	53184	36935	56224
1986	60894	34157	48503	34194	48555	40087	56923	39595	56224
1987	59700	37601	49103	37182	48555	44958	58710	43055	56224
1988	59715	39238	48031	39666	48555	47848	58571	45931	56224
1989	59903	40148	46999	41477	48555	48529	56810	48028	56224
1990	60097	42652	47965	43177	48555	51289	57677	49996	56224
1991	61015	44904	48829	44652	48555	54276	59021	51704	56224
1992	61677	47437	50403	45698	48555	56593	60131	52915	56224
1993	61741	50295	52244	46743	48555	57508	59736	54126	56224
1994	62184	52043	53314	47397	48555	57926	59341	54883	56224
1995	62757	54462	54462	48555	48555	60338	60338	56224	56224

5.6 The Pattern of Poverty in Norway 1979-1995

Before 1984 the Income Distribution Surveys were triennial. We therefore study the poverty trend for each of the years 1984-1995 in addition to the years 1979 and 1982.

Figure 5.1 shows the poverty rate for which the poverty lines are based on disposable income per unit of consumption. If the overall increase in prosperity is not taken into account, i.e. the poverty line is calculated in relation to the annual median, there was, most remarkably, an even and substantial increase in the poverty rate in the period 1984-1988. Between 1982 and 1984 there appears to have been a reduction in the poverty rate, while the poverty rate after 1988 has remained stable. Looking at the period 1979-1995 as a whole, there was only a slight increase in the poverty rate. For information about the uncertainties of the estimates see Table 5.A.1 in Appendix I.

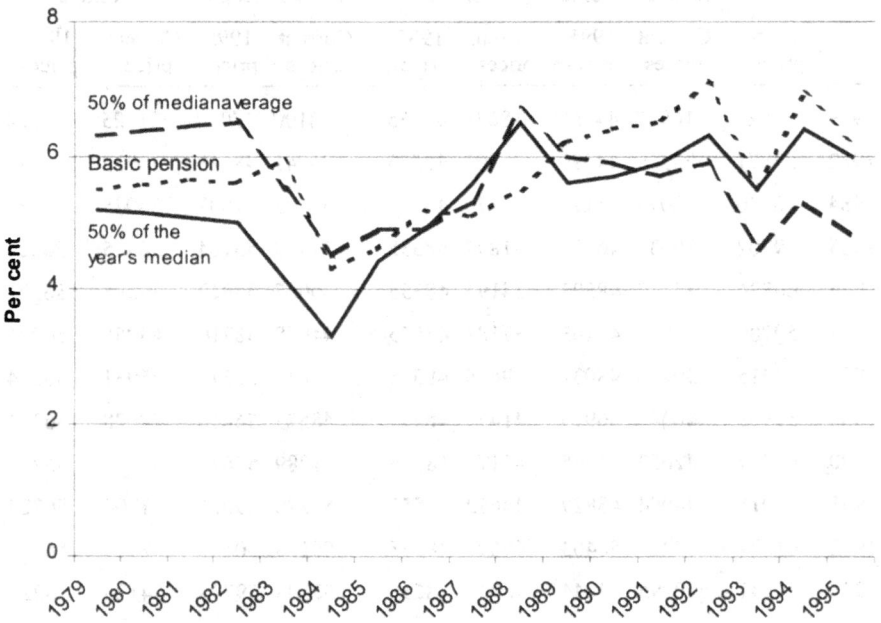

Figure 5.1 The trend in poverty rates in Norway according to alternative poverty lines based on disposable income per unit of consumption.

We also note that social assistance is not included in the income definitions used. It can seem surprising that the poverty rate increased so sharply during the boom in the mid-1980s, a period when employment also began to rise, and that the sharp increase in unemployment, particularly from 1988 to 1989, did not lead to any increase in the poverty rate. Despite the sharp increase in household interest expenses until 1988, it can be seen from Table 5.1 that the median in the distribution of disposable income per unit of consumption (in fixed prices) increased particularly in the period 1984-1987, and then again from 1992 to 1995. This latter change is primarily due to the fall in interest rates that started in 1993. The sharp increase in the poverty rate between 1984 and 1988 is primarily due to the increase in borrowing and the lack of balance between income and debt interest during this period.

When we take into account the general increase in prosperity and calculate the poverty lines from the median average for the years 1979-1995, we find largely the same trend. But the poverty rate was higher at the beginning and lower at the end of the period, so that for the entire period there was, as expected, a reduction in the poverty rate when based on this poverty line.

The extent and development of poverty above is based on the definition of disposable income. Disposable income is defined as an aggregate income less taxes and debt interest. From the middle of the 1980s and particularly from 1986, household borrowing increased. Together with an increase in the borrowing rate, this led to a sharp increase in household capital expenditure. A substantial part of borrowing was used to finance housing. The value of the services a home provides is, however, substantially undervalued in measuring disposable income. Because of this measurement problem, it is, as pointed out in section 5, important to use a complementary definition of income. We have chosen to use income after tax, which is different from disposable income in that debt interest is not deducted. The pattern in poverty given in Figure 5.2 is somewhat different when the poverty measures are based on income after tax per unit of consumption, i.e. debt interest is not deducted. As in Figure 5.1, a reduction in the poverty rate until the mid-1980s can also be seen here. After that, however, the poverty rate increased slightly from 3 per cent in 1985 to 6 per cent in 1995. This trend deviates somewhat from what we found on the basis of disposable income, where we saw a strong increase in poverty until 1988, with subsequent stabilisation.

This roughly fits in with what we know about the trend of overall income inequality, which diminished slightly from the beginning of the decade until 1987-88, largely as a result of the increase in employment during the economic boom of the mid-1980s. In 1989 the inequality increased, and then remained relatively stable at the new level. A corresponding increase in the poverty rate did not take place in 1989. It is natural to see the increase in inequality in 1989 in connection with the sharp increase in unemployment this year (Andersen et al., 1995). This indicates that the overall income inequality is more sensitive than the poverty rate to the functioning of the labour market.

The reduction in the poverty rate until the mid-1980s is remarkable not least since it was a period with strong growth in income after tax. At 1995 prices, 50 per cent of the median value of income after tax per unit of consumption increased from NOK 47,100 in 1979 to 58,700 in 1987, i.e. an increase in real income of 25 per cent. This also indicates that the poor, according to this definition, have had a real increase in income.

The other measure of poverty (50 per cent of the median) does not change over time. Figure 5.2 naturally shows that the poverty rate with this measure is higher than with the first measure in 1979, but lower in 1995. This measure shows that the poverty rate was 7.3 per cent in 1979 and 5.1 in 1995, i.e. a substantial reduction in the poverty rate during the entire period. The strong reduction in the poverty rate occurred in the first half of the period, and is thus primarily a reflection of the sharp increase in real income in the 1980s.

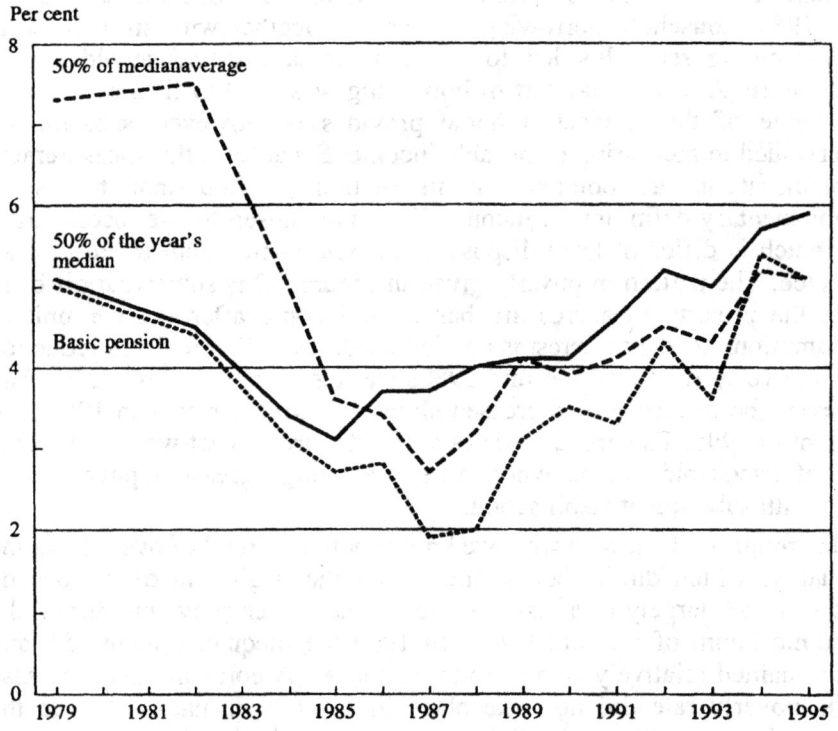

Figure 5.2   The trend in poverty rates in Norway according to alternative poverty lines based on income after tax per unit of consumption

Norway has no national standards for low income. Social assistance payments are set locally and information about them has not been available to us. Instead we have used the basic pension. This does not mean that we regard the basic pension as the poverty line, but it is possibly the only national income standard that can be interpreted as a low income level.

Figures 5.1 and 5.2 show that the poverty percentage is smallest when the definition of income is income after tax and the poverty line is determined by basic pension and family allowance payments.

The exclusion of social assistance is naturally a serious drawback to the definition of income when illustrating the trend in poverty, both because one has to expect to overestimate the extent of poverty and because disbursed social assistance has increased sharply during this period (sevenfold). From the 1991 survey, information on social assistance has been registered. When social assistance (and basic and supplementary benefit in the event of disability) are included as income, the poverty rate is reduced by about 1 percentage point, from 5.9 to 4.6 per cent in 1991 with a poverty line based on disposable income, and from 4.6 to 3.8 per cent based on income after tax. Because of the sharp increase in social assistance, we expect the poverty rate would not have been reduced by an equally large amount in 1979 if social assistance had been taken into account.

In delimiting the poor, one could argue that assets and whether the household is a student household should be taken into consideration. It is regarded as legitimate for students to have low incomes because education is viewed as an investment. Moreover, students receive student loans which are not regarded as income. There is relatively little impact on the poverty rate if student households (student households are households in which a student is the main breadwinner) are excluded. In 1991 the poverty rate delimited on the basis of disposable income went down from 5.9 to 5.5 per cent if student households were excluded.

In many ways it seems unreasonable to define the poor without taking assets into consideration. Particularly when using delimitations based on disposable income, there are a number of households with low equivalent incomes that have substantial assets, both real and financial. Largest is the gross finance capital among the poor with delimitations based on disposable income. If, for example, one said that poor people (delimited to 50 per cent of the median for disposable income per unit of consumption) with gross financial capital per unit of consumption of at least NOK 50,000 are not to be regarded as poor, the group of poor people would be reduced by scarcely 10 per cent, or around 0.5 percentage points.

In the above we have only used the percentage of people with incomes under a certain threshold (P_0) as a measure of poverty. As previously mentioned, this measure does not say anything about the income level and income differences among the poor. We will therefore supplement the poverty rate with the poverty measures P_1 and P_2 (see section 2). Note that P_1 is equal to the product of the poverty percentage and poverty gap, while P_2 is a poverty measure that also reflects income disparity among the poor.

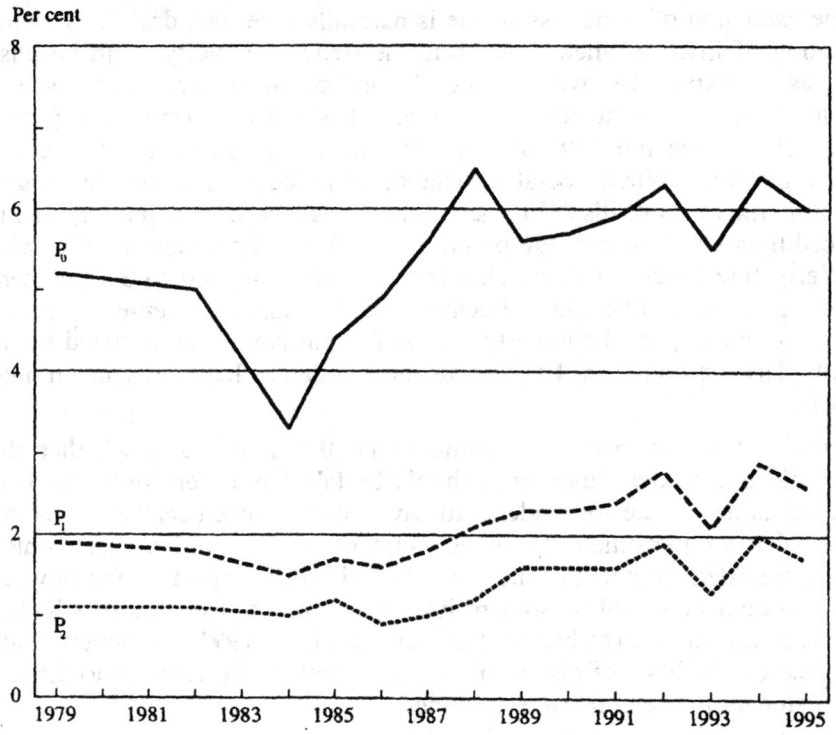

Figure 5.3 The trend in the degree of poverty measured by P_0, P_1, P_2 based on disposable income per unit of consumption.

For poverty measures based on disposable income, both P_1 and P_2 show relatively substantial changes in the distribution of income among the poor. Taking into account the uncertainties in the estimates (see Tables 5.A.2 and 5.A.3 in Appendix I) we cannot, either for P_1 or P_2, claim that changes have taken place in the course of the first half of the 1980s. On the other hand, the measures for the period 1986-1992 increased before remaining unchanged or declining. The increase in P_1 and P_2 is only a reflection of the increase in the percentage of the poor (P_0). The relative increase for P_1 and P_2 is, however, weaker than for P_0 and is due to a narrower poverty gap and income differences among the poor.

From the results in Figures 5.1-5.3 it follows that the low income/poverty structure has been relatively stable for the period 1979-1995 as a whole. In order to have a more detailed picture of the disparity in the distribution of income among the poor we will confine ourselves to describing the situation in 1993. By using income after tax as a basis and 50 per cent of the median income as the poverty line, we arrive at the distribution pattern shown in Table 5.2. Even if this table is based on income after tax and we therefore do not deduct debt interest, the poorest 10 per cent have on average negative income in 1993. This is because of the definition and measurement of net self-employment income. With exceptions, certain people in certain years can end up with losses from self-employment. Viewed over a long period this can, however, be outweighed by years of high income as a result of substantial profits. For such people or households, annual income provides an incomplete picture of their standard of living. Table 5.2 shows a large variation in the annual incomes of the poor. On average, the richest 10 per cent of the poor in 1993 have over four times as high an income after tax as the next poorest 10 per cent (second decile).

Table 5.2 Decile average (standard deviation in parentheses) of income after tax among people with an income lower than 50 per cent of the median income in 1993

Decile	Average income after tax, NOK	
1	-1969	(2101)
2	14120	(2861)
3	23178	(1799)
4	33146	(2759)
5	40876	(1378)
6	45129	(1285)
7	49269	(804)
8	52109	(819)
9	54868	(469)
10	61029	(2748)
All	37176	(1163)

5.7 Income Composition among the Poor

In this section we will examine the composition of income among the poor. This information will *inter alia* contribute to greater clarity as to whether certain processes are behind the observed pattern of poverty. For example, it will be important to know whether the poor are for the most part employed or whether they tend to live on transfers.

Table 5.3 Composition of income among the poor in 1982, 1986, 1990 and 1993. Percentage of gross income (income before tax)

Year	Employment income	Self-employment income	Capital income	Transfers	Total income	Taxes	Interest	Disp. income
1982								
All persons	70	12	4	15	100	24	8	67
The poor defined as: 50 per cent of median of disposable income per unit of consumption	36	32	8	23	100	8	51	26
50 per cent of median of income after tax per unit of consumption	45	9	8	38	100	11	31	36
1986								
All persons	68	12	6	15	100	23	12	64
Poor defined as: 50 per cent of median of disposable income per unit of consumption	51	20	6	23	100	11	42	47
50 per cent of median of income after tax per unit of consumption	45	7	7	42	100	14	12	74
1990								
All persons	66	10	6	17	100	24	14	62
Poor defined as: 50 per cent of median of disposable income per unit of consumption	50	15	6	28	100	9	47	44

	Year	Employ-ment income	Self-employment income	Capital income	Transfers	Total income	Taxes	Interest	Disp. income
50 per cent of median of disposable income per unit of consumption		48	8	6	38	100	10	24	66
	1993								
All persons		65	10	7	18	100	23	10	67
Poor defined as: 50 per cent of median of disposable income per unit of consumption		51	10	5	34	100	10	31	59
50 per cent of median of income after tax per unit of consumption		45	7	4	44	100	11	8	80

There are two important conclusions that we would like to draw from Table 5.3. Firstly, most of the income, including that of the poor, comes from income-generating work. When the poor are delimited on the basis of disposable income, around two-thirds of the income is occupational income. This is just a little less than is the case for the total population. Transfers only account for a small part of the income basis for these people: for poor delimited by disposable income transfers account for around one fourth of total income in 1982, 1986 and 1990 and about one-third in 1993 (compared to about 15 per cent for the entire population). When the poor are delimited on the basis of income after tax we find, however, that the transfers have greater significance and that transfers and wage income account for just under 50 per cent each of the income basis. People with large interest expenses are no longer regarded as poor.

The other conclusion is that interest is a dominant item for the poor delimited on the basis of disposable income. It makes up about half of the total income in 1982, 1986 and 1990 and about one-third in 1993, or about as much as employment income. This indicates that the poor according to this delimitation have substantial debt interest, and that an imbalance in the relationship between interest expenses and income leads to poverty according to this definition.

One also sees that the percentage of overall income from self-employment is not insignificant, particularly at the beginning of the 1980s.

150 Poverty and Low Income in the Nordic Countries

For the self-employed, interest on debt also includes interest on productive capital. The interweaving of business and personal finances among the self-employed and the far more complicated calculation of income from business activity provide special problems for interpretation. For this reason alone, one can raise the question of the relevance of using disposable income as the basis for identifying poor people or households.

5.8 Poverty in Different Population Groups

Although there have been only relatively modest changes in the percentage of the population that is poor, major changes may nevertheless have taken place in the composition of the poor. The results above could indicate that working people make up a significant portion of the poor, and that the poor in no way appear to be dominated by people living exclusively on transfers. We have also seen that students make up only a small portion of the poor.

Statistically speaking, one has to deal with the general problem that, with income statistics based on relatively small samples, the results for sub-populations are often quite uncertain. For that reason it is important to quantify the degree of uncertainty of the various estimates.

5.8.1 Age

Table 5.4 The poverty rate (standard deviation in parentheses) in various age groups when the poverty line is given at 50 per cent of the median for disposable income per unit of consumption

	1979	1985	1991
All	5.2 (0.27)	4.4 (0.26)	5.9 (0.25)
Under 18 years of age	4.5 (0.47)	6.0 (0.60)	8.2 (0.57)
18-34 years of age	6.9 (0.58)	5.7 (0.58)	8.9 (0.61)
35-64 years of age	3.6 (0.38)	2.6 (0.37)	4.3 (0.35)
65 and over	8.0 (1.00)	2.9 (0.51)	0.7 (0.23)

The clearest conclusion from Table 5.4 is that the risk of poverty among the elderly has been sharply reduced. Regardless of which of the delimitations of the poor one uses, the poverty rate among the elderly has fallen from nearly 10 per cent in 1979 to under 1 per cent in 1991. This also means that the elderly make up a diminishing proportion of the poor; in 1991 around 2 per cent of the poor were aged 65 and over. As seen from Table 5.1, both of these poverty lines are lower than the basic pension amounts. The conclusions for children are somewhat less clear. The poverty rate among children has increased when the poor are delimited on the basis of disposable income, from nearly 4 per cent in 1979 to 8 per cent in 1991. When the delimitation is based on income after tax, the change over the period as a whole is not statistically significant. The change in the percentage of poor children in the latter half of the 1980s is, however, significant.

In 1979-1991 families with children had an average income growth after tax that was somewhat above the trend in the general population. At the same time, however, there was a substantial growth in debt and interest payments owed by families with children. This growth applied to all parts of the distribution of income. It was also significant among households with lower incomes. This is presumably the reason why the poverty rate among children has increased so much when the identification of the poor is based on disposable income.

Among younger people between the ages of 18-34, too, we find a pattern similar to that for children, but slightly less pronounced. The poverty rate based on disposable income increased from 1979 to 1991, but somewhat more slowly than among children. When the delimitation is based on income after tax, the poverty rate drops from 1979 to 1985 and then subsequently increases, although with no overall change.

Middle-aged people between the ages of 35-64 occupy a position between the young and the old. The poverty rate based on disposable income did not change over the period as a whole. On the other hand, there has been a reduction in the poverty rate based on income after tax.

5.8.2 Gender

Regardless of delimitation, the poverty rate among *adult* men and women is quite similar through the entire period, with perhaps the exception of 1979.[2] The patterns of poverty basically follow the trend in the poverty rate for the whole population. The results could indicate that the poverty rate among

---

[2] The structure of the 1979 Income Distribution Survey deviates from later surveys. We will therefore not place too great emphasis on the fact that the poverty rate is different among men and women.

adult women has increased in the course of the 1980s. While in 1979 and 1985 there was a greater risk of becoming poor for men than for women, the risk was almost the same in 1991.

Table 5.5 The poverty rate (standard deviation in parentheses) among women and men over the age of 17 when the poverty line is fixed at 50 per cent of the median for disposable income per unit of consumption, per cent

	1979	1985	1991
Men	5.3 (0.72)	3.7 (0.39)	5.5 (0.38)
Women	3.3 (0.59)	4.0 (0.40)	4.9 (0.38)

5.8.3 Type of household

We will show how the risk of poverty varies by type of household, and also how the poor are distributed by type of household based on data for 1993. The table also serves as a basis for comparison with a similar distribution in the section on chronic poverty below (therefore we use the concept of after tax income).

The poverty rate is clearly largest among singles and single mothers. In these two groups every fifth and sixth person respectively is poor. Among younger couples without children the poverty rate is above average, but is still under the level for the two groups mentioned above.

Although the poverty rate among families with children is about average for the population, it is still worth noting that poor people in families with small children account for a significant portion (around one fourth) of the group of poor people. Nearly three-quarters of the poor are young singles, families with small children or single mothers.

Table 5.6 The poverty rate among people in various types of households, and the distribution of all people and poor people by type of household. The poverty line defined as 50 per cent of income after tax per unit of consumption in 1993

		Poverty rate	Distribution by type of household	
			All people	All poor
All		4.9	100.0	100.0
Singles	Under 45 years of age	20.7	6.9	28.6
	45-64 years of age	5.0	3.7	3.7
	65 and over	2.7	3.7	3.6
Couples without children	Under 45 years of age	8.1	3.5	5.6
	45-64 years of age	1.7	5.7	2.0
	65 and over	1.7	8.5	2.9
Couples with children. Youngest child	0-6 years of age	5.3	23.0	24.5
	7-19 years of age	1.6	22.5	7.3
	20 and over	0.5	9.1	0.8
Single mothers with youngest child	0-19 years of age	16.3	6.0	19.5

5.8.4 Region

With delimitations of poor people based on disposable income, the results show a significant increase in the poverty rate in Eastern Norway (including Oslo). There is a significant reduction in the poverty rate in Western Norway, while there is no significant change in other parts of the country. The increase in the poverty rate in the course of the last half of the 1980s is only true for Eastern Norway.

With poverty delimitations based on income after tax, the results show significant reductions in the poverty rate not only in Western Norway, but also in Trøndelag. In Eastern Norway and Southern Norway, no changes can be demonstrated in the poverty rate from 1979 to 1991. Using this delimitation we also see that the poverty rate in Eastern Norway increased at the end of the decade. The trend also shows that the risk of poverty in 1991 was greater in Eastern Norway than in the other regions of the country.

Table 5.7 **Poverty rate (standard deviation in parentheses) in various regions when the poverty line is set at 50 per cent of the median for disposable income per unit of consumption**

	1979	1985	1991
All	5.2 (0.26)	4.4 (0.26)	5.9 (0.25)
Eastern Norway	4.4 (0.36)	3.9 (0.35)	7.1 (0.40)
Southern Norway	4.7 (0.69)	6.0 (0.80)	4.4 (0.55)
Western Norway	6.5 (0.69)	4.5 (0.62)	4.7 (0.51)
Trøndelag	6.9 (0.95)	3.8 (0.75)	5.3 (0.78)
Northern Norway	5.7 (0.85)	4.8 (0.81)	4.7 (0.67)

5.9 Chronic Poverty

Empirical analyses of poverty are usually based on annual cross-sectional data. The choice of one year as the period of income is based on tradition as well as the availability of data. Of course, a one-year period gives limited information about the duration of poverty. If most people experience low annual incomes only a few times in their lives, the average duration of poverty will be short. In this case the transition in and out of poverty (measured by annual income) will be high. If, on the contrary, income mobility is low, there will be a strong tendency towards chronic poverty and hence a more serious problem of poverty.

Our definition of chronic poverty is based on individual income histories collected from repeated observations of annual income over a ten-year period, 1986 - 1995. For each person, the household income after tax per unit of consumption was calculated for each of the ten years in the period. We classify a person as chronically poor if he/she has a total income for the ten-year period 1986 - 1995 which is lower than 50 per cent of the median of the distribution of the total incomes for the same ten-year period for the entire population.

The data on which these statistics are based has been collected from repeated observations of a sample of 3,750 people resident in Norway in 1986 who were still living in 1995. The information about the households was for the most part gathered by means of interviews, whereas the information about income was gathered from tax records and from other public records.

Previous studies and analyses have indicated that there is a high degree of mobility among the poor, in the sense that only between 40 per cent and 60 per cent of the households that were registered as poor in a given year were still registered as poor the following year (Epland and Korbøl 1992). Even if we use the individual person, as opposed to the household, as the unit of analysis, the results shown in Table 5.8 still demonstrate the same degree of movement in and out of poverty as reported by Epland and Korbøl.

Table 5.8 **Percentage of people classified as poor in 1986, 1989 and 1992 who were still poor the following year**

Year	Percentage of poor people who were still poor one year later
1986	52.7
1989	40.8
1992	51.0

At first glance, the figures in Table 5.8 might appear to indicate that poverty is only a temporary state for roughly half of the people who are registered as poor on the basis of the traditional annual indicators.

Nevertheless, Table 5.8 does not really provide us with any real information about the question of the duration of poverty. First of all, we must ascertain whether the changes in status in focus here are the result of a marginal increase in income. Secondly, there is also the issue of whether it is in fact the same people who are slipping in and out of poverty over a longer period of time. If this is the case, then poverty would nonetheless appear to be chronic in its nature.

156 *Poverty and Low Income in the Nordic Countries*

In order to shed some light on these two issues, we intend to use the measure of chronic poverty mentioned earlier as our point of departure. The measure of poverty we will use is calculated on the basis of the sum of the annual incomes for ten years (1986 - 1995). As an alternative to the poverty lines that we have defined specifically for each individual year, we will now use 50 per cent of the median of the ten-year distribution as our poverty line. This measure yields the result that 1.5 per cent of the population are poor, whereas 6.4 per cent of the population have an income lower than 125 per cent of this poverty line. Note that the average annual poverty line for this ten-year period was NOK 58,976 (1995 rates), i. e. at the same level as the equivalent annual poverty line for 1995 (see Table 5.1).

Table 5.9 shows the number of times that the people registered as poor in the model based on income over the ten years were also poor in the corresponding year-by-year analyses for the years 1986 - 1995 (see section 6). This information has been further supplemented with corresponding information about the people whose annual income in the ten-year period was less than 125 per cent of the poverty line, i. e. people whose average annual income in the period 1986 - 1995 was less than NOK 73,719 (1995 rates). By way of a benchmark, the annual average income over the ten-year period for the whole population of Norway was NOK 127 188 (1995), and the average income per year among the poor was NOK 46,730 (1995).

The results indicated in Tables 5.9 and 5.10 demonstrate a clear tendency towards long-term poverty; as many as 67 per cent of the people whose ten-year income was below the poverty line were also registered as poor in more than half of the years in the period 1986 - 1995.

Table 5.9   Distribution of the chronically poor, according to the number of times they have appeared in the annual figures, per cent

Number of times	0	1	2	3	4	5	6	7	8	9	10
Below the poverty line	0.0	0.0	7.5	8.1	6.0	11.3	13.2	16.7	7.5	23.8	5.8
Below 1.25x the poverty line	31.8	13.7	16.3	9.9	8.6	4.1	3.0	3.9	1.7	5.4	1.3

Table 5.10 Proportion of chronically poor who are also poor in the figures from individual years, per cent

	1986	1987	1988	1989	1990	1991	1992	1993	1994	1995
Below the poverty line	45.1	58.2	76.4	66.1	60.1	64.5	77.4	75.2	65.8	59.7
Below 1.25x the poverty line	22.5	31.6	33.7	23.7	24.5	26.3	26.3	24.8	22.8	16.8

The low degree of mobility is further underlined if we raise the level of the poverty line by 25 per cent. Only a small fraction of the people whose income was in the interval between the poverty line and 1.25 times the poverty line experienced being poor in more than two of the ten years in our period of study.

Table 5.11 shows the variation in average annual income after tax for those with ten-year incomes below the poverty line in the ten-year income distribution and 1.25 times the poverty line.

Table 5.11 Average income after tax during the ten- year period 1986 - 1995, with the corresponding annual average for people whose ten-year annual income was lower than the poverty line and 1.25 times the poverty line in the ten-year distribution of income (standard deviation shown in brackets)

	Average ten-year income	Corresponding annual average income									
		1986	1987	1988	1989	1990	1991	1992	1993	1994	1995
Poverty line	467313 (22062)	50555 (4892)	47884 (3755)	46366 (3362)	48524 (5315)	41376 (4196)	45404 (4050)	42328 (3875)	47131 (5014)	42974 (4348)	54772 (4225)
1.25x poverty line	623928 (8682)	61772 (1649)	61332 (1643)	63362 (1455)	60958 (1622)	58879 (1559)	61864 (1392)	62671 (1651)	63789 (1648)	62510 (1648)	66793 (1495)

This table thus demonstrates that there is little variation in the annual average incomes for each year among those households that had a low ten-year income. This is in accordance with the conclusions drawn by Aaberge and Wennemo (1993), who also found a corresponding stability in the annual incomes of people with a high income. They also pointed out that stability in the person's participation in the labour force was a significant factor in low income mobility, and especially among the people with the lowest and highest incomes.

We call attention to the fact that children born and people who died later than 1986 do not belong to the population for the distribution of ten-year incomes. However they can be represented as being among the poor in the distribution of annual income.

Table 5.12 Composition of income after tax among the chronically poor. Percentage of income before tax

	Wages and salaries	Entrepreneurial income	Property income	Transfers	Total income	Tax	Interest paid	Disposable income
All persons	68	11	6	15	100	25	12	64
Below poverty line	43	18	3	36	100	14	8	78
Below 1.25x poverty line	40	9	4	46	100	13	10	77

Comparing Table 5.12 with the corresponding distributions based on annual income in Table 5.3 (based on 50 per cent of the median income after tax), we find the same pattern of composition of income among the chronically poor as among the sporadically poor. Wages and salaries and transfers constitute somewhat less than half of total income. We also see that a considerably higher percentage of total income is entrepreneurial income among people below the poverty line than in the Norwegian population as well as among the sporadically poor.

Table 5.13 Proportion of those people who are poor according to the annual distribution of income after tax, who also are chronically poor

	1986	1987	1988	1989	1990	1991	1992	1993	1994	1995
Below poverty line	15.7	24.6	34.7	32.0	31.5	41.8	41.8	42.3	45.9	40.8
Below 1.25x Poverty line	34.1	57.8	66.4	49.7	55.5	74.0	61.7	60.5	60.5	49.7

Table 5.13 supplements the information in Table 5.10. In interpreting the results, one should take into account that the group of chronically poor is much smaller (1.5 per cent of the population) than the groups of poor based on the annual income distribution (3.1-5.9 per cent). We refer to Table 5.10 which shows the proportion of the chronically poor who are poor according

to the annual income distributions.

Table 5.13 shows that more than half of the people who are poor according to the annual distribution are not poor according to the ten-year distribution. We found earlier that there is little income-mobility and little variation in the annual incomes among the chronically poor. Hence the results in Table 5.13 indicate that most of the people who are poor according to the annual distribution have low incomes only temporarily.

The results shown in Table 5.14 confirm this. The average ten-year income of people who appeared poor in the year-by-year figures, but not in the ten-year model, was almost double the figure for the average ten-year income of the people who were shown to be poor by the ten-year model. This proves that the year-by-year poverty indicators are unsuitable as a tool for identifying people who have a consistently low income. The reason for this is that the annual indicators capture people who have a low income for a limited period of time only, for example people in education or training, and people who are members of households in which the main income-earner is self-employed and has a low income in certain exceptional years. Alternatively, of course, it may also be due to measurement errors.

It is also noteworthy that a ten-year income of NOK 940 000 among the mobile poor corresponds to an average annual income of NOK 94 000, whereas the actual average annual income of the chronicly poor was NOK 46 730 in the period 1986 - 1995.

Table 5.14 Average ten-year income after tax of people classified as poor in the individual, year-by-year figures, but who are not chronically poor, 1995 NOK

Year in which poor									
1986	1987	1988	1989	1990	1991	1992	1993	1994	1995
Average income									
36197	38081	46582	39614	39535	41621	38447	43830	31748	37229
Average ten-year income									
940865	947699	827138	941214	874365	817968	860876	902997	859932	900439

So, what is it that causes a person to have an income below the poverty line in the ten-year model, and what characteristics do the people who are identified as poor have in common?

We know from other analyses that people who have a persistently low personal income generally also have a weak position on the labour market (see Aaberge and Wennemo, 1993). This group consists of students, school pupils, people serving compulsory military service, people working in the home, pensioners and recipients of national insurance benefits. This study, however, shows that pensioners and recipients of national insurance benefits constitute only about 15 per cent of the people whose income is less than 50 per cent of the median income in the ten-year measure. If, however, we raise the poverty line by another 25 per cent, we find that the group now contains almost twice the number of pensioners and recipients of national insurance benefits.

Since the civil status and family situation of people change over time, we shall look for a correlation between these factors and low income over the ten-year period, on the basis of civil status in each of the years in the period 1986 - 1995.

Table 5.15 Distribution of people whose ten-year after tax income was less than 1 and 1.25 times the minimum income level for chronic poverty, broken down according to civil status and family type. Average percentages for the period 1986 - 1995

Civil status and family type	Below poverty line	Below 1.25x poverty line
Single person, under 45 years	29.4	9.8
Single person, 65 years or over	0.0	11.3
Couple without children where head of household is 65 +	0.4	11.1
Couple with children aged 0 - 6 years	36.5	30.0
Couple with children aged 7 - 19 years	5.9	12.4
Single mothers with children aged 0 - 19 years	17.9	12.3
Other	10.5	13.2

Table 5.15 shows that 60 per cent and 55 per cent of the people registered as having a lower annual income for the ten-year period than NOK 589 760 and NOK 737 190 (1995 NOK) respectively were families with children.

With a poverty line based on annual income, we found that more than 50 per cent of the poor lived in households with children (Table 5.6). Based on incomes in a ten-year period the percentage is even higher, with 60 per cent of all poor people living in households with children. The percentage of the poor living in households with small children increases in particular when the poor are defined on the basis of ten-year incomes instead of annual incomes.

5.10 Summary and Conclusions

The purpose of this work has been to describe and discuss the incidence and degree of economic poverty in Norway in the period 1979-1995. Quantifying poverty requires precise definitions of population and income, and the determination of the scale for interpersonal comparability (equivalence scale) and poverty line. Since the choices made have normative implications, it is important to study whether and to what degree the relevant choices affect the results. The background for our choices is described in sections 1, 2 and 5.

Empirical analyses of poverty are usually based on distributions of annual incomes (converted to equivalent income) for separate years, and characterise poverty by the number of persons who have an income under a given limit called the poverty line. In our studies, we have used six different criteria for determining the number of poor. The results show that the choice of poverty criteria in particular have an impact on the level of poverty. For instance, we found that the poverty rate in 1993 varied between 3.6 and 5.5 per cent, depending on which of the six relevant poverty criteria we used. We found the lowest proportion when the definition of income is income after tax and the poverty line is determined by basic pension and family allowance payments. When social assistance and basic and supplementary benefit in the event of disability are included in income, the poverty rate is reduced by about one percentage point. Data on social assistance is only available after 1990.

Regardless of which poverty criterion was used, the poverty rate decreased in the first half of the 1980s, but rose again in the second half of the decade. The increase was, however, somewhat stronger for poverty measures based on disposable income than for measures based on income after tax. This difference is due to the strong increase in household borrowing and subsequent increased interest expenses in the period 1984-1988. The trend in the 1990s is more uncertain. The measures based on disposable income show no change, while certain measures based on income after tax indicate an increase in the poverty rate. Looking at the period 1979-1995 as a whole there is, however, no basis for asserting that the poverty rate has changed in Norway. By using poverty measures that also take into account relative income levels and income differences among the poor we find stability in the first half of the 1980s, a weak but steady increase in poverty from 1986 to 1992 and then keep steady on the 1992 level.

Even though the extent and degree of poverty are nearly unchanged, the demographic composition of the poor has changed. This is most clearly expressed by a sharp reduction in the poverty rate among the elderly. Among children and young single persons there was a slight increase in the poverty rate from 1979 to 1991.

The income composition for the poor shows that occupational income accounts for the major part of their income. This does however not mean that the working poor are typical of the poor in Norway. We interpret this to mean that those who are identified as poor in the annual distributions of income (distribution of annual income) are marginal both in relation to the labour market and the social security system. Another clear result is that, for poor people identified on the basis of disposable income, interest payments take up between 31 and 51 per cent of the combined incomes. This is partly due to an imbalance between income and interest expenses leading to poverty according to this definition and partly to problems related to measuring the income of the self-employed.

The results we have mentioned so far refer exclusively to analyses of annual cross-sectional data and naturally provide no facts as to whether poverty is chronic or not. To shed light on this question, we have studied individual income histories based on repeated observations of annual income for the period 1986-1995. As an alternative to the year-specific poverty lines we have used 50 per cent of the median in the ten-year distribution as a poverty line. We then find that only 1.5 per cent of the population were chronically poor, i.e. have a lower than ten-year annual income than this level, while 6.6 per cent have an income lower than 125 per cent of the poverty line. Moreover, we find that all of 67 per cent of the chronically poor were classified as poor in between 6 and 10 of the years in the period 1986-1995. The results also show that there was little variation in the annual income of the chronically poor. This is in strong contrast to the income history of the majority of those classified as poor according to the annual indicators. These people have only transient low incomes. They may be people who are going to school or those belonging to households in which the head is self-employed with a low net self-employment income in one single year. Consequently, the annual indicators are unsuitable as a tool for identifying those who have persistently low incomes.

5.11 Appendix I

Table 5.A.1. Proportion of people in Norway who are poor according to alternative poverty lines in 1979, 1982 and 1984-1995; Per cent (Standard deviation in parentheses)

	1979	1982	1984	1985	1986	1987	1988	1989	1990	1991	1992	1993	1994	1995
Disposable income per unit of consumption														
50 per cent of the year's median (z_1)	5.2 (0.12)	5.0 (0.14)	3.3 (0.23)	4.4 (0.26)	4.9 (0.20)	5.6 (0.25)	6.5 (0.27)	5.6 (0.27)	5.7 (0.19)	5.9 (0.25)	6.3 (0.26)	5.5 (0.26)	6.4 (0.15)	6.0 (0.18)
50 per cent of median average (z_2)	6.3 (0.29)	6.5 (0.16)	4.5 (0.26)	4.9 (0.27)	4.9 (0.20)	5.3 (0.24)	6.7 (0.27)	6.0 (0.28)	5.9 (0.20)	5.7 (0.24)	5.9 (0.25)	4.6 (0.24)	5.3 (0.13)	4.8 (0.16)
Basic pension (z_3)	5.5 (8.27)	5.6 (0.15)	4.3 (0.26)	4.6 (0.26)	5.2 (0.20)	5.1 (0.24)	5.5 (0.25)	6.2 (0.28)	6.4 (0.20)	6.5 (0.26)	7.1 (0.27)	5.5 (0.26)	6.9 (0.15)	6.2 (0.18)
Income after tax per unit of consumption														
50 per cent of the year's median (z_4)	5.1 (0.26)	4.5 (0.14)	3.4 (0.23)	3.1 (0.22)	3.7 (0.17)	3.7 (0.20)	4.0 (0.21)	4.1 (0.23)	4.1 (0.17)	4.6 (0.22)	5.2 (0.23)	5.0 (0.25)	5.7 (0.14)	5.9 (0.18)
50 per cent of median average (z_5)	7.3 (0.31)	7.5 (0.17)	5.0 (0.28)	3.6 (0.23)	3.4 (0.17)	2.7 (0.17)	3.2 (0.19)	4.1 (0.23)	3.9 (0.16)	4.1 (0.21)	4.5 (0.22)	4.3 (0.23)	5.2 (0.13)	5.1 (0.17)
Basic pension (z_6)	5.0 (0.26)	4.4 (0.14)	3.1 (0.22)	2.7 (0.21)	2.8 (0.15)	1.9 (0.15)	2.0 (0.15)	3.1 (0.20)	3.5 (0.15)	3.3 (0.19)	4.3 (0.21)	3.6 (0.21)	5.4 (0.13)	5.1 (0.17)

Table 5.A.2 Degree of poverty measured by P_1 (standard deviation in parentheses)

	1979	1982	1984	1985	1986	1987	1988	1989	1990	1991	1992	1993	1994	1995
Disposable income per unit of consumption														
50 per cent of the year's median (z_1)	1.9 (0.12)	1.8 (0.07)	1.5 (0.13)	1.7 (0.14)	1.6 (0.09)	1.8 (0.11)	2.1 (0.12)	2.3 (0.14)	2.3 (0.11)	2.4 (0.13)	2.8 (0.14)	2.1 (0.13)	2.9 (0.08)	2.6 (0.10)
50 per cent of median average (z_2)	2.2 (0.13)	2.1 (0.07)	1.6 (0.13)	1.8 (0.14)	1.6 (0.09)	1.8 (0.11)	2.1 (0.12)	2.4 (0.15)	2.4 (0.11)	2.4 (0.13)	2.6 (0.14)	1.8 (0.12)	2.6 (0.08)	2.2 (0.09)
Basic pension (z_3)	2.1 (0.13)	1.9 (0.07)	1.7 (0.13)	1.8 (0.14)	1.7 (0.09)	1.6 (0.10)	1.9 (0.12)	2.5 (0.15)	2.5 (0.11)	2.6 (0.13)	3.0 (0.15)	2.1 (0.13)	3.0 (0.08)	2.7 (0.10)
Income after tax per unit of consumption														
50 per cent of the year's median (z_4)	1.9 (0.12)	1.6 (0.07)	1.1 (0.10)	1.4 (0.13)	1.1 (0.07)	1.1 (0.08)	1.1 (0.08)	1.7 (0.12)	1.8 (0.09)	1.8 (0.11)	2.2 (0.13)	1.8 (0.12)	2.7 (0.08)	2.4 (0.09)
50 per cent of median average (z_5)	2.6 (0.14)	2.2 (0.07)	1.4 (0.11)	1.5 (0.13)	1.1 (0.07)	1.0 (0.08)	1.0 (0.08)	1.7 (0.12)	1.7 (0.09)	1.7 (0.11)	2.0 (0.12)	1.6 (0.12)	2.6 (0.08)	2.2 (0.09)
Basic pension (z_6)	2.0 (0.12)	1.6 (0.07)	1.1 (0.10)	1.4 (0.13)	1.0 (0.07)	0.8 (0.08)	0.8 (0.08)	1.5 (0.12)	1.6 (0.09)	1.6 (0.11)	2.0 (0.12)	1.5 (0.11)	2.6 (0.08)	2.2 (0.09)

Table 5.A.3 Degree of poverty measured by P_2[**]) Standard deviation in parentheses. In calculating P_2 negative income is set at nil

	1979	1982	1984	1985	1986	1987	1988	1989	1990	1991	1992	1993	1994	1995
Disposable income per unit of consumption														
50 per cent of year's median (z_1)	1.1 (0.09)	1.1 (0.06)	1.0 (0.11)	1.2 (0.12)	0.9 (0.07)	1.0 (0.09)	1.2 (0.09)	1.6 (0.13)	1.6 (0.09)	1.6 (0.11)	1.9 (0.12)	1.3 (0.10)	2.0 (0.07)	1.7 (0.08)
50 per cent of median average (z_2)	1.2 (0.09)	1.2 (0.06)	1.1 (0.11)	1.2 (0.12)	0.9 (0.07)	1.0 (0.09)	1.2 (0.09)	1.7 (0.13)	1.6 (0.09)	1.6 (0.11)	1.9 (0.12)	1.2 (0.10)	1.9 (0.07)	1.6 (0.08)
Basic pension (z_3)	1.2 (0.09)	1.2 (0.06)	1.1 (0.11)	1.3 (0.12)	1.0 (0.07)	1.0 (0.09)	1.2 (0.09)	1.7 (0.13)	1.7 (0.09)	1.7 (0.11)	2.0 (0.13)	1.3 (0.10)	2.1 (0.07)	1.8 (0.08)
Income after tax per unit of consumption														
50 per cent of year's median (z_4)	1.1 (0.08)	1.0 (0.05)	0.7 (0.08)	1.0 (0.11)	0.6 (0.05)	0.6 (0.07)	0.6 (0.06)	1.1 (0.10)	1.3 (0.08)	1.2 (0.09)	1.5 (0.11)	1.1 (0.09)	1.9 (0.07)	1.6 (0.08)
50 per cent of median average (z_5)	1.4 (0.10)	1.2 (0.06)	0.8 (0.08)	1.1 (0.11)	0.6 (0.05)	0.6 (0.07)	0.6 (0.06)	1.1 (0.10)	1.2 (0.08)	1.2 (0.09)	1.4 (0.10)	1.1 (0.09)	1.8 (0.07)	1.5 (0.08)
Basic pension (z_6)	1.1 (0.09)	1.0 (0.05)	0.7 (0.08)	1.0 (0.11)	0.5 (0.05)	0.5 (0.06)	0.5 (0.06)	1.0 (0.10)	1.2 (0.08)	1.1 (0.09)	1.4 (0.10)	1.0 (0.09)	1.8 (0.07)	1.5 (0.08)

5.12 Appendix II

5.12.1 Variance of FGT indices

Let $X_1, X_2, \ldots, X_n$ be n independent observations from income distribution F (cumulative distribution function) and let $I_i(z)$ be an indicator function defined by

(A1) $\quad I_i(z) = \begin{cases} 1 & \text{if } X_i \leq z \\ 0 & \text{otherwise} \end{cases}$,

in which z is the poverty line. It then follows that $\hat{P}(a)$ defined by

(A2) $\quad \hat{P}_a = \dfrac{1}{n} \sum_{i=1}^{n} \left(1 - \dfrac{X_i}{z}\right)^a I_i(z)$,

is an unbiased estimator for P_a. defined by (1)

The estimator $\hat{P}_a$ for P_a has the following properties:

Proposition 1. $\hat{P}_a$ is an unbiased estimator for P_a which has an asymptotic normal distribution with variance

(A3) $\quad \text{var } \hat{P}_a = \dfrac{1}{n}\left(P_{2a} - P_a^2\right).$

Proof. It follows directly from the Central Limit Theorem that

$$\dfrac{\hat{P} - P_a}{\left(\text{var } \hat{P}_a\right)^{\frac{1}{2}}} \xrightarrow[n \to \infty]{} N(0,1).$$

By using the rule for double expectation we see that

$$E\hat{P}_a = E\left[I_i(z)E\left[\left(1-\frac{X_i}{z}\right)^a | I_i(z)\right]\right] =$$

$$F(z)\int_0^z \left(1-\frac{x}{z}\right)^a d\frac{F(x)}{F(z)} = \int_0^z \left(1-\frac{x}{z}\right)^a dF(x) = P_a$$

Furthermore, by using the rule for conditional variance we see that

$$\text{var}\hat{P}_a = \frac{1}{n^2}\text{var}\sum_{i=1}^n I_i(z)E\left[\left(1-\frac{X_i}{z}\right)^a | I_i(z)\right]$$

$$+\frac{1}{n^2}nE\,\text{var}\left[\sum_{i=1}^n \left(1-\frac{X_i}{z}\right)^a I_i(z)|I_i(z)\right] =$$

$$\frac{1}{n^2}n\text{var}\left(I_i(z)\frac{P_a}{F(z)}\right) + \frac{1}{n^2}nEI_i(z)\text{var}\left[\left(1-\frac{X_i}{z}\right)^a | I_i(z)\right] =$$

$$\frac{1}{n}\left(\frac{P_a}{F(z)}\right)^2 F(z)(1-F(z)) + \frac{1}{n}F(z)\left[\frac{1}{F(z)}\int_0^z \left(1-\frac{x}{z}\right)^{2a} dF(x) - \left(\frac{P_a}{F(z)}\right)^2\right] =$$

$$\frac{1}{n}\frac{1-F(z)}{F(z)}P_a^2 + \frac{1}{n}\left[P_{2a} - \frac{P_a^2}{F(z)}\right] =$$

$$\frac{1}{n}\left[P_{2a} - P_a^2\right]$$

References

Aaberge, R. and T. Wennemo (1988). *Inntektsulikhet i Norge 1973-1985* (Income Inequality in Norway), Reports 88/15. Statistics Norway.

Aaberge, R. and T. Wennemo (1993). *Inntektsulikhet og inntektsmobilitet i Norge 1986-1990.* (Income Inequality and Income Mobility in Norway 1986-1990), Social and Economic Studies 82. Statistics Norway.

Andersen, A.S., J.E. Kristiansen, O. Skarstad and H.P. Wilse (1980). *Inntektsfordeling og levekår* (Income Distribution and Living Conditions), Socio-economic Studies 46. Statistics Norway.

Andersen, A.S., J. Epland, R. Kjeldstad and J. Lyngstad (1995). *Husholdningenes økonomi. 1980-tallet Fra vekst til innstramming* (Household Finances in the 1980s. From Growth to Belt-tightening), Statistical Analyses no. 8. Statistics Norway.

Epland, J. and L. Korbøl (1992). *Duration of Poverty in Norway in the 1980s. Some Longitudinal Results from the Norwegian Socio-economic Panel.* Report from Multidisciplinary Research Conference on Poverty and Distribution Oslo, November 16-17, 1992. Working paper from Department of Social Statistics. Statistics Norway.

Foster, J., J. Greer and E. Thorbecke (1984). A Class of Decomposable Poverty Measures. *Econometrica,* 52, 761-765.

Gulbrandsen, Lars (1991). *Fra forbruksfest til gjeldskrise* (From Consumer Spending Spree to Debt Crisis), Institute of Applied Social Research report 91:9.

Lunde, T.K. and C. Poppe (1991). *Ny-fattigdom i velferdsstaten* (Neo-poverty in the Welfare State), Report no. 3. National Institute for Consumer Research.

Ravallion, M. (1992). *Poverty Comparisons: A Guide to Concepts and Methods.* LSMS Working Paper, Number 88. The World Bank.

Rødseth, T. (1977). *Inntektsfordeling i Norge* (Distribution of Income in Norway), Official Norwegian Reports NOU 1977:44.

Statistics Norway (1972). *Lavinntektsundersøkelsen 1967* (Survey of Low Income 1967), Statistical Analyses no. 4.

Stjernø, S. (1985). *Den moderne fattigdommen* (Modern Poverty), Scandinavian University Press.

Strøm, S., T. Wennemo and R. Aaberge (1993). *Inntektsulikhet i Norge 1973-1990* (Income Inequality in Norway), Reports 93/17. Statistics Norway.

Townsend, P. (1979). *Poverty in the United Kingdom.* Penguin.

6 Poverty in Sweden: Changes 1975-1995, Profile and Dynamics

BJÖRN GUSTAFSSON

6.1 Introduction[1]

The Swedish economy has experienced many changes since the middle of the 1970s. Economic growth has slowed, both in itself and in comparison with many other industrialised countries. Sweden has therefore lost its high position in the ranking by GDP per capita. For example, while Sweden ranked number four amongst the OECD countries in 1970, it had fallen to number nine in 1990 and down to sixteenth position in 1995. (Lindbeck, 1997)

Also the business cycle has developed differently to that of many other countries. The downturn in the world economy, which was triggered by the first oil price shock in the early 1970s, affected the Swedish economy considerably later. The time lag was mainly due to economic policy. Unemployment rates started to rise in the early 1980s and culminated in a peak in 1983. Nonetheless, the level was much lower than that in most other OECD countries. The pattern for the rest of the 1980s was low unemployment, high economic activity, and relatively high inflation. This situation ended abruptly at the beginning of the 1990s.

The next downturn in the world economy coincided with decreased domestic demand and changed priorities for Swedish economic policy. The principal economic policy goal of maintaining low unemployment has been replaced by that of holding down inflation. The unemployment rate skyrocketed and reached its maximum in 1993, at a level much higher than ever experienced by the members of the present labour force. Labour force participation rates fell sharply. While there were many changes in the

---

[1] I thank Bengt-Olof Gert and Kjell Jansson, Statistics Sweden and Torun Larsson and Håkan Nyman at the Department of Economics, University of Göteborg for help during various stages of the research process. Financial support from the Swedish Council of Social Research (SFR) is acknowlegded.

macro-economy during the first half of the 1990s, this has not been true subsequently. There has been export-led growth in output and inflation has been low. Less positively, the employment level has not been restored.

Sweden has long been known for its comprehensive and generous social welfare programmes. It has also been known for its high level of taxation. The 1960s and 1970s were decades of rapid expansion. Ever larger proportions of the population became eligible to receive payments from various transfer systems and benefits tended to be increasingly generous. The expansion of pensions is of particular relevance to the question of poverty in the Swedish population. The level of the minimum pension increased more rapidly than the consumer price index and an ever larger proportion of the elderly became entitled to supplementary pensions.

The local level of the public sector in Sweden has become a major provider of social services. For example, there was an increase in the provision of public child care in tandem with an increased female labour force participation and this is generally considered to be a causal relationship. At the end of the 1980s the female labour force participation rates in Sweden were remarkably high by western standards.

In addition, the role of the Swedish welfare state changed at the beginning of the 1990s. Exploding public expenditure on unemployment benefits, high expenditure on active labour market policy measures together with a reduction in tax revenues led to large public sector budget problems. In the middle of the 1990s there were many reductions in levels of benefit and expenditure on other public programmes. There were cuts in the system of sickness insurance, in the system of parental leave benefits and in the unemployment insurance systems. For the first time since their introduction half a century ago child benefits were lowered in nominal terms. Also the pension systems underwent changes. The worsened financial situation of local government undermined their ability to provide social services.

Since the mid-1970s there have also been a number of demographic changes in Sweden. As in many other countries, the population is ageing. By international standards, Swedish families are small and they are becoming even smaller. While, in many countries in the south of Europe, young adults typically live with their parents, this is not the case in Sweden. Family stability has decreased. However, perhaps the most important demographic change in recent decades in terms of poverty is the rapid growth of the foreign born population. Many recent immigrants originate from distant countries and they have arrived in Sweden as asylum seekers or their relatives.

All the changes listed above can be assumed to have had an effect on the distribution of low income as well as on the profile of poverty. The purpose of this chapter is to investigate how economic poverty in Sweden has developed since the middle of the 1970s. We also analyse the poverty profile for Sweden and the way in which this has changed in order to see who is prone to poverty and who has a low risk of being poor. Data is presented for nearly every year between 1975 and 1995. As "poverty" can be defined and measured in different ways, we work with alternative definitions in order to provide firm conclusions.

One issue in poverty research which has attracted increased attention is the dynamics of poverty. Are the same people poor year after year, or is there a considerable rate of turnover? If the latter is true, then most spells of poverty are short. In this case, however, the related question is whether the same people experience frequent spells of poverty. Is mobility in and out of poverty affected by age? How do different demographic events and family events affect poverty status? In addressing these questions, we note that there have been few previous assessments based on data for a Nordic country.

The rest of this chapter is organised in the following way. In the next section we survey the literature on poverty in modern Sweden. Section 6.3 discusses data and assumptions. Time-based data showing how the extent of poverty has developed in the entire population are presented and discussed in Section 6.4. The poverty profile is described in Section 6.5 and the issue of the correlation between gender and poverty is discussed in Section 6.6. The design of the study of the dynamics of poverty is outlined in Section 6.7, and the results are presented and discussed in Section 6.8. Finally, Section 6.9 presents our conclusions.

6.2 The Literature on Poverty in Sweden

The literature on poverty in modern Sweden is not particularly extensive. For a long time, studies of those who received "poor relief", "social help" or "social assistance" dominated efforts to assess how many people of which type have experienced economic difficulties. Studies on social assistance recipients have continued to provide valuable knowledge. (See for example Bergmark (1991) and Salonen (1993)). However, in surveying the literature, we have chosen to exclude studies of welfare recipients. Instead we have tried to concentrate on attempts to identify those in financial difficulty which do not focus on households which receive a means-tested transfer.

Surveys on research often benefit from grouping contributions into categories, even though it is not always obvious in which category a particular contribution should be placed. We follow this approach, and summarise the contributions under three headings.

6.2.1 Contributions by sociologists

There is a long tradition of making level of living surveys in Sweden. Data is obtained by relatively long interviews of samples of the adult population. The results make it possible to see what resources people have and to see living conditions in the context of a large number of other dimensions. Most analyses have focused on one single dimension, but there are also attempts to consider several. An early attempt was by Erikson and Thålin (1984) studying "problematic states" according to seven dimensions (health, economic resources, housing conditions, social relations, leisure activities, political resources and work conditions) using data from 1968, 1974 and 1981. The proportion of those who had problems in at least three dimensions decreased from 22 to 12 and 8 per cent respectively. Tham (1994) shows that in 1991 the proportion had decreased to 5 per cent.

The approach of enumerating "problematic states" raises two questions. One concerns who should be given the task of defining those states and the other is how the definition should be applied. In the British sociological tradition of poverty research, there has been a shift from giving the task of defining states to a single researcher (for example, Townsend, 1979) to giving it to the public (Mack and Lansley, 1985). The latter approach parallels the tradition of "subjective poverty" originating from economists in the Netherlands as well as social scientists in Belgium. In this approach, survey questions are presented to a sample of the public. The answers to the questions, which can be differently phrased, result in answers which can be used to construct a poverty line.

In Sweden a group of researchers at the Department of Sociology at the University of Umeå was inspired by the work of Mac and Lansley to formulate questions, to a nation wide sample, concerning the respondents' opinion of necessary consumption at the beginning of the 1990s. The results have been used to provide one point of measurement of the poverty profile (Halleröd et al, 1993, Halleröd, 1994, Halleröd, 1995). The answers have also been used to make a comparison between Great Britain and Sweden (Halleröd, 1996) This study shows that deprivation is more prevalent and more unevenly distributed in Britain in comparison with Sweden. Other published work based on the same survey analyses questions based on the tradition of subjective poverty (Saunders et al,

1994).

To what extent do people with low incomes have problems in other dimensions? This is a very relevant question, and it has been the subject of empirical studies (Halleröd, 1991, Mayer, 1995, see also Statistics Sweden, 1997).

6.2.2 International comparisons of income poverty

The Luxembourg Income Study (LIS) makes international comparisons of income distributions by using the available harmonised data. Data for Sweden (the Household Income Survey, described in the next section) was included in the database at a very early stage. In studies based on LIS, poverty is most commonly defined based on the disposable equivalent income of a household and a poverty line. Most often persons living in a household with an income of less than 50 per cent of the median (or mean) equivalent disposable income for the country (and the year under investigation) are defined as poor. In this manner "poverty" is anchored to the contemporary general income level of the country being studied. One exception among users of LIS is Gustafsson and Lindblom (1993) who anchored their poverty line to the generosity of each country's welfare state.

In the first studies based on LIS, which referred to the beginning of the 1980s, Sweden appeared to be a country with low rates of poverty, and with a very low risk of the elderly falling below the poverty line (see, for example, Smeeding et al, (1990) for a study covering 7 countries and Smeeding (1991) where the comparison covers 10 countries). In comparison to the United States, few children in Sweden fall below the poverty line (see also Jäntti, 1993). From an international perspective poverty among single parents and their children in Sweden appears to be small (Wong et al, 1993). Another particular characteristic of poverty in Sweden is that females are not more poverty-prone than males (Sörensen, 1992, Wright, 1993).

As the observations from successive years were added to LIS it became evident that (relative) poverty in Sweden had been rising from 1981 to 1987 (Mc Fate, Rainwater and Smeeding, 1995). The increase in relative poverty over time, and the fact that datasets for more countries have been added to LIS has meant that in the most recent studies based on LIS Sweden no longer stands out as having a uniquely low relative poverty (Förster, 1993, Osberg and Xu, 1997, Smeeding, 1997). For example when Smeeding (1997) ranks 19 countries as they appear circa 1990 according to the extent of poverty, the United States takes the highest rank while

Sweden comes as number 11.

There are also international comparisons of income poverty based on sources other than LIS. A recent study based on the European Household Panel 1994 and Nordic Surveys of Living Conditions places Sweden together with Denmark, Norway and Finland among the EU countries having the lowest relative poverty in relation to the national average as well as to the EU average (Vogel, 1997). Gustafsson and Nivorozhkina (1996) compared poverty in urban Russia at the end of the 1980s with Sweden. In their study, Swedish poverty appears to be strongly concentrated amongst young adults.

All studies surveyed up to now in this section have classified people as poor or not poor based on their disposable income measured over a period of one year. How do the results change when the observation period is extended? In Duncan et al (1993, 1995) eight countries, including Sweden, are investigated. The study focuses on families with children and the results show that the proportion of the poor in any one year escaping poverty in the next is larger in Sweden than in most other countries investigated. The analysis also indicates that cross- country mobility in poverty status from one year to the next is affected by the extent of poverty. In countries with a high proportion, movement of the poor out of poverty is infrequent while the opposite is the case in countries with few poor.

6.2.3 A native tradition

In Gustafsson (1984) minimum levels in the Swedish transfer and tax system were investigated with the purpose of establishing a politically determined poverty line. The results showed a remarkably large agreement in levels for families without children. The levels coincided with recommendations which the National Board of Health and Welfare issued somewhat later. These recommendations were intended for local governments to use when adopting guidelines as a tool for processing applications for social assistance. Gustafsson (1984) also used alternative poverty lines to estimate the extent of poverty in 1979 - 1981 as well as to investigate the poverty profile. That study preceded those based on LIS.

Basically the same approach (but using the guidelines issued by the National Board of Health and Welfare) was used by Gustafsson (1987) to obtain a time series on poverty spanning 1975 to 1985 (8 measurement years). This time series was linked to an estimate for 1967 based on the Level of Living Survey in Gustafsson and Uusitalo (1990). That study compared the development of poverty in Finland and Sweden and found striking similarities. A later update brought the time series forward to 1991

(Gustafsson, 1994). This series attained a semi-official status when it was included in the first Social Report of the National Board of Health and Welfare (Socialstyrelsen, 1994) and had been updated in the second Social Report (Socialstyrelsen, 1997).

6.3 Data and Assumptions

This study uses two alternative poverty lines. The first is based on recommendations to local governments issued in the middle of the 1980s by the National Board of Health and Welfare for guidelines to be used when processing social assistance applications. The guidelines cover all expenditure necessary for maintenance, with the exception for housing costs. The latter are computed using a formula which uses information about the number of household members and current rents (There is a certain regional variation in these).

This poverty line is updated using the consumer price index (components excluding housing, for more details see footnote 1 in Gustafsson, 1996). In this aspect it resembles the poverty line used in the United States for producing the official estimate of the extent of poverty. This poverty line thus represents a more or less constant purchasing power, and later we refer to the time series obtained by using it as "absolute".

The "relative" series of poverty starts from 50 per cent of the median for equivalent disposable income in each year of measurement. The actual amounts are listed in an appendix to this chapter. An often applied equivalence scale is used. According to this, a single adult assumes a value of 1.0, for each additional adult the value 0.7 is added, while for each additional child a value of 0.5 is added. The main difference between the absolute and the relative series is that the former implies a constant purchasing power while the second includes a variable one, which in most cases increases from one year to the next.

The estimates are based on the household income survey (HINK) made by Statistics Sweden which contains about 10,000 households each year. Information is obtained by telephone interviews (previously this was done by mail questionnaires), from tax returns and from registers on public transfers received. The target population is people who have resided in Sweden during at least six months. People living in institutions are excluded. The adult with the highest personal income is the reference person for the household.

HINK started during the first half of the 1970s, and subsequently the survey has been carried out every year. The first surveys are difficult to compare, and data for the years with a low comparability are very difficult to access. Consequently, we have only worked with the surveys of 1975 and 1978 from the 1970s. Starting in 1980 and until 1995 (the latest year available) we have derived results for each year. Our period of analysis thus covers two decades. There are few examples of time series on poverty for such a long period, the one for United States is an exception.

One problem in analysis for users of HINK can be traced back to the large tax reform which took place towards the end of the period under observation. This meant that from 1991 some incomes which were not previously recorded became visible. To bridge the gap between the new and old definitions, Statistics Sweden imputed values based on incomplete information and produced synthetic surveys for 1989 and 1990. This is the reason why we report two estimates for those two years.

Even if HINK has many advantages it also has some less attractive features. A well known issue is the definition of a household or family. In HINK a household or family contains one or two adult persons of opposite sexes and there can be one or more children. A person changes from being considered a child to being classified as an adult at the age of 18 years. As in reality a household can have more than two adults, and adults of the same sex can live in the same household, this definition of a household is very narrow. When assessing poverty from HINK it is mainly the situation of young adults living with their parents which is problematic, as they are considered to be separate households. The possibility that many young adults living with their parents have access to housing and maintenance at a low cost or for no cost at all is not considered in HINK. Thus there is an obvious risk that our estimates of poverty among the 18 - 29 year olds are too high at every point of measurement. As HINK does not record transfers from parents to adult children there is also a risk that poverty among the middle-aged is underestimated at each point. However, it is less clear whether, and in what way the time series presents a misleading picture of the development over time due to the definition of a household or family.

Another questionable issue is the definition of the population under study. From the start HINK includes people who have been living in Sweden for most of the measurement year, thus including those who have resided in the country for a period of less than a year. Examples of the latter are recent immigrants and emigrants. Further examples are the newly born and the deceased. As the shorter period of residence is not considered when assessing poverty there is a risk that misleading results are produced. However, for a single year in the latter parts of the measurement period it is possible to investigate how important the definition of the population is. Nevertheless, it is not likely that changes over time would appear fundamentally different when applying the most appropriate definition of the population under study.

The poverty estimates reported here are all based upon the disposable income of a household. This means that the wealth of a household does not affect who is classified as poor, which can be perceived as less than satisfactory. Below we give an example showing that such considerations affect the appearance of the profile of poverty at any one point in time. However, results from an earlier study (Gustafsson, 1994) indicate that the picture of the change in poverty is not seriously affected if one considers personal wealth in the definition of poverty.

We represent the extent of poverty by showing estimates of the proportion of families and individuals below the poverty line. In addition we apply two indices, members of a family suggested by Foster, Greer and Thorbecke (1984). These indices also consider how poor the poor are, by taking into account the difference between the disposable income of a family and its poverty line ("the poverty gap" or the "income deficit"). By normalising the deficit with the poverty line, one obtains (in case of income not being negative) a value which is bounded by 1 and 0. When computing one of the indices (FGT (I)) the proportion of the poor is multiplied by the average (normalised) poverty gap. The second index (FGT (II)) also starts from each family's (normalised) poverty gap, but it is raised to the power of 2 before the average is taken. The second index thus places more emphasis on larger than smaller poverty gaps. It is thereby sensitive to how the poverty gaps are distributed among the poor. Using three indexes gives a more complete picture of poverty than applying only one. An attractive feature of the FGT indices is that they are additively decomposable. Poverty in the entire population is a weighted sum of poverty within each category and the population shares are the weightings.

6.4 The Development of Poverty

Figure 6.1 shows the results when using the poverty line which is based on guidelines issued by the National Board of Health and Welfare as it was formulated in the middle of the 1980s for all the years of observation. This figure also shows how large are the proportions that can be considered as "very poor" because they fall under 75 per cent of the poverty line. In the figure there is also a curve indicating the proportion of people living in households with an income below 125 per cent of the poverty line. The difference between this curve and the curve derived from the poverty line shows the proportion of the "nearly poor".

An interesting conclusion from Figure 6.1 is that at a given point in time the estimate is very sensitive to the level of the criterion. There is a lack of symmetry when the level is changed. An increase in the poverty line of 25 per cent results in a larger increase in the rate than does a decrease by 25 per cent. Figures for 1995 show this. When the poverty line is increased by 25 per cent the proportion of the population more than doubles from 9.4 per cent by 11.4 per cent to 20.8 per cent. When the poverty line is decreased by 25 per cent the proportion of the population decreases by slightly less than half to 5.2 per cent.

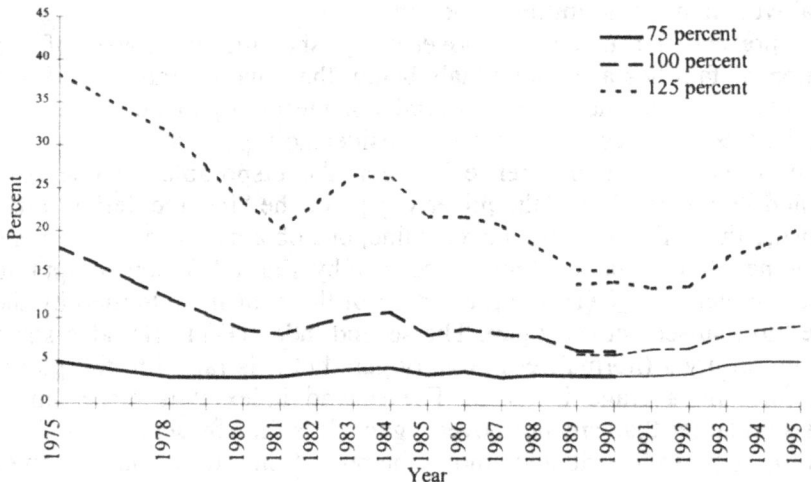

Figure 6.1 Proportion individuals below 75 per cent, 100 per cent och 125 per cent of the poverty line (absolute serie) 1975-1995

The long term development differs between the three alternatives. This can be illustrated by estimates from running regression models using time as the right hand variable. The estimates reported in Table 6.1a clearly show a negative trend for that proportion which falls under the higher alternative.[2] This is also the case for the negative trend for the main alternative ("the absolute series") where the t-statistics are larger than 2.0. The figure shows that the decrease in the "absolute series" took place at the beginning of the period under observation. However the proportion falling below 75 per cent of the poverty line has not decreased from the beginning of the period to its end, as the estimates for 1975 and 1995 are very close.

---

[2] The estimates are based on 20 observations, and among the right hand side variables there is also a variable indicating whether the observation belongs to the new or old series.

All curves in Figure 6.1 point upwards at the end of the observation period. During the first half of the 1990s an ever larger proportion of the Swedish population fell under a poverty line which represents a constant real income. Taking the very rapidly deteriorating situation of the labour market into consideration, this is not surprising. Perhaps more surprising is that the increase has not been larger. However, attention should be paid to the fact that while the unemployment rate peaked in 1993, the curves in Figure 6.1 do not subsequently turn downwards.[3]

Table 6.1 Estimations of the time effect on the extent of poverty defined in different ways and expressed as a proportion of households and FGT (II)

a.

Poverty series	Absolut serie			Relativ serie	FGT(II)
	75 per cent	100 per cent	125 per cent		
Proportion poor	0.15 (2.44)	-0.25 (1.61)	-0.62 (2.34)	0.23 (6.37)	0.06 (2.44)

t-value in parenthesis, n=21

b.

Poverty series	Absolut serie			Relativ serie	FGT(II)
	75 per cent	100 per cent	125 per cent		
Unemployment	0.24 (3.59)	0.40 (2.44)	0.82 (2.68)	0.11 (1.83)	0.13 (4.04)
Serie (t-1)	0.50 (4.16)	0.67 (6.04)	0.73 (5.24)	0.32 (1.99)	0.26 (1.71)

t-value in parenthesis, n=21

---

[3] While the fraction below the poverty line increased from 9.0 per cent in 1993 to 9.4 per cent in 1995 the proportion below 125 per cent of the poverty line increased from 18.7 per cent to 20.8 per cent.

The implication of the results is that the Swedish distribution of income (at its lower tail) has become more unequal. While during the two decades under observation the average living standard of the Swedish population has increased, there have not been fewer poor. A further observation from Figure 6.1 is that the effects of the business cycle during the 1980s are visible as the two upper curves peaked in 1983 and 1984 respectively. Table 6.1b is based on regression analyses, which indicate that the unemployment rate has a positive effect on the extent of poverty. In the estimated model the right hand side includes a variable which is also the dependent variable with a time lag of one year.[4] In every case the coefficients for this variable are positive and have a value lower than 1.0. A possible interpretation of this is that a considerable proportion of one year's poor continue to be poor the next year. We will investigate this phenomenon below using panel data on households.

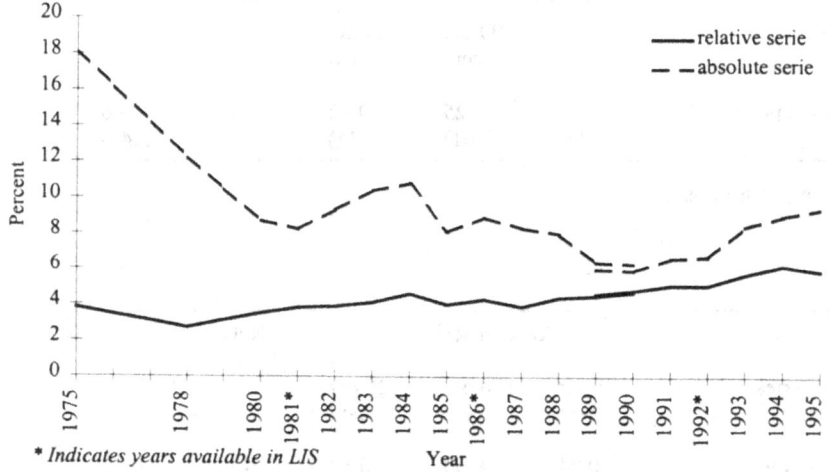

Figure 6.2 Proportion of individuals below the poverty line, "relative serie" and "absolute serie" 1975-1995

The ever more unequal distribution of income at the end of the period under study (see Gustafsson and Palmer, 1997) means that a poverty line which only considers the distribution of income and not the general level

---

[4] We estimate the model for a time series, which has one value for each year 1975 to 1995. This time series is obtained by linking the new series to the one using the two values observed during two years. In addition values for 1976, 1977 and 1979 have been added by interpolation.

shows a different development to that we have seen. Figure 6.2 illustrates how large proportions of the population that fall below 50 per cent of the median equivalent income for the year under observation. Figure 6.2 shows an increase since the end of the 1970s, and there is also a positive trend for the entire period of observation (see Table 6.1a).[5]

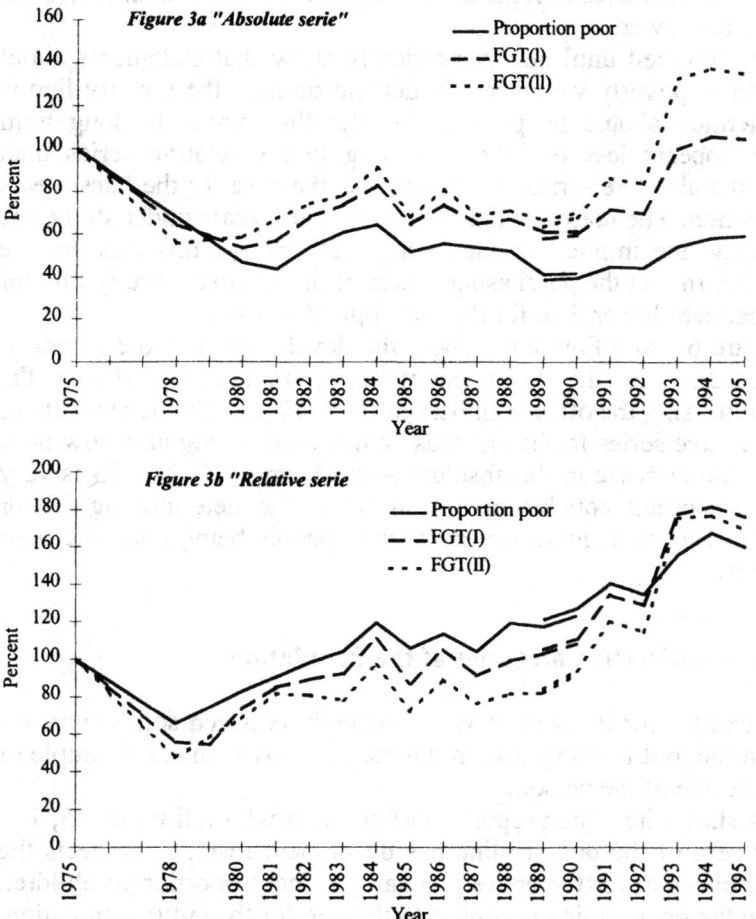

Figure 6.3a and 6.3b. Poverty trends 1975-1995 according to different poverty index. 1975=100

---

[5] The coefficient for the trend variable is positive and the t-statistics are higher than 2.0.

From a low of 2.7 per cent of all persons falling below the relative poverty line in 1978 the proportion increased up to 5.9 per cent at the end of the period under study. Also for this alternative we have investigated whether unemployment and the poverty rate during the preceding year affects the poverty rate. The results reported in Table 6.1b are similar to the ones for the absolute series as regards the sign of the coefficients. However, the t-statistics are lower.

The results reported until now very clearly show that statements about the proportion in poverty very strongly depend on how the poverty line is updated. Attention should be paid to the fact that while the long term development appears less positive according to the relative series than according to the absolute series, the opposite is the case for the latest years under observation. The reason is that, while for most years under study, the relative poverty line implied an increasing real income, this was not the case after 1992. In fact the purchasing power of the relative poverty line for 1995 is 8.6 per cent lower than for the one applied in 1992.

While Figure 6.1 and Figure 6.2 show the development of the extent of poverty according to the head count ratio, Figure 6.3 shows the development utilising the other members of the FGT-family, the absolute as well as the relative series for households. When considering also how poor the poor are, the increase in the absolute series from 1992 to 1993 is very abrupt. The important conclusion is that while the deteriorating labour market did not lead to a significant number of people being poor, the poor became poorer.

6.5 Poverty in Different Categories of the Population

The risk of being poor in Sweden varies strongly between some divisions of the population, but less so between others. We start with one example of the former, the age of the person.

Figure 6.4 shows how the proportion of children who fall under 75, 100 and 125 per cent of the poverty line has developed. In many respects the picture resembles that for the entire population. The proportion of children falling below the poverty line is similar to the one for the entire population. Childhood in modern Sweden does not imply a particularly high or low risk of being poor. The figure also shows that the risk of being poor has increased from 4.8 per cent in 1990 to 8.3 per cent in 1995. The deteriorating situation for families with children in Sweden during the 1990s is shown through rapid increases in the proportion of children that are under 125 per cent of the poverty line. While in 1992 the proportion was 13.4 per cent it had increased to 24.5 per cent in 1995.

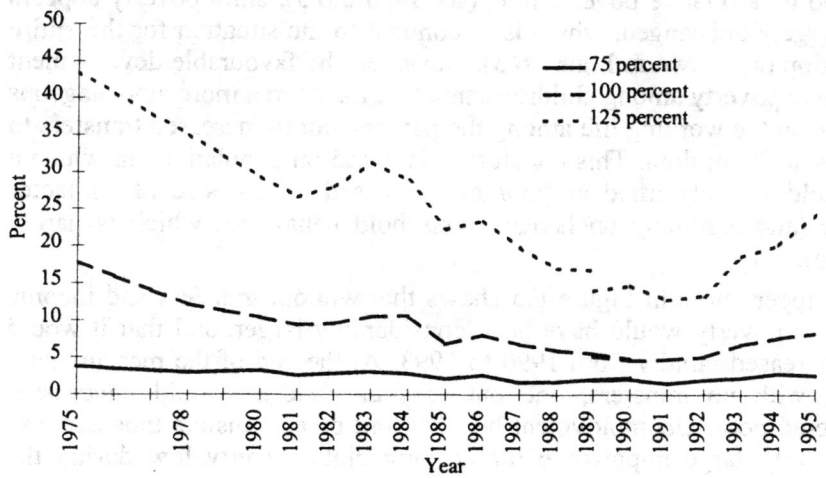

Figure 6.4 Proportion of children below 75 per cent, 100 per cent and 125 per cent of the poverty line (absolutet serie) 1975-1995

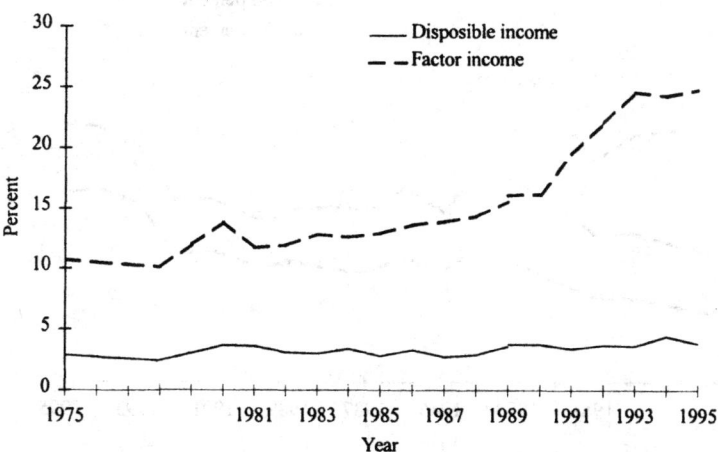

Figure 6.5 Proportion of children below 50 per cent of the median (relative serie) when estimates are made on the disposible income and factor income respectively 1975-1995

Based on a relative poverty line, (see Figure 6.5), child poverty appears to be largely unchanged, which is in contrast to the situation for the entire population (as shown in Figure 6.3). However, the favourable development of relative poverty among children cannot be traced to a more advantageous situation in the working life among the parents, but to increased transfers to families with children. This conclusion is based on simulations in which a household was classified as poor or not based on the size of its factor income (and assuming unchanged household behaviour, which is hardly realistic).

The upper curve in Figure 6.5 shows that without transfers and income tax, child poverty would have been considerably larger, and that it would have increased rapidly from 1990 to 1993. At the end of the measurement period, with no transfers, one out of four children would have been considered poor. Unemployment benefits and other transfers thus came to have a very large importance for keeping child poverty low during the 1990s.

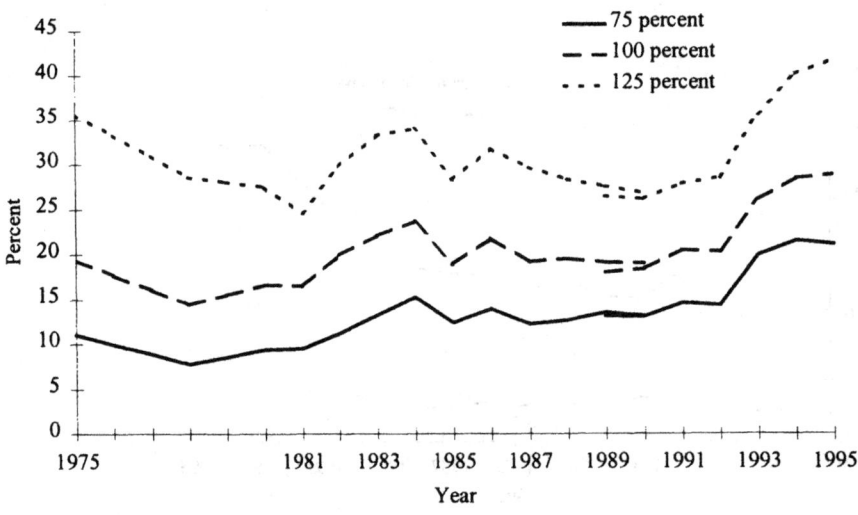

Figure 6.6 Proportion young individuals (18-29 years) below 75 per cent, 100 per cent and 125 per cent of the poverty line (absolute serie) 1975-1995

One part of the development in child poverty is that single parent families have become more common, and transfers are particularly important to reduce poverty for them. From the first year of observation to the last the number of single parent families increased from 159,000 to 252,000, or by 58 per cent. Roughly one out of two single parent families have a factor income lower than the poverty line. However, transfers reduce the proportion of single parent families below the poverty line dramatically (See also Gustafsson, Tasiran and Nyman, 1997).

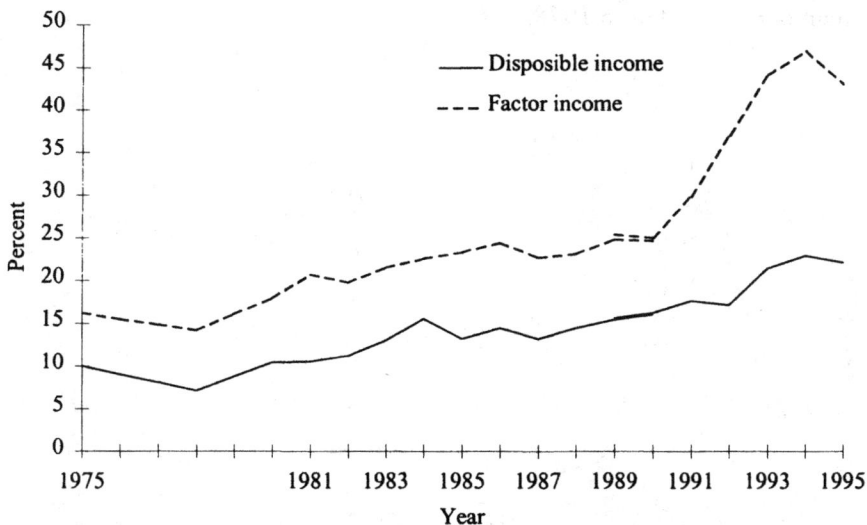

Figure 6.7 Proportion young individuals (18-29 years) below 50 per cent of the median (relative serie) when estimates are made on the disposible income factor income respectively 1975-1995

Poverty in present day Sweden is to a very large extent concentrated amongst young adults. Figure 6.6 shows high poverty rates among people aged 18 - 29 and also a large proportion which is very poor. While seen over the entire period under observation the proportion of people who fall below the poverty line has decreased in the entire population, the opposite is the case among young adults. In 1995 the poverty rate among young adults was 28.8 per cent. We have estimated regression models with specifications as shown in Table 6.1 but with the proportion of poor young adults as a left hand variable. The results show that the poverty rate among young adults is strongly affected by the condition of the labour market. The higher the unemployment rate, the higher the poverty rate among young adults.

When applying a relative poverty line, the increase in poverty among young adults since the beginning of the 80s appears to be dramatic, (Figure 6.7).[6] The same figure also shows how many would have been regarded as poor if only factor incomes were observed. Also this proportion has increased, and at an extremely rapid pace from 1990 to 1993. During these years employment among young adults decreased rapidly. Based on factor income only almost one out of two young adults would fall below the contemporary relative poverty line at the end of the period, compared to less than one out of ten in 1978.

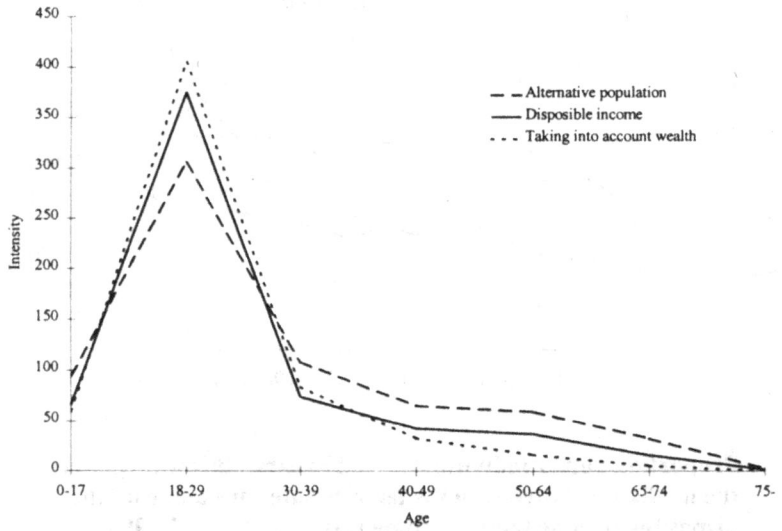

Figure 6.8   Poverty intensity according to age and when different assumptions are made year 1993

In work active ages the risk of being poor diminishes with age, as shown in Figure 6.8. This figure illustrates results based on various assumptions for the year 1993. The figure shows the proportion of people in an age

---

[6]   The rate increased from 7.1 per cent in 1978 to 22.9 per cent in 1994.

category who fall below the poverty line as a percentage of the entire population ("intensities").

If one excludes young adults living with their parents, people who have not lived in Sweden for the entire year of measurement and people drafted into military service from the population investigated – i.e. if one looks at the socalled alternative population in Figure 6.8 - poverty among young adults does not stand out as highly, and the poverty intensity among other adults is higher. Nevertheless the proportion of those considered poor among young adults is three times as high as for the entire population.

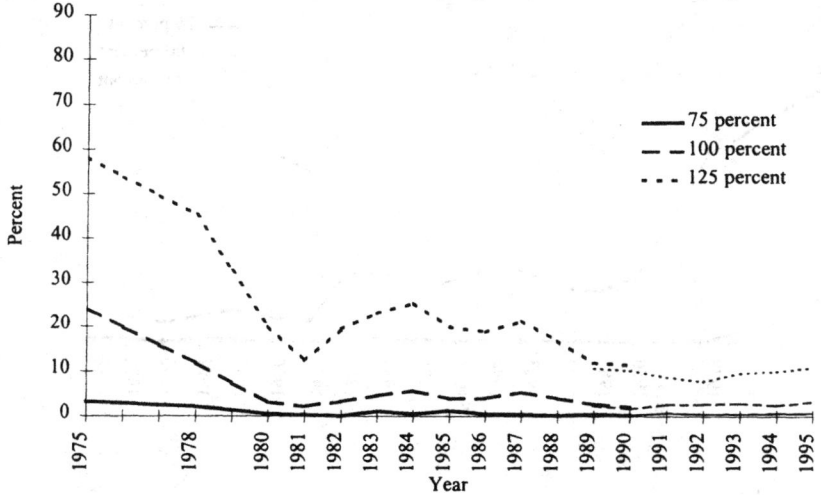

Figure 6.9a Proportion individuals aged 65-74 below 75 per cent, 100 per cent and 125 per cent of the poverty line (absolute serie) 1975-1995

However, if we base poverty assessments on the household's ability to spend, defined as the sum of income and net worth (valued at market prices) the age profile is even more marked. Then young adults have an intensity to be considered poor which is four times as large as for the entire population, while the intensity for the middle-aged falls considerably. Because almost all elderly people receive the basic pension, very few elderly are very poor. Measured by a poverty index which incorporates the poverty gap for each household, poverty among the elderly in Sweden is currently insignificant. Very few elderly people have an income which places them under a relative poverty line.[7]

---

[7] In 1995 it was 0.8 per cent of those 65 - 74 and 1.1 per cent of those 75 and older.

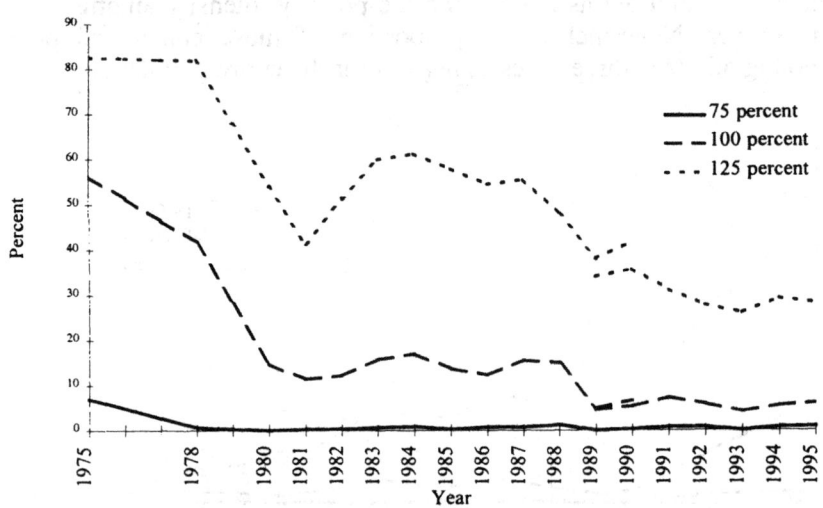

Figure 6.9b Proportion individuals age 75- below 75 per cent, 100 per cent and 125 per cent of the poverty line (absolute serie) 1975-1995

However, many aged have an income which is just over the poverty line. Figure 6.9 for people aged 65 to 74 and Figure 6.10 for those 75 and older show that in the beginning of the observation period most of the elderly were actually considered as poor or almost poor. Those proportions decreased rapidly until 1981, then increased somewhat and continued to decrease at a slower pace from 1984 over the rest of the 1980s. As very few people over 65 have earnings this development was driven by increased pension payments. Compared to the rapid changes during the 1970s and 1980s, changes in rates among the elderly during the 1990s were small.

Table 6.2 The composition of poverty after age in 1975, 1985 and 1995

Age	Composition of the population below 50 per cent of the median		
	1975	1985	1995
0-17	11.8	11.0	10.2
18-29	40.8	52.0	59.6
30-39	9.0	11.4	10.8
40-49	7.3	9.4	8.6
50-64	12.2	8.7	5.7
65-74	10.2	5.9	2.2
74-	8.6	1.6	3.0
Total population	100	100	100

We summarise the findings on the relation between age and poverty by inspecting the age composition of those who fall below a relative poverty line. Table 6.2 shows the situation in 1975, 1985 and 1995. The general pattern is the same for all years. However, it is also clear that the poor population has become younger. While two out of five poor were young adults (18 to 29 years of age) in 1975, the proportion had increased to three out of five in 1995. On the other hand, the proportion of people aged 50 and more among the poor had decreased from almost one third in 1975 to one tenth in 1995.

Table 6.3 Relative poverty among households in different H-regions during the periods 1980-87 and 1988-95

	1980-87	1988-95
Stockholm	5.0	7.6
Göteborg/Malmö	5.4	7.2
Larger cities	5.7	7.3
South, cities	5.2	7.0
North, cities	4.9	7.1
North, sparcely populated	5.2	7.4
Total population	5.3	7.3

While in some European countries such as Italy and Germany (after unification) contemporary poverty varies considerably by region, this is not the case in Sweden. Table 6.3 shows results obtained when applying relative poverty lines and dividing the country into six regions and pooling estimates for several years. There is virtually no variation worthy of comment across the regions.

Table 6.4 Relative poverty during the period 1980-87 and 1988-95 according to the citizenship of the reference person, and the proportion below the poverty line taking into account the factor income of the household

Citizenship	Disposible income		Factor income	
	1980-87	1988-95	1980-87	1988-95
Swedish	5.2	7.0	36.0	39.9
Nordic	6.6	8.8	26.0	34.3
European, not Nordic	12.2	16.4	35.0	47.4
Other	13.6	19.2	49.2	69.6
Total population	5.3	7.3	35.8	40.4

The situation of immigrants in the Swedish labour market has deteriorated during later decades. (See for example Aguilar and Gustafsson, 1994) In Table 6.4 we report relative poverty rates according to the citizenship of the household head and pooling surveys for various years. The poverty rates for people living in households headed by someone having a Nordic (but not Swedish) citizenship are only marginally higher than for natives. However, the situation is rather different among other foreign households where the poverty rates are considerably higher.

While very few immigrants to Sweden before 1980 originated from countries outside Europe and North America the immigration flows to Sweden during the 1980s and 1990s led to a rapid increase of the category. At the end of the period households with a foreign non-European head numbered 89,000, which is equal to 1.9 per cent of all households in the population. The factor income of a remarkably large proportion of such households was not sufficient to place its members over the poverty line. Actually this was the case for every second household in the first period of the 1980s and almost 70 per cent during the most recent period, (see Table 6.4). This proportion is remarkably large because, as opposed to the native population, almost all non-European household heads are of work active ages.

In HINK it is also possible, for the later survey years, to study how poverty rates vary by country of birth. In many respects country of birth is a better indicator of immigrant status since many foreign-born inhabitants naturalise and the rate of naturalisation varies across origins. Pooling data for 1993 and 1994 Gustafsson (1997) reports poverty rates (the "absolute series") for the category of households with all adults foreign-born and the category of households with one adult foreign-born and the other native. The poverty rate was much higher in the former category (19.8 per cent) than in the latter (6.0 per cent) which actually was slightly lower than for the third category of all adults in the household native born (7.7 per cent). This study also showed poverty rates to be highest among recently arrived immigrants and to decrease, with few exceptions, with the number of years since immigration.

We now turn to a breakdown which considers how much market work adult household members perform or alternatively if the household has pensions as the main source of income. Table 6.5 indicates that being a pensioner or performing a lot of market work leads to a very low risk of being poor. Here, all estimates of the poverty rate are below 2 per cent. The other extreme with a very high poverty rate is when a household lacks pension incomes and also performs little or no market work. One in two people living in such households are classified as poor.

Table 6.5 **Proportion of households below 50 per cent of the median according to retirement status of household head and working hours of adult household members**

	Disposable income	
	1980-1987	1988-1995
Retired	1.1	1.9
Working hours (per cent of full time)		
0 - 24	49.5	49.6
25 - 74	6.2	7.5
75 -	1.3	1.3

There have been considerable changes in the size of the four categories which are reported in Table 6.5. Households with pensions as the main source of income increased during the first part of the period, which pushed the poverty rate in the entire population down. From 1990 to 1993 the number of people living in households with no or only a low working time and without pensions doubled. Here we see a very clear illustration of the fact that the abrupt fall in employment at the beginning of the 1990s led to increased poverty.

6.6 Gender and Poverty

It is well known that females in the United States are more poverty prone than males. For example, the official estimates for 1995 shows that while 12.2 per cent of males were poor, this was the case for 15.4 per cent of females. Thus females run a risk 26 per cent higher than males of being poor. This gender gap in poverty risk has not changed much since the series started at the beginning of the 1960s. However, a larger and larger proportion of the poor households are "families with a female householder, no spouse present" (mainly single mothers). While in 1960 there was no adult male in somewhat less than one out of five poor families, this was the case in two out of five families in the middle of the 1990s. This development is driven by the increased frequency of female headed households. Many black Americans (two out of five) now live in single mother families with high poverty rates. The social policy discussions in the US are also very much focused on single mothers. Looking back in history, one sees that females, most often elderly, were predominant amongst those receiving poor relief in Sweden. Thus, when referring to earlier periods, it is not inappropriate to talk of poverty as feminised in Sweden. However, as we have seen above, poverty rates among the elderly have fallen drastically. The fact that women live longer than men and often have lower pensions no longer means that poverty is feminised in Sweden. Many single mothers in Sweden earn enough to make them non-poor and others are lifted out of poverty by receiving transfers. Thus there are no strong reasons to expect poverty in present day Sweden to be feminised.

Table 6.6 **Proportion of men and women below 75 per cent, 100 per cent and 125 per cent of the poverty line and below the relative poverty line, 1980-87 and 1988-1995**

		1980-1987			1988-1995		
		Men	Women	Total	Men	Women	Total
"Absolute serie"	75	4.1	3.2	3.6	4.6	3.6	4.1
"Absolute serie"	100	9.3	8.9	9.1	7.3	7.3	7.6
"Absolute serie"	125	21.9	24.2	23.1	15.9	17.6	16.8
"Relative serie"		4.4	3.6	4.0	5.7	4.7	5.2

In Table 6.6 we report estimates of how many males and females fall below 75 per cent, 100 per cent and 125 per cent of the poverty line, pooling surveys over two periods. There is very little difference between males and females in the proportion falling below 100 per cent of the poverty line. However, the fraction of males considered very poor is somewhat higher than the corresponding fraction of females. On the other hand, the figures indicate that there are somewhat more nearly poor females than nearly poor males. For example, the numbers in Table 6.6 mean that while during the later period 8.6 per cent of males were nearly poor, the corresponding proportion among females was 10.3 per cent.

However, there is one problem with the estimates presented in Table 6.6 which is shared with almost all other estimates of poverty by gender. They all start from the assumption that spouses pool their income equally and thus share the same income situation. This assumption is not necessarily correct. Simulation studies (Borooah and Kee,1994, Findlay and Wright, 1996) have shown that as soon as one abandons this assumption and assumes that poverty status is influenced also by how much each spouse earns on the market, the results change dramatically and females appear to be more poverty prone.

But what evidence do we really have about the pooling of resources between spouses in industrialised countries? In fact, very little. One exception is Lundberg et al (1996) who present a "natural experiment" of a policy change in the United Kingdom that transferred a substantial child allowance to wives in the late 1970s. The results indicate that some expenditures were affected when the income share of wives increased.

An alternative to investigating whether spouses pool resources is to ask them, keeping in mind that the answers may not always reflect reality. This strategy can be used for Sweden by using the Family Survey conducted by Statistics Sweden in 1992. It is based on interviews of more than 3,000 women born in 1949, 1954, 1959, 1964 and 1966 and more than 1,500 men. The samples of men and women are independent. Married and cohabiting respondents were asked if they had a shared economy, alternatively, partly shared the economy or had completely separate economies. As many as 78 per cent (among 2,441 females as well as among 1,195 males) responded that they had a shared economy. Thus pooling is a good first approximation. Slightly less than one out of five responded that they partly shared income with their spouses. Only 4 per cent of females (3 per cent of males) responded that the incomes of spouses were totally separate.

What does this mean for estimates of poverty by gender? Assuming no sharing among respondents who did not indicate full sharing, we arrived at estimates of those falling below a poverty line set at 50 per cent of median equivalent income. This showed that in this category female poverty rates were twice as high as male poverty rates (10.4 per cent in comparison to 5.1 per cent). However, as this applies to less than every fourth couple, differences in total poverty rates by gender are small (5.4 per cent for males compared to 5.7 per cent for females).

From this exercise we can conclude that if one believes what the respondents say, a group of poverty prone women has been identified, which probably has not been identified as poor in earlier research in any industrialised country. This category consists is of married or cohabiting women who do not share incomes with their spouse. However, the result of the exercise also shows that this does not lead us to think of women in Sweden as generally more poverty prone than men.

6.7 Designing a Study of Swedish Poverty Dynamics

How long-lasting is the state "poverty"? Is a family poor one year after another? Or is poverty a short event meaning that the poor during one period are not poor in the next? Among which categories is poverty more long-lasting and among which is poverty more transitional? Which events makes a household fall into poverty and which allow a poor household to escape poverty? The answers to these questions are central for the understanding of poverty. However, answering the questions put high requirement on data.

The Household Income Survey (HINK) makes it possible to shed light on the dynamics of poverty. This is the case because the survey was made as a rotating panel. Each year half of all respondents were rotated out, which means that it is possible to follow a respondent and the family he or she lives in for two years (year t and year t + 1). In total there are 11 pairs of years (1980/81 to 1990/91) available for analysis. Because of a limited sample size we have chosen to pool data from several panels in order to raise the level of precision of the estimates. The disadvantage with this approach is that in doing so we have limited the possibilities to say something about the changes in mobility during the period under observation.

Our study makes it possible to investigate short-term mobility in poverty-status. Its design draws on Duncan et al (1993, 1995) but is more general, as it is not restricted to families with children and in addition it uses data from three more pairs of years. There are nevertheless limitations, for example, patterns of poverty-mobility might be rather complicated. For example, people who are poor one year and non-poor the next might run a higher risk than other non-poor to fall back into poverty. It is not possible to study this pattern of behaviour directly from our data. However, there is an additional possibility of analysis which we have exploited. With the purpose of evaluating the large tax reform, about 10,000 households which were surveyed in HINK in 1989 were also surveyed in 1992. Therefore the data make it possible to analyse the relationship in poverty status between year t and year t + 3.

In the mobility analyses we use households as the unit of analysis, and we base poverty assessments on a relative poverty line set to 50 per cent of contemporary median equivalent disposable income (applying the same equivalence scale as above). This makes it possible to study how large a fraction of people poor in year t became non-poor in the next year under study ("exits") as well as the proportion of non-poor in year t who became poor in the next year ("entries").

One possible objection to this approach is that very small observed income changes from one year to the next (which might be caused by measurement errors) can define mobility in poverty status. To avoid this, we imposed a restriction: mobility out of poverty requires that disposable equivalent income in the later year is at least 60 per cent of the median. In the same manner mobility into poverty requires that equivalent disposable income during the first year is at least 60 per cent of the median, and has to be less than 50 per cent of the median the second year.

Behind mobility in poverty status there can be demographic changes as well as changes in how much market work the adult household members perform. We measure such changes by comparing the status of the household in the two years under observation. The demographic changes are that the number of adults increases (from one to two) or decreases (from two to one) and that the number of children increases or decreases.

A household is classified to have had experienced "job gain" if the total hours of work increased from being less than 500 in the first year to being more than 750 in the latter year. Conversely "work loss" is defined as being that the household has changed from over 750 hours of work during the first year to less than 500 hours of work in the latter year. The event of "more work" means that the number of hours of work for the family increases from a higher level of at least 500 in the first year by at least 250 hours. In the same manner "less work" means that the number of working hours have reduced by at least 250 hours while still being at a level of at least 500 hours in the second year. The events "job gain" and "more work" are mutually exclusive and this is also the case for "job loss" and "less work".

We assume that the poverty effects of changes in work vary by age of the reference person. By time, and thus by age, people qualify for social security benefits such as unemployment benefit and pension payments. Therefore we expect that the poverty consequences of a job loss and of less work can be expected to decrease with age.

6.8 Results on Poverty Dynamics

We start the description of results by looking at exit rates and entry rates for the entire population. The estimates of the exit rate between year t and year t + 1 based on 3,871 observations obtained by pooling the 11 pairs of panels is 38.8 per cent. There is thus considerable mobility out of poverty.[8] However, the estimate also means that three out of five households that were poor in year t remained poor during the following year. Whether this is a low or high proportion depends very much on expectations.

Basing the estimates of exit-rates on the first six pairs, or alternatively the last five pairs, gives almost identical results. Thus it does not seem as if exit-rates changed during the period studied, which is also the impression obtained when studying estimates based on each single panel. Our results also show that out of 606 poor households observed in 1989, four years later 65.7 per cent were non-poor. Thus, only one out of three initially poor were also in poverty four years later.

Turning to entry-rates, they are, of course, much lower. The estimate based on the 47,336 non-poor observations obtained by pooling 11 pairs of

---

[8] This would have been still larger if we also included those poor who had an equivalent income between 50 and 60 per cent of the median in year t + 1. This would give a proportion of 52.4 per cent.

panels is 1.06 per cent. Thus among one hundred non-poor observed during one year, 99 continue to be non-poor during the next year. However, we find evidence that the entry-rates have increased over time although the increase is far from dramatic. Basing estimates on the first six panels results in an entry-rate of 0.98 per cent, while the one made on the last five panels is 1.17 per cent. Thus it seems that the increase in the relative poverty series reported above has been generated by increased inflow into poverty, not by decreased outflow. Results from analysing the 9,445 households that were not poor in 1989 shows that only 1.5 per cent were poor four years later.

On the one hand our results indicate that there is considerable mobility out of poverty, and that periods of poverty are often short. On the other hand they also show a very strong correlation in poverty status between the years of observation. To take one example: the risk of being poor in year t+1 is 58 times as large for those who were poor in year t compared to those non-poor the same year.[9]

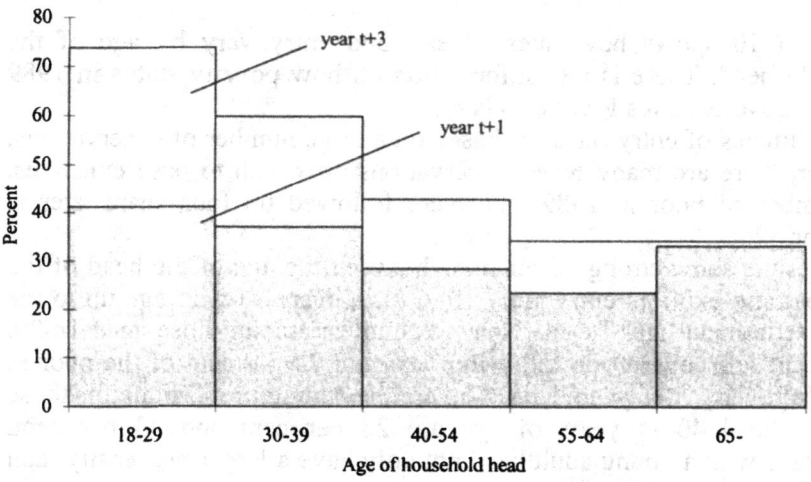

Figure 6.10a Exit rates according to age of household head

---

[9] Estimates are based on 11 pairs of observation. The relative risk is calculated as (100 - 38.8) / 1.06. The risk of being poor in year t+3 among those poor in year t is 23 times as large as for those non-poor the same year.

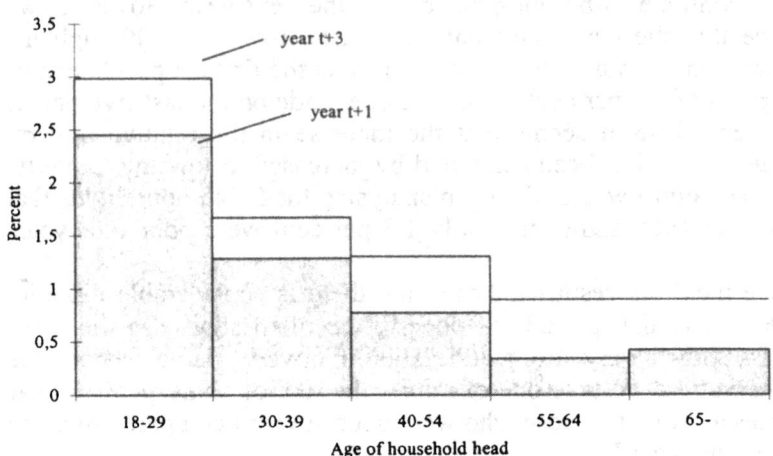

Figure 6.10b Entry rates according to age of household head

Figure 6.10 shows how rates of exit and entry vary by age of the household head. There is also information on how poverty status in 1989 relates to poverty status four years later.

All estimates of entry rates are based on a large number of observations. However, there are many fewer observations on which to base exit rates. The number of poor in 1989 who were followed up four years later is particularly low.[10]

The results show strong correlations between the age of the head of the household and exit and entry rates. Both rates decrease with age up to the general retirement age. To take some examples: among those aged 18-29, 41 per cent left poverty the following year and 74 per cent of the poor in 1989 left poverty four years later. The corresponding proportions for those having a head 40-54 years of age are 28 per cent and 43 per cent. Households with a young adult head not only have a larger propensity than the middle-aged to leave poverty, they also have a higher propensity to enter poverty. While the entry rate among those 18-29 is 2.5 per cent, that for those 40-54 is only 0.8 per cent.

---

[10] The smallest number of observations is 84 among those poor in 1992 aged at least 55. In the panel data there are 151 poor aged at least 65 who are followed up the next year.

We now turn to the relation between events and rates of entry into poverty, as reported in Table 6.7. Starting with demographic events we notice an entry rate among those experiencing childbirth or an increase in the number of children in other ways which is relatively similar to all non-poor households. This is consistent with findings from the cross-sectional analysis, namely that the risk of being poor among children is rather similar to the population as a whole. On the other hand, among spouses who have separated, the risk of entering poverty is three times as high as average.

Table 6.7 Changed household composition and working hours and the mobility into poverty among those who experienced changes

	Proportion not poor households that experienced the event (percentage)	Proportion not poor that became poor year t+1 (percentage)
Total		1.02
Number of adults decreased from two to one	1.86	3.07
Number of children in the household increased	3.31	1.29
The household lost a job; Total	3.24	11.23
According to age of reference person (years)		
-35	1.37	20.57
36-45	0.31	19.96
50-64	0.82	1.68
65-	0.74	1.46

As many as 11 per cent of those non-poor who had experienced job loss entered poverty. This is a rate much higher than for the much larger category who worked less in year t + 1. Nevertheless, this category has an above average risk of entering poverty. The poverty consequences of the events of job loss vary very much by age of head of household and according to the expected pattern. The entry rates are highest among the youngest, lowest among the oldest. For example: as many as one in five non-poor aged 18 - 35 who experienced a job loss entered into poverty. But among those non-poor aged 50 and 64 who experienced the same event only one out of 60 entered poverty.

Attention should also be paid to the fact that the events of job loss and less work are much more frequent among households with a young head than among others. The high entry rate among young adults shown in Figure 6.10 can therefore be explained both by such people experiencing a reduction in paid work more often and to the larger poverty consequences of such an event.

Finally, we turn to the relation between the event of an exit from poverty. The estimates reported in Table 6.8 show the following: among those who have experienced a decrease in the number of children, the exit-rate is fairly similar to the one for the total population. On the other hand, marriage or partnering for a poor household means a very high exit rate. As many as three out of four one-person households or single parents experiencing this event exited poverty.

Table 6.8   Changed household composition and working hours and mobility out of poverty among those who experienced changes

	Proportion poor household experiencing the event (Percentage)	Proportion poor households that became not poor the following year.
Total		38.16
Number of adults increased from two to one	7.23	74.16
Number of children in the household decreased	1.35	39.69
The household became employed	26.25	56.26
The household increased its working hours	14.99	69.66
The household neither became employed nor increased its working hours	58.76	22.04

A surprisingly large proportion of poor households experienced job gain (26 per cent) and more work (15 per cent). Thus as many as two out of five poor during one year have experienced one of these events. The majority of such households exit poverty. This is the mechanism by which many non-poor escape poverty from one year to the next. On the other hand, the result for those almost three-fifths of the poor who have not experienced a job gain is much darker. No more than 22 per cent of such households exit poverty the following year.

6.9 Conclusions

The Household Income Survey (HINK) provides a good opportunity to shed light on the development and structure of Swedish poverty. Compared to earlier studies using the same data we have here added more years of measurement and arrived at a time series spanning two decades. It has also been possible to shed light on the dynamics of poverty.

Poverty in present day Sweden is often transitory. A large proportion of those who are poor during one year have left poverty the next, and three years later most initially poor are no longer in poverty. The reason for this is often that someone in the household has taken up a job or increased hours of work. However, these results also mean that, seen over several years, the experience of poverty is widespread in the population.

The average real income of the households increased during the two decades studied. However, income inequality has grown since the first half of the 1980s. Therefore it is hardly surprising that results showing how the extent of poverty has developed in the entire population strongly depend on how the poverty line is updated. Since the beginning of the 1980s ever larger proportions of the Swedish population have fallen below a poverty line based on median contemporary income. The share of individuals and households who fall below a poverty line which represents a constant purchasing power have not decreased since the mid 1980s, and such households were actually poorer at the end of the period.

As employment decreased rapidly in the beginning of the 1990s, it is hardly surprising that our figures show increasing poverty during the first half of the 1990s. Perhaps more surprising is that the initial increase in the poverty rate has not been larger than actually recorded. Undoubtedly the transfer system has had a large initial effect on reducing poverty. We have shown curves and numbers which indicate large reductions in poverty among children, young adults and households headed by a foreign non-Nordic head. For the first category, but not the two latter, there was no substantial difference in the poverty risk to the entire population. Another victory for the system of transfer in reducing poverty occurred at the beginning of the period, when the maturation of the pension system meant that the elderly were ever less poverty prone.

The risk of being poor in present day Sweden is very large if one lives in a household with a weak attachment to working life and which does not receive pensions. This description fits many young adults and many families with a foreign, non-Nordic head, categories which have high rates of poverty. The fact that many poor escape poverty quickly should be viewed from a background of many taking up a job or increasing their number of working hours. Movements into poverty are often the consequence of work loss or less work. Young adults make up a disproportionately large part of all the poor in Sweden. Young adults have a remarkably high risk of becoming poor. This in turn can be traced to the events of job loss and less work being more frequent among them and also to the fact that the poverty consequences of such events are higher for the young adults. The extent of poverty among young adults is strongly linked to the business cycle and has increased during the period of our observation. However, we have also found that poverty among young adults is more transitory than among others. While poverty in Sweden varies strongly with employment, age of the person and citizenship of the head of the household, gender differences are small. Present day poverty in Sweden has no regional variation.

6.10 Appendix

Table 6.A.1 Median for disposible income per consumption unit (for individuals)

	Nominal	In 1995 years value (index 1975=100)
1975	21068	21068
1976		
1977		
1978	29084	21518
1979		
1980	37108	22551
1981	40541	21981
1982	42701	21320
1983	46934	21514
1984	51047	21654
1985	56107	22174
1986	59278	22480
1987	64390	23421
1988	69743	23985
1989	77520	25046
1990	87768	25701
1991	99066	26504
1992	102116	26703
1993	101300	25307
1994	102803	25701
1995	102504	24406

References

Aguilar, R. and Gustafsson, B. (1994).Immigrants in the Swedish labour Market During the 1980s, *Scandinavian Journal of Social Welfare*, 3, 139-147.

Bergmark, Å (1991). *Socialbidrag och försörjning. En studie av bidragstagande bland ensamstående utan barn*, Stockholm: Stockholms universitet. Rapport i Socialt arbete nr 55.

Borooah, V.K. and McKee, P.M. (1994). Intra Household Income Transfers and Implications for Poverty and Inequality in the U.K. In: Creedy, J. (ed.) *Taxation, Poverty and the Distribution of Income*, London: Edward Elgar.

Duncan, G., Gustafsson, B., Hauser, R., Schmauss, G., Jenkins, S., Messinger, H., Muffels, R., Nolan, B., Ray, J-C and Voges, W. (1995). Poverty and Social Assistance Dynamics in the United States, Canada and Europe, in McFate, K., Lawson, R., and Wilson, W. J. (Eds) *Poverty, Inequality and the Future of Social Policy. Western States in the New Social Order*, New York: Russel Sage.

Duncan, G., Gustafsson, B., Hauser, R., Schmauss, G,. Messinger, H., Muffels, R., Nolan, B., Ray, J-C (1993). Poverty Dynamics in Eight Countries, *Journal of Population Economics*, 6, 215-234.

Erikson, R.and Thålin, M. (1984). Samgång mellan välfärdsproblem in: Erikson, R. and Åberg, R. (red) *Välfärd i förändring. Levnadsvillkor i Sverige 1968-1981*. Arlöv:Prisma.

Findlay, J. and Wright, R. (1996).Gender Poverty and the Intra-Household Distribution of Resources, *Review of Income and Wealth*, 42, 335 - 351.

Föster, M (1993). *Comparing Poverty in 13 OECD Countries: Traditional and Synthetical Approches*, Luxembourg Income Working Paper No. 100.

Foster, J., Greer, J. and Thorebecke, E. (1984). A Class of Decomposable Poverty Measures, *Econometrica*, 52, 761-766.

Gustafsson, B. Tasiran, A. and Nyman, H. (1997). Single Parent Families and Social Security – the Case of Sweden, In De Jong, P. and Marmor, T. (Eds) *Social Policy and the Labour Market*, Aldershot: Ashgate. International Studies on Social Security vol 2.

Gustafsson, B. and Lindblom, M. (1993). Poverty Lines and Poverty in Seven European Countries, Australia, Canada and the USA, *Journal of European Social Policy*, 3, 21-38.

Gustafsson, B. and Nivorozhkina, L. (1996). Relative Poverty in Two Egalitarian Societies. A Comparison Between Taganrog Russia During the Soviet Era and Sweden., *Review of Income and Wealth* 42, 321 - 334.

Gustafsson, B. and Palmer, E. (1997). Changes in Swedish Inequality. A Study of Equivalent Income 1975-1991, In Gottschald, P., Gustafsson, B. and Palmer, E. (Editors) *Changing Patterns in the Distribution of Economic Welfare – An International Perspective*, Cambridge: Cambridge University Press.

Gustafsson, B. and Uusitalo, H. (1990). The Welfare State and Poverty in Finland and Sweden from the mid-1969 to the mid 1980s, *Review of Income and Wealth* 36 (3), 249-266.

Gustafsson, B. (1984). *En bok om fattigdom*, Lund: Studentlitteratur.

Gustafsson, B. (1987). *Ett decenium av stagnerade realinkomster*, Stockholm: Statistiska Centralbyrån (Levnadsförhållanden. Rapport 54).

Gustafsson, B. (1994). Ekonomisk fattigdom i Sverige sedan mitten av 1970-talet, *Socialvetenskaplig Tidskrift*, 1, 267-285.

Gustafsson, B. (1995). Assessing Poverty. Some Reflections on the Literature, *Journal of Population Economics*, 8, 361 - 381.

Gustafsson, B. (1996). Fattigdom i Sverige. Förändring åren 1975 till 1993, struktur och dynamik in: Puide, A. (Ed) *Den nordiska fattigdomens utveckling och struktur*, Köbenhavn: Nordiska Ministerrådet, Tema Nord 1996:583.

Gustafsson, B. (1997). Invandrarnas försörjning pages 78-85 *in Statens Invandrarverk Mångfald och ursprung*, Norrköping.

Halleröd, B (1991). *Den svenska fattigdomen*, Lund: Arkiv.

Halleröd, B., Marklund, S., Nordlund, A. and Stattin, M. (1993.) *Konsensuell Fattigdom. En studie av konsumtion och attityder till konsumtion*, Umeå: Umeå Universitet, Umeå Studies in Sociology, No 104

Halleröd, B. (1994). *Poverty in Sweden: A New Approch to the Direct Measurement of Consensual Poverty*, Umeå: Sociologiska institutionen, Umeå Universitet, Umeå Studies in Sociology, No 106.

Halleröd, B.(1995). The Truly Poor: Direct and Indirect Consensual Measurement of Poverty in Sweden, *Journal of European Social Policy*, 5, 111 - 129.

Halleröd, B.(1996). Deprivation and Poverty: A Comparative Analysis of Sweden and Great Britain, *Acta Sociologica*, 39, 141 - 168.

Jäntti, M. (1993.) *Essays on Income Distribution and Poverty*, Åbo: Åbo akademis förlag.

Lindbeck, A. (1997). The Swedish Experiment, *Journal of Economic Literature*, XXXV, 1273 - 1319.

Lundberg, S., Pollak, R. and Wales, T. (1996). Do Husbands and Wives Pool Their Resources? Evidence from United Kingdom Child Benefit, *Journal of Human Resources*, XXXII, 461 - 480.

Mack J. and Lansley, A. H. (1985). *Poor Britain*, London: Georg Allen and Unwin.

Mayer, S. (1995). A Comparison of Poverty and Living Conditions in the United States, Canada, Sweden and Germany, in McFate, K., Lawson, R., and Wilson, W. J. (Eds) *Poverty, Inequality and the Future of Social Policy. Western States in the New Social Order*, New York: Russel Sage.

McFate, K, Smeeding, T. and Rainwater, L. (1995). Markets and States: Poverty Trends and Transfer system Effectiveness in the 1980s, McFate, K., Lawson, R., and Wilson, W. J. (Eds) *Poverty, Inequality and the Future of Social Policy. Western States in the New Social Order*, New York: Russel Sage.

Osberg, L. and Xu, K. (1997). *International Comparisons of Poverty Intensity: Index Decomposition and Bootstrap Inference*, Luxembourg Income Study, Working Paper, No. 165.

Salonen, T. (1993). *Margins of Welfare. A Study of Modern Functions of Social Assistance*, Torna Hällerstad: Hällerstads Press.

Saunders, P., Halleröd, B. and Matheson, G. (1994). Making Ends Meet in Australia and Sweden: A Comparative Analysis of the Consensual Approach to Poverty Line Methodology, *Acta Sociologica*, 37, 3-22.

Smeeding, T. (1991). Cross-country Comparison of Inequality and Poverty Positions, In Osberg, L. (Editor) *Economic Inequality and Poverty. International Perspectives*, New York, London: M. E. Sharp.

Smeeding, T. (1997). *Financial Poverty in Developed Countries: The Evidence from LIS - Final Report to the UNDP*, Luxembourg Income Study, Working Paper, No. 155.

Smeeding, T., Rainwater, L., Rein, M., Hauser, R. and Schaber, G. (1990). Income Poverty in Seven Countries: Initial Estimates from the LIS Database. In Smeeding, T, O'Higgins, M. and Rainwater, L (Eds) *Poverty Inequality and Income Distribution in Comparative Perspective*, Harwester Wheatsheaf, Hemel Hempstead.

Socialstyrelsen (1994). *Social Rapport 1994*, Stockholm, SoS-rapport 1994:10.

Socialstyrelsen (1997). *Social Rapport 1997*, Stockholm, SoS-rapport 1997:14.

Statistics Sweden (1997) .*Välfärd och ojämlikhet i 20-årsperspektiv 1975 - 1995*, Stockholm, Levnadsförhållanden Rapport 91.

Sörensen, A. (1992). Zur geschlechtsspezifischen Struktur von Armut. *Kölner Zetschrift für Soziologie und Sozialpsychologie, Sonderhefte, 32* ("Armut im modernen Wohlfartstaat" Eds. Leibfried, S. and Voges, W), 345-366.

Tham, H. (1994). Ökad marginalisering i Sverige 1968-1991? in Fritzell, J. and Lundberg, O. (red) *Vardagens villkor,* Stockholm: Brombergs.

Townsend, P. (1979). *Poverty in the United Kingdom,* Penguin, Harmondsworth.

Vogel, J. (1997). Living Conditions and Inequality in the European Union 1997 Eurostat, *Population and social conditions E/1997-3.*

Wong, Y-L., Garfinkel, I and McLanahan, S. (1993). Single Mother Families in Eight Countries: Economic Status and Social Policy, *Social Service Review,* 67, 177-197.

Wright, R. (1993). *Women and Poverty in Industrialised Countries,* The Luxembourg Income Study, Working Paper 96.

7 Conclusions

BJÖRN GUSTAFSSON AND PEDER J. PEDERSEN

7.1 The Study

In this book we have surveyed and analysed the development and structure of economic poverty or low incomes in Denmark, Finland, Iceland, Norway and Sweden. Our approach has been to work on data sets for the individual countries which have been made as comparable as possible. We have applied an economic definition of "poverty" based on household disposable income. For each country we have used the same equivalence scale to adjust for differences in household size, and the same poverty line, i.e. 50 per cent of the median in the distribution of household-size-adjusted disposable incomes. For the individual countries, this has been supplemented by the use of alternative poverty lines. Furthermore, data has also made it possible to investigate movements in and out of poverty and the duration of poverty in Denmark, Norway and Sweden, by following individuals and households for more than one year.

In an comparative context, the extent of poverty in the Nordic countries is considerably smaller than that found in many other industrialised countries. Despite this, problems related to poverty and low income have attracted considerable attention in the Nordic countries. One reason for this is increased problems of unemployment which first appeared gradually in Denmark, and much more abruptly in Finland and Sweden at the beginning of the 1990s. A second reason for studying poverty in the Nordic countries is that social programmes in those countries were considerably expanded during the 1960s and 1970s, while this was not the case during the 1980s. Finland and Sweden even saw considerable cuts in programmes during the 1990s. Yet another reason for our study is evidence for some of our countries, especially Sweden, which indicates increased income inequality, pointing to the possibility that economic growth has not benefited everyone. Finally, the proportion of people living on means-tested social assistance has increased in the Nordic countries.

Considerable efforts have been made to standardise data and sampling periods across countries. Despite this, the levels of the poverty rates are not comparable across countries. This is due to problems regarding available data. The definition of a household differs across countries and some income components are not included in the data for some of the countries.

For example, in Denmark we have access to information for two adults in a household only if they are married, not if they are cohabiting. Data for Norway does not include social assistance before 1991, while the Danish data does not include rent support. Another example relates to differences in the data collection method, where information on incomes in the sample for Iceland is collected using telephone interviews, while mainly register information is used in the other countries.

7.2 The Development of Poverty over Time

One of the motivations for the present study was to analyse the question of whether the very different profiles of unemployment in the individual countries have had an impact on the level of and the change in the poverty rates. The prior expectations, conditional on a strong impact from unemployment on the aggregate poverty rate, would then be to observe an increasing poverty rate in Denmark and strongly increasing rates in Finland and Sweden since 1990. The level and the changes in unemployment have been moderate in size for Iceland and Norway, meaning that equally strong expectations do not exist for those two countries.

Summarising the development in the aggregate poverty rates, using 50 per cent of the median current disposable income as the poverty line, those prior expectations were clearly not fulfilled. In Denmark, we find, using 1980-1995 data, that the aggregate poverty rate is stationary with a counter-cyclical sensitivity that is reduced during the period. In Finland, the aggregate poverty rate declines very much between 1971 and the mid 1980s. After that, the level is low and stationary, reacting surprisingly little to the explosive increase in unemployment from 1990. The dramatic increase in unemployment – from 3 to 20 per cent in a year- is, however, as expected, reflected strongly if the calculations are made using factor incomes instead of disposable incomes. For Iceland, survey based evidence is available for the years 1986-1997. There is a trend towards increased inequality in the distribution of an income concept consisting of earnings, unemployment insurance benefits and pensions. The aggregate poverty rate relative to this income concept shows a counter-cyclical sensitivity. For Norway, the data refers to the period 1979-1995. The aggregate poverty rate is nearly stationary, and tends – surprisingly – to behave pro-cyclically, i.e. the poverty rate goes up in the boom years of the mid 1980s and it is more or less constant in situations with higher unemployment later in the period. For Sweden, data has been available for 1975, 1978 and annually for the period 1980-1995. Sweden differs from the other Nordic countries in showing an increasing trend in the poverty rate. The increasing inequality in the Swedish income distribution is thus related to the finding that an increasing part of the population is in the low end of the distribution.

In the individual chapters, results can be found concerning the development in the low income rate both by using absolute poverty lines instead of the relative lines, the results from which are summarised above, and concerning the results from using more elaborate measures of poverty than the results regarding head count summarised here. A fairly general and understandable observation is that during periods of economic growth there is a difference for poverty assessments if the poverty line is updated with the consumer price index only, or by the development of median disposable income.

The cyclical sensitivity of the aggregate poverty rate has been mentioned above. For Denmark, Iceland and Sweden we find a counter-cyclical sensitivity. For Norway the poverty rate is pro-cyclical while the cyclical relationship is weak in the case of Finland. Regarding the specific impact of unemployment, there is evidence in the Danish and the Swedish cases that individual unemployment has a significant impact on the low income risk. In the case of Denmark, this is especially true for women in the 1990s.

7.3 The Poverty Profile

The analyses of the aggregate poverty rates were followed by looking into poverty or low income for different groups in the population in each of the countries. Regarding the poverty rate in different age groups, the most striking development is found for those older than 60 and for those younger than 30. For the age group in between, fairly small changes occur. For those older than 60, poverty has decreased, indeed it has nearly disappeared, in the four large Nordic countries. The reasons behind this development are a set of common factors. A greater proportion of people in this age group has become eligible for various early retirement options. Labour market pensions and private pension schemes have been expanded, and the relative benefit levels in public sector pensions have been increased. This is reinforced by the delayed effect from the increase in labour force participation among married women, who have increasingly become eligible to benefits from different retirement schemes. The experience of Iceland is however an exception to this general conclusion. The retired in Iceland have a fairly high poverty rate, also in the 1990s, reflecting the less comprehensive character of the Icelandic welfare state in comparison with the other Nordic countries.

At the other end of the life cycle, the poverty rate among those younger than 30 is relatively high and increasing in all our countries. A number of factors are relevant to this development. Firstly, a number of young people of 18 and older still live with their parents. In spite of the fact that part of this group receives transfers – in cash and in kind – from their parents, they are treated according to a statistical convention as separate households. Secondly, an increasing share of young people are students in a broad range of types of education, implying that their current low income status for the great majority is only temporary from a life cycle perspective. Finally, pulling in the other direction, youth unemployment has been a serious problem in the Nordic countries too. While we generally find that poverty is a temporary problem for the young, there is a risk that a part of the young generation will face long-term difficulties providing for themselves with an income from an ordinary job, due to long term unemployment at the time they entered the labour market.

High poverty rates among young adults presents a challenge to public policy. The success in reducing poverty among the aged in the four large Nordic countries was achieved by increased transfer payments to that section of the population. This strategy cannot be carried over as a major strategy for combating poverty among young adults. Effective measures to combat poverty among young adults who have a potentially long working career ahead of them have to affect their possibilities to find a job and thereby receive an income. Thus strategies have to affect their human capital and measures are thus found among programmes on education and training.

The recorded high poverty rates among young adults also offer a challenge to statistical systems and research. The transition from parental home to an independent adult life needs to be better monitored and understood. For example, there is a need to understand better the role financial transfers from parents to adult children play in different parts of the population.

Regarding variations in poverty rates by gender and by family types, we find in general only small differences in the poverty rate between women and men. The phenomenon of the "feminisation of poverty" known from the literature on other countries is thus not found for the Nordic countries. Among the explanatory factors behind this result are the high participation rates in the labour market for married women, the fairly small female-male wage gap, and the mainly universal character of welfare benefits. Once again, Iceland is an exception because of less generous social programmes, implying that relatively many of those with low incomes are older single women or single mothers.

To be married or cohabiting reduces the risk of poverty significantly. Having children in the family implies a significantly higher poverty risk in Denmark, Iceland and Norway. For couples, too, the risk of low income increases with the number of children in both Denmark and Iceland. In Norway, 60 per cent of the – very low – share of the population living in long term poverty are families with children. In Finland, single parents are no more exposed to low income than others, and in Sweden the "absolute" poverty rate of families with children is unaffected by the big increase in unemployment from 1990. This, however, is completely dependent on public sector benefits, as the poverty rate regarding factor incomes goes up strongly after 1990 for families with children.

The regional variation in poverty rates is affected by growth differentials, internal migration and by the coverage and scope of the welfare state. An impact from these kinds of mechanisms is found in Finland, with a strong convergence in regional poverty rates during the period. In the mid 1990s regional differences in poverty rates are small in the Nordic countries, or as in the cases of Denmark and Sweden, virtually non-existent.

Immigrants have always been considered more exposed to the risk of low income, at least during their initial stay in the host country. This risk has increased in recent years, as the composition of immigrants and refugees has shifted towards non-European groups with greater difficulties in finding employment, due to language problems and cultural distance from the host country. At the same time aggregate unemployment has been high, in the Nordic countries too. Sweden has by far the greatest immigrant population – both in absolute and relative terms – among the Nordic countries. Immigrants are included in the Swedish data and the analysis shows a clearly higher poverty risk among non-Nordic immigrants.

7.4 Dynamic Aspects of Poverty

A final part of the country analyses was to study the dynamics of poverty. Although in no Nordic country has a household panel been set up with the purpose of monitoring poverty dynamics, it was possible to find register information for Denmark, Norway and Sweden which was useful for dynamic poverty analysis. When studying poverty dynamics, several methodological issues arise which are not relevant to cross-section analyses. It is a very demanding matter to try to compare poverty dynamics across countries, and we have not entered into it. Nevertheless a number of interesting findings on poverty dynamics from the three country chapters can be assembled.

For all three countries it was found that a considerable proportion of people who are poor one year have escaped poverty the next. The proportion depends on the definition used, but varies roughly between two and three out of five. Nordic poverty is thus definitively not a situation where all the poor stay poor year after year. On the other hand, the results also show that the risk of being poor one year is very much affected by poverty status in the preceding year.

Among the main results in the Danish case was the finding of higher entry rates to low income and lower exit rates among women compared with men. Another interesting finding was that the fairly stationary aggregate poverty rate is the net result of a decline in both the entry rate to and the exit rate from a low income state. The Norwegian analysis relies on an alternative methodological approach by using 50 per cent of the median in the ten-year distribution of income as a line for cronic poverty. The results show that only 1.5 per cent of the population were chronicly poor. However, in contrast to the income history of those classified as poor according to the annual indicators the cronic poor had persistently low annual incomes. The exit rate in Sweden is at the same level. The Swedish analysis relates changes in individual circumstances to the entry and exit rates relative to a low income state. It is found that losing a job or a partner significantly increases the entry rate. Becoming a couple, working more hours and getting a job all have a significant positive impact on the exit rate from poverty.

7.5 Concluding Remarks

Overall, the poverty rates are fairly low and fairly stable in the Nordic countries. It is demonstrated, however, that the aggregate near-stability is the net result of major changes occurring regarding the poverty risk for particular groups in the population. Furthermore, it should be emphasised that the low and fairly stable poverty rates apply to disposable incomes. The picture is quite different concerning factor incomes. A major challenge to the Nordic welfare states is consequently to narrow the gap between the low income shares relative to factor incomes and to disposable incomes. A narrowing effected by cutbacks of major welfare state programmes will meet political resistance. The alternative, to reduce unemployment, is obviously a more attractive option, making it at the same time possible to continue to finance central welfare state programmes in the future.

Presentation of the Authors

Rolf Aaberge, cand.real. from the University of Oslo 1976, is Senior Reseach Fellow at the Research Department, Statistics Norway. His research activities covers labour supply, taxation, unemployment, local government economics, poverty, income distribution and social welfare.
E-mail: roa@ssb.no

Arne S. Andersen, mag.art. in sociology from the University of Oslo in 1972, is Adviser at Department of Social Statistics, Statistics Norway. Main research area is welfare research, in the later years with emphasis on analysis of household economy.
E-mail: arne.andersen@ssb.no

Björn Gustafsson has a PhD in economics, and holds a position as professor at the Department of Social Work, University of Göteborg, Sweden. He is a senior researcher at the Swedish Council of Social Research (SFR). Gustafsson's research covers empirical studies on poverty, social assistance, the distribution of economic well-being and the welfare state as well as the economics of immigration.
E-mail: bjorn.gustafsson@socwork.gu.se

Markus Jäntti received a PhD in Economics at Åbo Akademi University in 1993. He is since 1996 a Senior Research Fellow with the Academy of Finland. Major research interests are income inequality, mobility and poverty in comparative perspective, applied labour economics and statistical inference for income distribution analysis.
E-mail: markus.jantti@abo.fi

Stefán Ólafsson has a D.Phil. degree in social studies from Oxford University. He is a professor in the faculty of Social Sciences at the University of Iceland. He is also a director of the University's Social Research Institute. Ólafsson's research is primarily in the field of welfare studies, industrial sociology and societal development.
E-mail: olafsson@hi.is

Peder J. Pedersen is professor of Economics at the Department of Economics, University of Aarhus and research director at the Centre for Labour Market and Social Research. Main research interests are incentives and labour market behaviour, income distribution and pensions and retirement.
E-mail: ppedersen@econ.au.dk

Veli-Matti Ritakallio, Ph.D., is Senior Research Fellow in Social Policy at the University of Turku. Currently he works as visiting fellow at the Research School of Social Sciences, Australian National University (Canberra). His major research topic has been poverty, especially measurement issues, cross-national comparisons and the role of the social policy in combatting poverty. He is currently doing research on changed nature of the connections between life-cycle and risk of poverty.
E-mail: Veli-Matti.Ritakallio@utu.fi

Karl Sigurðsson has a degree in political sciences from the University of Iceland and is a researcher at the University's Social Research Institute. His work is mainly in the field of survey reaserch, especially labour market surveys, political surveys and media ratings.
E-mail: karls@hi.is

Nina Smith is professor of Economics at the Aarhus School of Business and research director at the Centre for Labour Market and Social Research. Her main research interests are labour supply, income distribution and poverty, gender wage gap and applied welfare economics.
E-mail: nina@hdc.hha.dk

Tom Wennemo, cand.mag. from the University of Oslo 1983, is EDP-adviser at the Research Department, Statistics Norway. He has been involved in empirical projects on labor supply and taxation, unemployment, income distribution and poverty.
E-mail: wen@ssb.no

Presentation of Nordiska Ministerrådet

The Nordic Council of Ministers was established in 1971. It submits proposals on co-operation between the governments of the five Nordic countries to the Nordic Council, implements the Council's recommendations and reports on results, while directing the work carried out in the targeted areas. The Prime Ministers of the five Nordic countries assume overall responsibility for the co-operation measures, which are co-ordinated by the ministers for co-operation and the Nordic Co-operation committee. The composition of the Council of Ministers varies, depending on the nature of the issue to be treated.

The Nordic Council was formed in 1952 to promote co-operation between the parliaments and governments of Denmark, Iceland, Norway and Sweden. Finland joined in 1955. At the sessions held by the Council, representatives from the Faroe Islands and Greenland form part of the Danish delegation, while Åland is represented on the Finnish delegation. The Council consists of 87 elected members - all of whom are members of parliament. The Nordic Council takes initiatives, acts in a consultative capacity and monitors co-operation measures. The Council operates via its institutions: the Plenary Assembly, the Presidium and standing committees.